MUSLIMS OF METROPOLIS

MUSLIMS OF
METROPOLIS

The Stories of Three Immigrant
Families in the West

KAVITHA RAJAGOPALAN

RUTGERS UNIVERSITY PRESS
NEW BRUNSWICK, NEW JERSEY, AND LONDON

Library of Congress Cataloging-in-Publication Data

Rajagopalan, Kavitha, 1977–
Muslims of metropolis : the stories of three immigrant families in the West / Kavitha
Rajagopalan.
    p. cm.
  Includes bibliographical references and index.
  ISBN 978–0–8135–4344–4 (hardcover : alk. paper)
    1. Muslim families—England—London—Social conditions—Case studies. 2. Muslim
families—Germany—Berlin—Social conditions—Case studies. 3. Muslim families—
New York (State)—New York—Social conditions—Case studies. I. Title.
  HQ525.I8R34 2008
  306.85086'912091821—dc22

                                                                2007044902

A British Cataloging-in-Publication record for this book is available from the British
Library.

Visit our Web site: http://rutgerspress.rutgers.edu
Manufactured in the United States of America

For my family:

Amma and Appa, my foundation and inspiration;
Srikanth, my twin and my best friend;
and Matthew, the love of my life.

CONTENTS

PART III

Alienation and Acceptance

8   Sukriye Finds Love   209

9   Nishat Lets Go   239

    Epilogue   262

    Characters   265
    Pronunciation of Characters' Names   267
    Sources   269
    Index   277

PREFACE AND ACKNOWLEDGMENTS

One chilly, breezy afternoon in late autumn 2000, I rushed to meet Sukriye Dogan, who eventually became one of the main characters of this book, at Morena, a homey little neighborhood café near Goerlitzer Park in Kreuzberg, Berlin. The regular scenesters were there, sipping *Milchkaffee* and hand-rolling cigarettes with thick, stringy tobacco leaves. I shook off the damp cold and made my way toward a broad wooden table by the front window. Sukriye was already there with her friend, a French dramaturge, and she waved me over with a warm smile on her face.

I was in Berlin on a Fulbright scholarship to study political identity and lobby formation within the city's large and increasingly vocal Turkish community, whose cultural and spiritual home was here in Kreuzberg. Rather than sit in lectures and libraries, I planned to report on the process of lobby formation from the ground, and had gotten involved with a number of projects as one way to plug myself into the community and personally invest myself in its issues. I had also begun taking Turkish language courses, and hoped to gain enough conversational proficiency to speak with those members of the community who, for want of German fluency, remained marginalized not only from German society but also from the upper echelon of Almanci (or Turkish German) society seeking to establish itself in the German political process. I had gotten involved with a project Sukriye was leading at the Freie Universitaet about gender relations and diasporic consciousness within one Kurdish minority community, and through this project and her contacts, hoped to focus one section of my research project on the concerns and issues facing the Kurdish subminority within the Turkish minority population in Berlin.

I was running late to our meeting today from my Turkish language class, and as I slid into the booth across from Sukriye, I heartily greeted her in Turkish. And her face froze. She politely nodded and then said, "I don't speak Turkish. We are Kurds." I only realized some months later that my attempt at demonstrating my sympathy for her culture had been at best a social blunder and at worst a crass insult. It was one of the first "Ah-ha" moments I had during my research in Germany, a realization that the image of the Turkish community in Berlin had been grossly simplified not only by the German public but also by the very people who were creating the Turkish collective identity in German public consciousness. The Kurds were not a Turkish minority, but a frustrated nation with little cause to celebrate the rising influence of the Turkish community in Germany. Although I continued to report and write about the Kurdish community in Berlin, I kept my primary research focus on the Turkish community and its leadership's efforts to define a clear sociopolitical platform from individual planks as diverse as education policy and senior care.

At the end of my research term, I returned to the United States to pursue my master's degree in international affairs at Columbia University's School of International and Public Affairs (SIPA) in New York City. I set out to educate myself about comparative approaches to migration policy, to understand the varying barriers and avenues to socioeconomic and political integration of immigrant communities in the major immigration destinations of the world, and to learn to write about these issues in a way that would appeal to a broad readership. I intended to research and write about these issues for the rest of my professional life, and I hoped through study to deepen my understanding of political economy, urban planning, regional conflict, and immigration policy so as to better understand the reasons why people migrated, what they hoped to achieve, and what barriers they had to overcome in the process. The September 11, 2001, attacks in New York City and Washington, D.C. took place one week after the program had begun, and immigration policymaking throughout the West changed almost overnight. Within weeks of the attacks, reports of mass detentions and deportations began to filter out from ethnic neighborhoods and Muslim communities across the tri-state area, and I set out to research how the residents in these communities were coping with the immigration sweeps. After I met several families who were variously affected by the sweeps and the changes in policy, I realized that Muslim immigrants were now facing a wholly different set of barriers to becoming a part of society than I or any other immigrant had dealt with. And I began to see the beginnings of a book.

Over the course of my program at SIPA in New York, I made intermittent trips back to Berlin and to London, always taking the same approach to reporting that I had during my first trip in Berlin. I first plugged into the network of community-based organizations in order to meet some of the community's leading voices and to familiarize myself with their primary concerns. Then I hit the streets, going to the immigrant neighborhoods and ethnic enclaves themselves, approaching strangers on the streets, in shops, in the subways, and outside of mosques, asking them their stories and dragging them into long conversations over tea and coffee. I spoke with imams, police officers, lawyers, teachers, politicians, grocers, and editors of ethnic press, all of whom worked with or came into regular contact with members of these communities in some way or another. Meantime, I scoured the Internet, monitoring dozens of periodicals and blogs, and read hundreds of pamphlets, studies, analyses, policy papers, histories, and novels that related directly or indirectly to immigration, migration policy management, Islam in the West, the immigrant communities I was researching, the homelands they had left behind, the host countries in which they had settled, and the cities in which they lived. After graduating from SIPA, equipped with some journalistic training and some education in international policy, along with reams of contacts, interviews, and research material, I set out to write the book you find here.

This book would not have been possible without the help of many people, who have variously taught me, encouraged me, guided me, and supported me for what has become my most ambitious undertaking to date. My greatest debt of gratitude is owed to the main characters of this book and their tremendously warm and giving families, who took me into their confidences, their homes, and their hearts for the many years that it took to research and write this book. They have sheltered me and fed me, opened up their albums and diaries, told me things they had never before shared, and introduced me to everyone they knew. This book may never foster a lasting peace, win a nation its independence, or gain a family amnesty, but these three families have invested in this book the same courage and faith that they have in these, the guiding passions of their lives. My special thanks go to Sharif and Muna Nashashibi, along with their family members in London, Jerusalem, and Ramallah who broke fast with me, took me to protests, and welcomed me as a lifelong friend; to Sukriye, Mehmet, and Adla Dogan, to Nezir Suleiman, and to the dozens of Sukriye's siblings, cousins, nieces, nephews, aunts, and uncles who tore *nane* with me, taught me how to dance in a circle, and treated me like a member of their family; and to Nishat and Rafiqul Islam, who showed me how to eat sweets in the morning, let me witness the intimacies of their joys and sorrows, and allowed me to continue to telling their story even when they had lost all hope of a happy ending.

Although I officially began working on this book in 2003, the journey toward becoming a writer began long before, and I would like to extend a special thanks to all of the teachers, editors, professors, and fellow journalists who nudged me toward striking out onto this path. In particular, I would like to thank Samuel G. Freedman, for whose words of wisdom, unwavering confidence, and continuing interest in the book, its characters, and its progress I will be eternally grateful. I owe a special gratitude to Marlie Wasserman, my editor and publisher, who, between the demands of directing the press, took the time to provide me with numerous insights and thoughtful critiques, and gave me the opportunity to realize a long-standing dream.

The Institute for International Education's Fulbright program, the US Department of Education's Foreign Language and Area Studies grant, and the American Council on Germany's John J. McCloy fellowship provided me with the precious funding I needed to travel and research, and I am indebted to them. I also would like to extend a special thanks to my various employers

over these years who have afforded me the flexibility and time off to concen-
trate on a project of this magnitude.

Many people gave generously of their time to sit with me in exhaustive
interviews, open their private collections of literature and legislation, to help
me develop my network of contacts and experts, and to inform my travels in
unfamiliar places. I am deeply indebted to the following people, who, among
countless others, gave generously of their valuable time and insights over
these many years. In Berlin, I would like to extend a special thanks to Aso
Agace, Katrin Arendt, Metin Aktas, Riza Baran, Ahmed Berwari, Jochen
Blaschke, Selim Bicuk, Halil and Nuran Can, Cemalettin Cetin, Safter Cinar,
Martin Duespohl, Edda Eisenhardt, Barbara Guegold, Siamend Hajo,
Barbara John, Sanem Kleff, Ute and Michael Koepp-Wilhelmus, Uta Kural,
Neriman Kurt, Filiz Mueller-Lehnhartz, Mustafa Mih, Rainer Muenz, Ozcan
Mutlu, Ertekin Ozcan, Shakh Sagna, Eva Savelsberg, Ali Ucar, Yunus and
Nuersel Uyger (and their lovely children), and Metin Yilmaz. In London and
in the Palestinian territories, I would like to express my gratitude to Zeina
Ashrawi (and her wonderful friend Rana), Muhammed Aziz, Subhi al-Azzawi,
Abdesselam Ben Daoud, Chris Doyle, Abdurraheem Green, Anna Habib,
Abdel Halim, Mosab Hassan, Ismail Jalili, Ghada Karmi, Abdul Karim Khalil,
Riddah Nijabat, Afif Safieh, Safaa el-Sawy, Said Shehadeh, Mordechai
Vanunu, and Lucas Welch, along with dozens of other Palestinians both in
Ramallah and in London who expressed a wish to remain unnamed. In the
United States, I would like to express my sincerest thanks to Irfan Ahmed,
Judy Brandwein, Adem Carroll, Louis Abdellatif Christillo, Namita Chad,
Yvette Clark, David Cole, Shoshi Doza, Asghar Choudhry, Emily Gildersleeve,
Maha Hilal, Syed Hussain, Saira Kazmi, Samira Khan, Monami Maulik, Naiem
Mohaimen, Anwari Rajput, Ahmad and Mohammed Razvi, Saurav Sarkar,
Michele Steinbuch, Kani Xulam, Azar Zedi, along with various members of
the Islams' family and community who chose not to be named in the book.

Dozens of friends and colleagues have helped me to edit the text and have
served as an invaluable sounding board for the ideas presented here. I owe
a debt of gratitude to Lisa Anderson, Noah Angell, Gal Beckerman, Kim
Bylander, Brad Fox, and Joanne Hawana for taking the time and care to offer

their comments and feedback on sections of the text. I would also like to offer my special thanks to the "Dark Side," my friends and fellow writers who have talked me through many a crisis of form and faith, and to my legions of wonderful friends and relatives who have offered their love, moral support, and encouragement through countless gifts of meals, shelter, literature, and drinks, and through countless hours of conversation. Thanks are also owed to the dozens of helpful executive assistants and research assistants, grant administrators and educational program coordinators, data recovery technicians and software salespeople, librarians and student group organizers who have offered their assistance at the right times.

Most of all, I would like to thank my beloved family for being my greatest champions, my true believers, my bedrock of unwavering support and enthusiasm. They have all read and reread the many drafts, and brainstormed with me about style and narrative choice, and taken care of me when I was too absorbed in my work to take care of myself. My parents taught me to pursue my passions with absolute faith and total conviction, and raised me to always approach my life's work with curiosity, compassion, and perseverance. My twin brother and best friend, Srikanth, has been a part of my inner dialogue since childhood, and without him I never would have been able to develop or clarify many of the ideas in this text. Matthew, my husband, has inhabited the worlds of this book since we first met, and as my tireless editor, my voice of reason, and my greatest comfort during my darkest moments, has embraced my project as his own. My eternal gratitude goes to them, and to the goddess Parashakti, who sent them to me.

NOTE ON THE TEXT

As there is no exact system for transcribing words and names from Arabic, Bangla, or Urdu into English spellings, I have used spellings that I believed were easiest to read as the closest approximation to the actual pronunciation of the word or name in question, and have spelled characters' names as they themselves did, where applicable. For example, in Arabic convention, it would be common to see "Rafiq ul-Islam," but one of the book's characters wrote his name as "Rafiqul Islam," to which I held. Please note that, although Turkish and Kurmanci employ phonetic variants of the Latin alphabet, there are certain letters that are not found in English. In typing the text of this book, I did not have access to keyboards containing these specialty letters, and so have not included them. These letters were not altered to approximate actual pronunciation.

MUSLIMS OF METROPOLIS

INTRODUCTION

In the last decade, widespread discussion of Muslim countries, immigrants, religious practices, social customs, and political beliefs has rendered Muslims far more visible than they have been at any other time in Western history. But more often than not, the rhetoric of these public discussions conflates diverse and unrelated communities into one group, and associates Islamic identity with largely negative social stereotypes. In countries throughout the West, Muslim immigrants live under the scrutiny of the rest of society, and at times of the government. They are regularly suspected of sympathizing with movements characterized as sociopathic, terrorist, and anti-Western. Frequently, they are accused of outrageous designs on Western democracy and values, and of attempting to replace tolerant Western secularism with Islamist theocracy. Some commentators have even gone so far as to say that the West's very tolerance of Islam in its midst will be its undoing. The debate surrounding Muslim immigrant communities in the West and Muslim majority countries abroad has often been confused by misinformation, reduced to stereotype, and degraded by fear.

Fear of Islam is not new to Western society. Throughout the second half of the twentieth century, as different revolutionary groups employed similar Islamic rhetoric or militant tactics to advance their separate goals, the image of the Muslim terrorist became a common trope in Western news media and pop culture. Despite the unique histories, players, and implications of these revolutionary movements, there emerged a single image—the Islamist militant, the face of Islamic terrorism. Media and pop culture images of this one-dimensional, interchangeable Islamist militant have rarely been offset with narratives reflecting the true complexity and diversity of Muslim communities and their political history. Over thirty countries today have majority Muslim populations, which belong to hundreds of ethnic, linguistic, and religious sub-communities. Yet even as many academics, journalists, and policymakers work against the growing snowball of generalization, other prevalent voices in Western academic, media, and policy settings have justified and facilitated the conflation of Muslims from all over the world and the political spectrum into one group. When many different peoples can be seen as one, as fundamentally different from and essentially antipathetic to the rest of society, then they can easily be feared.

Until recently, the fear of Islam had little impact on the prospects and opportunities of Muslim immigrants living in the West. Driven from home by the same forces as other immigrants, in search of the same things as other immigrants, they tended to exist in the Western public arena as immigrants rather than as Muslims. Islam remained a private religious practice rather than a public political category. Where communities formed, they formed along ethnic or national lines, and where mosques were built, prayer was held in the language of one group only. Different Muslim communities rarely comingled, and Muslim identity was considered secondary to ethnic or national identity.

But in recent years, many Western governments have begun to regard Muslim immigrants not as immigrants first, but as Muslims. Countries with vastly different political systems and immigration histories have begun to develop a shared rhetoric to explain how Islam stands in conflict with Western social and political values. Whether the dominant concern of a given Western government is national character, public secularism, or national security, Muslim immigrant communities and their interests stand at the center of discussion. The discussions may state a desire to "win the hearts and minds" of Muslims by promoting multiculturalism and social integration, to expand parameters for citizenship, or to partner with Muslim immigrant community leaders to address national security concerns and increase political participation. In practice, however, Muslim immigrants may find they face greater hurdles at borders, from social service providers, and from law enforcement officials than other immigrants. Political rhetoric that brands Muslim immigrants as a single suspicious, culturally antagonistic, and destabilizing group of people has compromised many Muslim immigrants' sense of belonging and acceptance in places where they have lived for up to three and four generations.

As an immigrant myself, although not Muslim, I drew on a complex narrative of family culture, national myth, political and social realities, religious imperatives, and personal experience to construct my own identity and to locate myself in society. Regardless of religious or ethnic background, all immigrants and children of immigrants negotiate their own identities from a similar set of influences, and I always imagined that Muslim immigrants must face the same challenges and opportunities that my own family had faced. But after the Cold War, a fundamental shift in political attitudes toward Muslims and Islam began to occur as political theorists rushed to describe the new world configuration. As a student of international relations theory, I read the works of opinion leaders all over the world who, it seemed, were increasingly seizing on the idea of an essential cultural divide between Islam and the West. The earliest references to a so-called clash of civilizations consistently failed to include discussion of the role and place of what could be called the Muslim diaspora, the Muslim world *within* the West, and the West's fastest growing religious community.

Although religious conversion has drawn many adherents to the Islamic faith, this Muslim world within the West largely comprises immigrants. Of the estimated six million Muslims in the United States and the nearly twenty million in Europe, the overwhelming majority are immigrants, whose remittances have contributed significantly to public and private expenditures in their home countries, and whose tax contributions have accounted for considerable portions of the public revenue available in the West. These were millions of people from dozens of communities who were a part of the West, who had been for some time now. Migration has long been severely neglected aspect of international relations and international development debates. Without poverty and political instability throughout the world, migration would never have reached the high levels it has, and it is immigration that continuously changes the face of the so-called West. Immigrants, more than policies or institutions, are the foremost agents of social change, both in their host societies and in their countries of origin. In a so-called conflict between the West and Islam, Muslim immigrants are an untapped potential resource for cultural mediation, social integration in the host society, and economic development at home. To a certain extent, the level of integration an immigrant achieves depends on individual psychology and circumstances. But it cannot be denied that systemic ignorance and prejudice can create both tangible and intangible barriers to prevent immigrants from achieving full socioeconomic integration in their host societies.

I felt that it was time for a book that would address the underlying causes of ignorance and prejudice toward Muslim immigrants by showing the true diversity and complexity of this Muslim world within the West. This book would show that even as the societies of the West understand Muslim immigrants as Muslims first of all, most Muslim immigrants still construct their identities on the basis of the experiences of their families, their people, and themselves. I decided to write that book, following the immigration histories of three families from the homeland to the host country, from one generation to the next, through the experience of migration, adjustment, and finally identity formation in the host country. I would show how incredibly fragile a sense of social belonging really is. With a few hasty policy changes or rash media reports, social opinion can change drastically, threatening immigrants' opportunities for social belonging.

The three families you will meet in this book come from three very different places, and live in three different countries in the West, all major immigrant destinations with large Muslim immigrant communities. These families come from different socioeconomic, political, and ethnic backgrounds, but they are all Muslim. It should be noted, however, that this is not a book on theology or Islamic history. Although the stories in the book will refer to the ways in which the characters relate to Islam as they construct their identities, cope with adversity, or understand their roles in the world, this is not ultimately a book about Muslims but about immigrants. I am not concerned with religious practice so much as with social identity; I have chosen to write about Muslim immigrants rather than another group of immigrants simply because I believe that the social identity of Muslim immigrants stands under the greatest pressure of misunderstanding and mistrust throughout the world.

Nor is this book a piece of political advocacy. Some of the stories you will read here deal with politically sensitive or disputed histories. I have decided to let the characters of the book dictate how this material is presented, in order to illuminate how their interpretation of political history in their home countries has contributed to how they construct their identities, and I have only included events explicitly relevant to the personal histories of each character. I have chosen to use the names and terminology they used to describe political events and places, many of which have been named differently by people with differing interpretations of the history and politics. This book should not be read as an exhaustive discussion of histories and policies, nor as a piece of original scholarship that offers new historic interpretation or in-depth political analysis. It examines, rather, the narratives that individuals develop from their understanding of political events, policy changes, economic opportunities, and cultural life. This book is a forum for the individuals who appear here, for their opinions and experiences, and I have tried to show how they have interpreted their world in reaching a conclusion about their own place in it.

I set the book in three of the Western world's great metropoles: London, Berlin, and New York City. Although many immigration scholars and journalists have shown that, for a number of reasons, immigration to the West is no longer as city-oriented as in previous eras, I felt that placing the stories in cities was imperative to the narrative force of the stories themselves, and to illuminate the broader themes of the book. Nowhere is the theory of a conflict between Islam and the West more likely to founder than in a Western super city. In the modern world, civilizations do not have discrete borders. Instead, the content and shape of civilizations change within cities, where immigrant communities from all parts of the world are forced to rub shoulders, share neighborhoods, and develop an understanding of themselves relative to others. Additionally, the cities described here are home to the largest numbers of the immigrant communities I focused on in each of the three countries, and as such are a common element in the experiences of the broadest numbers in each community.

There are other major cities in the West with large Muslim immigrant populations, but I chose to focus on these three because they each act as the immigration capital in three countries whose immigration histories pose a particular contrast with one another. On the basis of its geopolitical history, each of these three countries offers a different social contract to its immigrants, and it is this social contract that immigrants consider, consciously or subconsciously, in formulating their expectations of their host society. The United Kingdom, as the preeminent imperial power of the nineteenth and early twentieth centuries, traditionally offered a social contract to former colonial subjects, or to members of its Commonwealth, and has only recently begun to devise an immigration and integration concept to cope with social cohesion and national security concerns. Germany lacked this ready channel of migration and never saw itself as an immigration destination. It has had to come to terms with long-standing social and economic cleavages between its native and non-native populations, the largest of which grew out of temporary guest worker populations staying on in the country long after the period of guest-worker recruitment had ended. The United States has long been held as an immigrant utopia, a place where individuals willing to work hard to achieve economic freedom were gladly welcomed, but has periodically had to address economic and national security concerns in the face of consistent and high levels of illegal immigration. In this book, you will see how the policy changes each government has introduced to cope with emerging social cohesion, national security, or economic stability concerns have affected the opportunities of individual immigrants, and have led immigrants to question the place in society they have carved out for themselves. The stories are not intended as a direct criticism or complete analysis of the policymaking processes in each of these countries, but rather to show how immigrant destinations have changed their social contracts in order to cope with political realities, how short-term vision in immigration policy formulation can have unforeseen long-term outcomes, and how a change in the social contract offered affects the social consciousness of individual immigrants.

I have also chosen to focus on three particular communities in order to highlight a set of contrasting community circumstances. I focused on the Arab community in London, itself a collection of several ethnic communities, whose activist core is upper middle class and secular. Britain's, and by extension London's, Arab population is dwarfed by the large, visible, and active South Asian Muslim community, which has taken the lead in defining British Muslim culture and setting its political agenda. I followed a Palestinian man from a powerful Jerusalem family and his strong, independent Syrian wife, and their son who, in spite of his relative wealth and high level of socioeconomic integration, struggles with feelings of alienation and anger over the hardships of the Palestinian people in Israel and its neighbor states. In Berlin, I wrote about the Turkish Kurdish community, a middle-class community composed of long-present guest workers and more recently arrived war refugees, whose collective character is defined largely by its nationalist struggle in the homeland. The Kurdish community has existed in a state between invisibility within and animosity toward the city's large and increasingly politically influential Turkish community. Indeed, many Kurds found their experiences with ethnic hostility and forced assimilation in Turkey replicated in Germany until the arrival of a later wave of Kurdish refugees fleeing the war between the Turkish government and Kurdish militants began to assert itself on Germany's immigrant political landscape. I followed a pioneering Kurdish farmer and his traditional, family-bound wife, and their daughter, the first woman in her family to graduate from a university, determined to forge a life based on the principles of humanitarian service, cultural pride, and feminism. In New York, I wrote about the South Asian Muslim community, a predominantly working-class, new community with a large undocumented population that suffered under mass security sweeps and detentions in the wake of September 11, 2001. I followed a gentle, scholarly Bangladeshi man and his individualistic, ambitious daughter, who married an undocumented Pakistani man in New York, going against cultural and legal mandates in order to pursue her version of middle-class American happiness. Although the experiences of the main characters depart from the majority experiences of their communities in many instances, all of them drew from their understanding of their communities' social and political standing to construct their identities.

My research methodology was largely journalistic, but I employed a number of different research techniques to help me variously fill out the narrative, place the stories in historic context, and provide them with a thematic framework. In order to reconstruct past events and frame the major issues facing each family, I relied heavily on in-depth biographical interviews with the members of the three main families, but also conducted extensive interviews with community political and cultural leaders, social-justice and activist organizations working on issues facing these communities, and with academics and political experts in each of the three countries who have focused on the related histories and political issues. I translated and interpreted all texts and interviews originally in German into English myself. I spent a good deal of time with each of the main characters, immersing myself in their lives and activities, and have included certain scenes derived from immersion reporting and observation. I compiled a bibliography of books and articles on history, political theory, and legal analysis relating to the regions, countries, and communities where each of the families moved, which I have included at the end of the book. I also tracked media reports on the leading immigration debates and analyses of Muslim communities published in each of the three cities, attended several conferences and public debates on these issues, and reviewed literary and film accounts of the experiences of members of these communities. In order to provide narrative or literary detail in instances where I was not present, I sometimes relied on the characters' memories and descriptions, as related in taped interviews and written accounts, but I often extrapolated from my own research and travels, and from my own understanding of the culture, geography, and practices of the sites and communities in which the book is set.

The book is divided into three sections, each dealing with different major themes. The first section addresses the themes of migration and memory. In this section, I describe the first generation's process of migration from home, and then trace its return migration through memory in old age. I explore how a conscious decision to migrate from circumstances of poverty or economic oppression, as opposed to a forced expulsion resulting from war or political change, shapes the first generation migrant's sense of optimism and self-determinism, and show how self-doubt and regret on the one hand, or success and contentment on the other, can color how immigrants view and narrate their own histories. How much autonomy an immigrant feels in making the decision to migrate determines whether or not the new life is embraced or whether it is seen as a long-term exile. Longing for home constitutes the basis for a family's ideal of home; the immigrant's stories and experiences become the foundation for the second generation's national myth, and later become crucial elements of the second generation's identity. Migration is often an incremental process, taking the migrant farther and farther from home in a series of small, calculated steps. Although immigration policy systems usually classify immigrants by category as either economic or political, this section will show how migrants can be both many times over during the course of their long journey from home.

The second section deals with the themes of integration and identity, tracing the process of identity construction among the second generation of immigrants, the children of the immigrants themselves. In this section, I introduce the concept of social contract between host country and immigrant, exploring the opportunities for or barriers to integration offered by each of the three destination countries. This section shows how the children of immigrants draw from their family culture and national myth to locate themselves in society, and how they use their own experiences to form a narrative of belonging in or exclusion from a host society. The section culminates with one moment of crisis for each of the characters, either in the homeland or in their personal lives, that changes their lives. Whether the crisis threatens their actual physical livelihood or compromises intangible feelings of purpose or belonging, each character will be faced with a decision on how to reconstitute professional goals, hopes for the future, and understanding of the social contract with the host government.

The final section deals with the themes of alienation and acceptance, faced by the individuals themselves, as well as across the societies in which they live. In this section, the reader will encounter the main characters coping with the aftermath of the crisis of either livelihood or faith that they faced in the previous section. This section takes place in the midst of an era in which the idea of a fundamental clash between Islam and the West has credence, making Muslim immigrants the subject of national scrutiny or security legislation. As they cope with their new understanding of their places in society, of their personal and professional values, and of their hopes for the future, the characters find that they must overcome new legal challenges or take risks that lift them out of their comfort zones. The characters ultimately seek help and security through a number of social institutions, be it family, religion, community, or the political system itself. Here I explore how the main characters' identities, opportunities, or senses of purpose have changed because of the laws, limitations, and prejudices they encounter.

This is a book of personal journeys, but it is also a book about the search for personal foothold during a major shift in the political paradigm of the day. Since the beginning of the twenty-first century, a new global paradigm has emerged, which has changed the way we understand our world. The concept of a fundamental clash between Islamic and Western culture, ideals, values, and politics has emerged, and the force of this ideology is undeniable. It often appears that the language of this so-called clash has seeped into the way cultural identity worldwide is produced, understood, and promoted. Recent immigration policy scholarship in Europe and in the United States has emphasized the importance of incorporating policies that promote long-term integration into immigration policy frameworks. But a global paradigm that glorifies the divisions between communities thwarts the fundamental force behind integration. Integration cannot occur through policy solutions alone. Fifty years after the introduction of racial desegregation policies in the United States, which ultimately have had little visible effect in the poor cities and rural areas across the country, it is clear that the core element of integration is emotional—people must feel they belong in a larger society, and the different subgroups in a society must feel a shared sense of destiny. With this book, I hope to offer an insight into the personal experiences and emotional lives of three Muslim immigrant families in the West. The one common sentiment that emerged in my travels within each community and in my conversations with each family was the desire for visibility and recognition on their own terms. The characters you meet here do not seek special treatment or privilege, just acceptance of their histories and concerns in the societies where they live, work, raise their families, and plan their futures. Whether these are read as simple stories or broader narratives, I hope to add their voices to the many speaking against the generalization, pre-judice, and fear that has so far surrounded Muslims living in the West.

PROLOGUE

A sporty black BMW rolls into the narrow alley shiny with rain far in London's southwest corner, and pulls up in front of the office for the Palestinian ambassador. It is November 16, 2004, just five days after Yasser Arafat, chairman of the Palestinian Liberation Organization, died, and Sharif Nashashibi and his mother Muna, both prominent British Arab activists, are coming to pay their respects and to meet with the ambassador. Sharif steps out of the driver's seat, wearing a fitted black shirt, his hair styled to look effortlessly groomed, trailing the faintest scent of fine cologne. As he stands beside the car, he looks almost like an advertisement with his chiseled features, his cool blue eyes, and his regal bearing. He scans the wet pavement and his lip curls in a slight sneer of distaste. He has just returned from a three-month-long consultancy in Ramallah, the capital of the Palestinian Authority in the West Bank, and he is not pleased to be back in London. It has only been four days since he returned, and already he feels the cold seeping into his bones and the hectic pace of London life knotting his shoulders. The sunlight and simple pleasures he had discovered in Palestine have taken on the qualities of a fantasy in his mind.

Sharif clicks the remote lock on the car door. His mother, a statuesque woman from whom her children inherited their attention to appearance and aura of breezy glamor, takes his arm. Wet gravel crunches beneath their shoes, echoing in the empty alleyway. They make their way toward the narrow, nondescript building, far removed from the grand embassy district in

Kensington, near their own home. As Sharif presses the buzzer on the unim-
pressive edifice, he reflects on the surreality of Arafat's death the day before
his arrival back home. Just yesterday, he attended a memorial put together by
members of a local Palestinian cultural organization, but he didn't stay for
long. He has spent much of the last three months railing against this man,
this icon, who remained firmly situated as the figurehead of the stillborn
Palestinian state until his death. But his feelings toward the man himself are
complicated. After all, Arafat was still the internationally recognized leader
of the Palestinian people, who spent his last years living like a rat under siege
in a destroyed compound, and whose death was surrounded by mystery and
speculation. Sharif knows people now who will be simultaneously elated and
saddened, hopeful and fearful of what might come next in Palestine.

Sharif is a descendant on his father's side of one of Jerusalem's oldest and
most powerful clans, the Nashashibis, who held positions of power in
Jerusalem from the fifteenth century right up until the creation of Israel, an
historically Western-educated, professional, literary, and political coterie
who still have prominence in Jerusalem and in the Palestinian government.
Sharif, however, was born in Kuwait thirty years after his father had been
exiled from Palestine, and did not find out he was Palestinian until he was
ten years old. He grew up in a stately three-story home in Knightsbridge,
tucked away in a little neighborhood of tree-lined cobblestone lanes and
tastefully decorated homes in central London, attending prestigious private
schools and vacationing in places like Cannes and Marbella. But as he educated himself about the history of Palestine, he cultivated an identity as an
outsider, finding his own good fortune meaningless unless he made himself
a voice for people who had been ignored and oppressed. When the second
Intifada broke out, he founded a media watchdog group in London, monitoring for discrimination and bias. But as Britain joined in on the global war
on terror declared by the United States, he found it harder and harder to
secure funding for an organization that published arguments in support of
controversial Palestinian and Arab figures. After a long struggle with depression and a mounting sense of purposelessness, he moved to Palestine on a
lark, and there found a sense of community and direction he had never

before imagined. When his consultancy there ended, he decided that he would return. He didn't know whether he would want to settle permanently in Palestine, but he was ready to make Ramallah his home.

Now he walks slowly up the stairs to the office of the Palestinian ambassador. The stairs are a mousy gray-brown color, spongy in texture, and the walls exhale stale cigarette smoke. They enter the ambassador's office, a small brown room with utilitarian furniture, low ceilings, and fluorescent lighting. The ambassador is alone in the building with just one older man, who lets the guests in downstairs. No security guards, pomp, or bon-vivant style normally seen among the diplomatic corps. Inside the office, the ambassador, a diminutive, tired-looking man in a pale blue shirt with rolled-up sleeves, hunches over his cluttered desk, clutching a pack of Marlboro Lights. Shrink-wrapped fruit baskets and cards, the remnants of a memorial reception for Arafat, clutter table-tops and chair seats. As Sharif and Muna enter the room, the ambassador rises to great them. He is distracted and weary, but offers them his usual hospitality. After a brief chat, Muna and Sharif take their leave, and Muna remarks that the ambassador's talents are wasted here, in a ceremonial role in a marginalized office on the outskirts of London. Sharif can't help but think that the corrupt and ineffective prime minister of the Palestinian Authority, for whom he has just been consulting, has it better than this. He himself can't wait to go back.

A cold, blue mist spills through Sukriye Dogan's bedroom window, just before nightfall on a dank Berlin afternoon in November 2003. She lies under three quilts, drowsing lightly, a shock of her black hair fanned across her white pillowcase. Her cell phone is tucked lovingly beneath her chin and her cordless phone receiver clutched in her right hand. On her bedside table sits a small bowl piled with different colored rocks—each one taken from the different lands of divided Kurdistan, which she has united in this small symbolic home far from Kurdish soil. At the top of the heap sits a rock from her childhood village, which was destroyed by Turkish military tanks in 1994, in the thick of the Turkish-Kurdish civil war. Until last month, Kurdistan had been the love of Sukriye's life, but now, for the first time, she is head over heels in love with a man, a man who lives in Syria and comes to her only through her telephone. Every night for the last two weeks she has spent at least four hours on the phone, and has been reduced to snatching sleep in naps. Now she dreams, her eyelids twitch, and she nestles closer to her cell phone. As she breathes in and out, its display screen fogs lightly.

Every window in her apartment is wide open. The walls and floor are cold. A small pot of water with jasmine oil simmers on the kitchen stove, coating the stale smoky air with a cloying sweetness. Last night, there had been intense conferences in this kitchen; bottles of wine were emptied, bags of olives eaten, a half-dozen packs of cigarettes were smoked. Sukriye had summoned a small crew of close friends and confidantes to her house for a planning session. Heads bent close together over a single candle and an ashtray in the middle of a scuffed wooden table, they discussed until nearly 3:00 a.m. the matter at hand—how she might sustain love with a man who lived in Syrian Kurdistan, surrounded by people who knew both of their families and who had little else to do but gossip, and under the scrutiny of a government hostile to the community in which he lived. But first, she had to break the exciting news: she was in love. First surprise, then disbelief, and finally whooping and teasing. The people gathered here had never before seen this particular combination of peace and hysteria in Sukriye's eyes. There was no doubt about it, their beloved Sukriye was indeed in love! After all these years, she had stepped onto the treadmill of joy and pain that had kept the rest of them running ragged for years.

"Who is it?" asked a young Kurdish man whose face was adorned with rectangular glasses and a picturesque mole. He was an acclaimed novelist from Syrian Kurdistan, himself soon to marry a young Kurdish woman whom he called the Zin to his Mem, after the Kurdish epic love poem. And he was also from the same hometown as Nezir, Sukriye's new beloved.

"Guess," Sukriye said, sucking on a pumpkin seed husk. "You know him."

"I know him?" asked the novelist.

"Yes."

Another man, a haggard-looking poet, who had once tutored a teenaged Sukriye in the Kurdish language and had since become one of her dearest friends, erupted in giggles, because he had already learned who the mystery man was. A Yezidi man who had barely escaped from Syria with his life many years before and had literally carried his mother on his back into Germany, the poet had broken his heart in a tragic love affair with a Muslim Kurdish woman. He had called Sukriye countless times over the years during emergencies of the heart, and now could hardly contain his delight at finally returning the favor. He grinned at the novelist and pulled another cigarette from his pack. Sukriye reached over and took it from his hand without taking her eyes off of the novelist's face.

The novelist sat silent for a moment, fingering his wine glass. "Nezir would be good."

"You're right." He and Sukriye regarded each other, expressionless. "It's him." Two beats. "Nezir." Sukriye's face broke into a broad smile.

Then, she planted both her elbows on the table and asked them to help her develop a strategy: how and where can I see him? There were two major obstacles to a rendezvous. First, Nezir was, like both the novelist and the poet, a stateless Kurd from Syria. Without a passport, he could only travel to a limited number of places. Second, they were not married. They discussed and dismissed possibilities. He could sneak across the border to Turkey, but she couldn't come there without her family finding out. The same if she went to his village in Syria. He could ride in a goods transport truck into Iraq, but the war there continued to pound away with increasing violence and bloodshed. He could smuggle himself into Iran, but unmarried couples risk stoning if they are caught there. The novelist, a hopeless romantic, suggested they get married, and Sukriye scoffed as she poured herself a healthy serving of wine. "Please, after two months of telephone calls I should marry him? Come on." The poet, an even more hopeless romantic, and with a fatalistic streak to boot, suggested that Nezir smuggle himself to Germany in a shipping container. Of course, he might die, but he might not, and what a romantic miracle it would be if he didn't!

Sukriye didn't even answer him, just lit another cigarette and rested her chin on her palm. When the United States had launched its invasion of Iraq earlier in the year, she, like most Kurds, was elated at the possibility that at least one part of Kurdistan might become free. And when she had visited

Iran as a student, she had enjoyed the connection she had felt as a speaker of a Persic language. But now, when she contemplates these places, she sees only obstacles.

She has been neglecting her job and neglecting her health, and last month alone she spent nearly 1,000 euros on phone calls to Syria. She has practically stopped eating or sleeping, has all but given up entertaining, and has taken up smoking. This is most definitely not like Sukriye, a strong and stable feminist, activist, social worker, and scholar, but also a gifted cook and hostess. She has just finished her master's degree in educational sciences and pedagogy, and for years now she has worked as a counselor and interpreter in psychotherapeutic institutions for refugees surviving rape, torture, and other violent instruments of war. For the better part of her life, she has been the one everyone else came to, teary-eyed, with their dramatic love stories and their epic refugee tales. She was the eye of the storm, the one no one could shake, the first to put a kettle on for tea and sit down for a good listen. But now she has found herself the most perfect and most unlikely partner. And she is the one who isn't eating, isn't sleeping, who is interested in only one topic and obsessing about immigration laws.

In her heart, she knows she will marry him. But she also knows that she will have to take on two of the most rigid governmental structures she can imagine. The Syrian government won't want to let him go, for fear that if empowered he might bring some sort of action against the government for its forty-year-long persecution of stateless Kurds living without rights or freedoms in their land. And the German government won't want to let him in, fearing that he might have ties with some militant organization on its antiterrorism watch list, and that as a stateless person he could not be deported. But for the time being, Sukriye just snuggles in a little bit deeper to enjoy her nap. Soon, she'll have to do battle for this man, but for now, she just wants to love him.

It is August 18, 2004, and tomorrow is the eighth anniversary of Nishat Islam's arrival in America from Dhaka, Bangladesh. The late summer air boils off the sidewalk and wafts into her apartment in Queens, New York City. As she drops herself into her chair to eat some warmed-up egg curry, she mutters half to herself, half to God, that she has nothing to celebrate. She bends low over her plate, and the fingers of the setting sun stroke her head. Her henna-streaked red-black-brown hair glows like heated wires. She silently thrusts a palmful of balled-up egg curry and rice into her mouth and gags. It is her first meal of the day. She hasn't seen her husband in over two years, since he offhandedly told her he was going to stop off to register with the United States government on his way to the work one spring morning. Like her, he was an illegal immigrant. But he was a perfume seller, and not a terrorist. Still, that day he was locked up in an immigration detention center, and Nishat hasn't seen him since. She often forgets to eat and can't make herself sleep at night. She spends most of her days in this apartment, brooding about the future, obsessing about the past.

Behind her, her three-year-old daughter Ayesha yelps and howls, and her one-year-old son Rasha begins to whimper from his crib. Nishat turns and barks roughly over her shoulder, "Hey, shut up! Shut up!" Ayesha stops and stares at her mother, her chubby arms limp at her sides, her round gourd of a tummy hanging over the top of her panties. Fat tears fill her great round eyes. She theatrically sticks her thick lower lip out and furrows her brow. "Mommy?" she pleads. Nishat sighs impatiently, pushes the still full plate from her, and sits back in her rickety metal and vinyl chair. Then she gets up, steps over the short plywood child-gate her father has built in the kitchen doorway and washes her hands. She pulls a bag of betel nut, some loose tobacco, some lime paste and betel leaves from a cabinet with ill-fitting doors. She smears the lime paste on the leaves and rolls herself a *paan*, which she thrusts in her mouth. She sets some tea on the stove and leans against the counter, studying her hands with a scowl.

Nishat, her two children, and her father live on the state assistance her daughter receives for her rehabilitation from a congenital birth defect, on food stamps and a housing subsidy, from a small stipend she's gotten from a social justice organization, and from the money her father earns peddling drawings in Central Park. Her life is beholden to the state and the weather. She has no future ahead of her, no promise for financial success, and almost as little hope for saving her marriage. She hasn't worked in over a year, and she is beginning to understand that her husband will never be able to come back to the home they've built here. The choice she faces is this: she can either leave America and give up her chance of coming back in order to be with him, or she can hold out for some legal miracle that she can get amnesty, citizenship, and sponsor her husband back to her. If she is honest with herself, she knows that if she stays she has to sacrifice her marriage. She is still looking for a way to keep both America and her husband, consulting with social justice organizations, giving interviews with major newspapers, and talking to other people who are in her situation. But most days, she only feels bitter, cheated, and utterly alone. She wants someone to tell her what to do, because right now her life is at a standstill.

She has been cagey and irritable every day this week. This morning, she left her apartment to visit an Indian palm reader just down the road in the heart of Jackson Heights, Queens, partly for diversion, partly for answers. Past the cash-and-carry grocery stores, the sweet shops, the *dhabas* selling greasy Punjabi fast food, past the sari shops and jewelry emporiums, all full of things she could not afford, and up a dark staircase she went to the palm reader. She carried these questions clenched in her hands: What should she do? Should she just give up and go back to Bangladesh? Should she stay and wait for something to change? If she stayed, would she be able to find work and have a good life? If she left, would her husband take her back and join her in Bangladesh? After two years apart, her husband would certainly doubt her fidelity. Should she choose him, or should she choose America?

She sat with the palm reader for over an hour and waited for her answers. She has asked lawyers and counselors and God, and finally she asked this short, balding Indian man before her. The palm reader told her that her heart line, which forms a ladle in her palm, indicates that she has the capacity for great success in business, if only she could learn to control her emotions and approach life with greater rationality. Then he gave her some boilerplate personality analysis and asked for his payment. She complained loudly to herself the whole way back home. As she leans over her counter, Nishat snorts derisively and gulps down her tea, thick with condensed milk. It's not her emotions standing in the way of her success, it's the laws of this land, she says sharply to the stuffy air. She heads into the bathroom; it's time for prayer.

She removes her gold bracelets and fat costume jewelry rings, she removes her thick imitation gold necklace and washes the makeup from her face. She changes out of her cheaply made beaded dress and into loose turquoise pajamas and a long fuchsia housecoat. She wraps an embroidered cotton scarf around her head and neck and unrolls a prayer mat in the narrow space between her bed and the wall. But she doesn't kneel down to pray just yet. She walks over to her wardrobe and pulls out a sheer pink lingerie set with a flouncy robe she's bought for when she sees her husband again. It too is cheaply made. She holds it up against her body, against her prayer clothes, and preens for the mirror. She tortures herself like this every day—neither rejecting her hope for married happiness nor completely embracing life in America. She hangs up the lingerie and sits on the bed for a short, harsh cry. Then she kneels down to pray.

PART I

MIGRATION AND MEMORY

CHAPTER 1

THE NASHASHIBIS' FAIRY TALE

In the cozy, chaotic den on the second floor of her central London home, Muna Nashashibi moves slowly between the couch and the low coffee table cluttered with newspapers in Arabic and English. It is a cold winter evening, and she is looking for her last pill of the day. The television broadcasts an Arabic news channel, and the news is of bloodshed in Iraq, of bloodshed in Palestine. Every few minutes she sits back down on the couch and, as she catches her breath from the exertion of minor movements, she squints at the television screen, her face angry and sad. She grabs a stack of papers and begins leafing through them, then restlessly changes the channel, her pill for the moment forgotten. Even though her body is tired, her mind refuses to rest. She was born in Iraq, raised in Syria, and married to a Palestinian, and on the news, she sees the places of her past burning. She gathers her news from British and European news channels as well, but she prefers the Arabic broadcasts; although her English is flawless, she often finds that European news channels get the story wrong, sometimes missing the important story altogether.

Outside her window, night has fallen velvety and quiet over London, which has been her hometown for twenty-three years, and every street she turns here is crowded with memories, landmarks of her past. She moved to London, into this very home, at the peak of her husband Hikmat's success, after she had taken a break from her own thriving career to have her first two children. Now, her three children are grown, and although they all still live at home, the house seems to grow quieter every year.

23

The downstairs is elegant and cold and still, like a museum of Arab objects d'art after hours. To the right of the front door is a ceramic tile with "Hikmat & Mona Nashashibi" printed on it in both English and Arabic calligraphy. The door opens into a broad foyer of mirror and marble, which leads to an opulent sitting room full of ornate pieces of brass and silver and fine inlay work, glinting now even in the darkness. But the family never enters through the front door and rarely spends time in the living room, unless they are entertaining the many intellectuals, activists, and Arab community leaders who often come to visit. Instead, Muna, her children, and her sister Maha congregate upstairs, in this room which serves as a den, a workroom, a library, and a conference room for Muna and her eldest son, Sharif, to plan their projects together.

Earlier this year, Muna underwent three heart surgeries, first to unblock her coronary artery, then to address complications and then still more complications. She knows she should rest more, but the news from the Middle East is relentless and, as a lifelong activist, Muna can't let herself just sit still. Muna has never been good at letting illness dictate what she can and cannot do, and she has spent her life dealing with complications.

Her family and Hikmat's family both struggled through the ravages of war, political turmoil, and exile before the two of them found each other. Together, they turned their backs to the struggles of the past and built a fairy-tale life, complete with annual Cannes vacations, nannies for the children, and the best home money could buy. She knows she has been the target of envy—for her life, her home, her love. But she also knows that she has fought for these things—through market crashes and her husband's depression, through her own illness, and through devastating family tragedies. She has fought with self-confidence and absolute determination, and with fierce protectiveness of her family. And so, even though she is ill and tired, even though she is steadily approaching old age, she cannot quite leave off the habit of worrying and planning and taking charge. In fact, just yesterday, she coordinated a group of friends to participate in a protest on behalf of the besieged families in Falluja, Iraq in front of the Parliament building, standing in a cold, misting rain for much longer than she should have.

Muna loves her homeland and thinks often and warmly of her happy childhood in Syria. But she keeps herself too busy to miss it for long. She thinks of her memories as old friends; she enjoys having them to visit, is not opposed to lingering with them over tea, but she would not want them to move in and take over her life. She knows she will never feel completely at home in London, but it is the only home her children know. And as long as her children are happy and near her, she is content to live her life far from the sun. For Muna, home has always been where her family is. For Hikmat, who lost his own homeland as a child, home became Muna.

Hikmat Nashashibi was six years old when his family fled Jerusalem in April 1948. When they crossed into Lebanon, never to return, he was asleep on his mother's lap. They planned to stay with his mother's family in Beirut for a couple of months, just until the violence between Jewish and Arab militias settled down. But just weeks after the Nashashibis left, when the British Mandate ended, Israel declared itself an independent Jewish state and the violence between militias exploded into a full-scale war between the new state and its Arab neighbors. When the war ended, hundreds of thousands of Palestinians were homeless, and the Nashashibis' palatial home was left straddling the line dividing Jerusalem between Israel and Jordan. The Nashashibi family had become exiles.

As they fled, the night sky above Jerusalem was purple, mottled and bruised from the explosions that shook their neighborhood every day now. Hikmat's father, Sharif Aref Nashashibi, rode beside the driver in silence, the deed to his house and his diploma from Oxford tucked into the inner lining of his jacket. His mother, Inaam, sat huddled between her two daughters, Aisha and Aida, with Hikmat on her lap. She carried the key to their home in her bra. How they must have flinched every time they heard gunfire or another explosion, as they raced away from home with their three sleepy children. They would have had no thought to look back at the home they would never see again, on a gentle slope surrounded by rose bushes, jasmine vines, and orange trees, its stained-glass windows dark. There had been no time to think about the future or commemorate the past, just to gather the "basic necessities" and rush to the car. Yet years later, as she lay dying of cancer in Beirut, Inaam described in precise detail the ornate stonework of their home and the exact fragrance of their garden in summer to her son. Although she died a widow in a country that had denied her exiled husband opportunity or hope, she would always see herself as the proud wife of a gentleman, a scholar, and a Nashashibi.

Sharif and Inaam never discussed permanent migration as an option. In fact, they never considered it. Sharif, an Oxford University graduate who was headmaster at a prestigious school and a scion of an elite Jerusalem family, had no intention of leaving his life behind. They were simply exercising their privilege, as well-situated people, to protect their three young children from the misery of war. Yes, the roads were unsafe, but staying had become far more dangerous. During the last year, Jerusalem had suffered under riots, a siege, and terrorist attacks on British offices and civilian neighborhoods. Schools and British administration offices closed. Armed Jewish and Arab militias clashed in nearby villages and sniped at each other across city streets. Reports of massacres in Arab villages and rumors of worse spread to induce widespread panic, and even before the war broke out, thousands of Arabs began fleeing to family and friends in the neighboring Arab states. By the end of the war, some 800,000 Arabs had fled Palestine to become one of the world's largest permanent refugee populations. Only after the war had ended would Sharif realize that neither he nor any of the generations that followed him could return home.

The same war that made Hikmat Nashashibi an exile made six-year-old Muna Abdelahad, his future wife, a Syrian. She was born in Iraq to Arab Christian parents—an Iraqi father and a Lebanese mother. At the time of her birth, those lands were not yet nations, but rather strategic territories divided among the victorious Western powers after the First World War. Muna's father, Jamil, had been given a Syrian passport to work for the Syrian Petroleum Company in Tripoli, and retained it when he had gone on to work as a wireless engineer for Syrian Airlines. When Syria went to war with the newly declared state of Israel, all airline personnel at once became Arab soldiers. Jamil belonged to a generation of well-educated, liberal-minded Arabs who yearned for the haphazardly divided Arab lands to be reunified, even if by war. More than Iraqi or Syrian, he saw himself as an Arab, so when joining the war effort meant pledging unswerving allegiance to Syria and foreswearing his Iraqi citizenship, Jamil didn't think twice.

Israel's declaration of independence was one of the pivotal events to inspire the nascent pan-Arab consciousness sweeping through the Arab upper middle class. It gave the infant movement a cause and sense of purpose. The defeat of the Arab states in the in the 1948 war as came to be known in Arabic as *al-Nakba*, "the disaster." That defeat and the Palestinian refugee crisis became the greatest symbol of shared Arab loss, and the greatest single fuel of pan-Arab consciousness.

Pan-Arabism drove many political changes in the region, but it also fostered the creation of a regional migration sphere that would alter regional socioeconomic dynamics and heavily influence two generations of middle-class Arab identity. As many Arab states stagnated under political turmoil and economic instability, many members of this middle class, including Hikmat Nashashibi and Muna Abdelahad, would pursue opportunities first within the Arab region, then in the cities of the West. And there, their pan-Arab ideology would dominate the cultural identity of the Arab diaspora. Even as the Arab states themselves forged and broke alliances, developing post-pan-Arab policies, members of the Arab diaspora would feel the influence of pan-Arab thinking. Pan-Arabism would bring Hikmat and Muna together, and would later shape the cultural identity and life work of their firstborn son, Sharif, as a media and political activist in London.

But it was not pan-Arabism that brought Hikmat and Muna, separately, to Kuwait. Jamil Abdelahad, Muna's father, was driven from Syria for his political beliefs, from his chosen home by his own people, and he sought refuge in Kuwait. Hikmat's family had been driven from their ancestral home by foreigners, and had failed to find hospitality and opportunity in Lebanon, so he looked to Kuwait as a refuge from that refuge. When Hikmat and Muna married, they came together as exiles, both committed to political and economic reform as a way to reclaim their lost past. Their marriage was a union of wills and a shared vision for the economic and political rebirth of the Arab region.

Jamil Abdelahad fled Syria in 1967 as an enemy of the state, after twenty years of life as a Syrian. His involvement with a right-wing party had put him at odds with the leftist Ba'ath regime that had taken over the government. As the Ba'ath regime grew in power, it grew in intolerance toward opposition, and Jamil soon became the target of a campaign of police terror. He escaped with his life to Kuwait, but his wife Nura stayed behind with his two daughters, Muna and Maha, while Maha completed her schooling. Syria was the only home Jamil's daughters had ever known, and their loyalty to Syria would never waver despite the resentment they must have felt for their father's troubles. Later, on cozy evenings in London, the two aging sisters would speak with effusive warmth and nostalgia of Syria, giggling over pictures and anecdotes, and proud of their Syrian dialect and heritage.

The same year Jamil fled, Israel launched a strike against Egypt, and in the war that followed, Israel annexed the Gaza Strip and Sinai Peninsula from Egypt, the West Bank from Jordan, and the Golan Heights from Syria. The war was sudden and acute. It seemed that one moment radios blared with rousing announcements and reports that the enemy was swarming in the skies like insects, only to fall silent in defeat mere days later. Life in Aleppo, the northern Syrian town where the Abdelahad family lived, remained largely unchanged, but Syria's loss was symbolic and profound. Although the tight-knit Abdelahad family weathered the separation and was reunited shortly afterward, the Levant remained divided. Later in life, Muna would remember an idyllic childhood, followed by a painful but brief family crisis that served as a sort of crucible for her personal growth. After her family was reunited, they enjoyed many years of shared joy and happiness, and so the sadness of their separation grew manageable in retrospect. But the division of the Arab lands was a wound that always caused her pain.

Muna grew up in a household and a nation dedicated to the cause of Syrian nationalism and Arab unity. After Syria's first military coup in 1949, the two main parties dominating the political landscape offered two different visions of Arab unity. The Ba'ath party called for the liberation of the Arab nation from narrow, parochial state boundaries, and was influenced by Marxist socialism. Its opposition party, influenced by German fascism, was the Syrian Socialist National Party (SSNP), which called for the creation of one "Greater Syria" from the union of Lebanon, Syria, Cyprus, Palestine, Jordan, Iraq, and Kuwait. But both parties spoke to the same national spirit and competed for the favor of Syria's large and growing middle class. Jamil and Nura became active in the SSNP in Damascus after the 1948 war ended, and remained involved with the party after moving to Aleppo, in the north of the country, in 1951.

For some time, the family's life in Aleppo was peaceful and prosperous. Jamil held a prestigious job as sales manager at Ford Motors, and Muna attended the only English-medium school in town, St. Paul's. Nura's parents lived close by, and they stopped by every day to spend time with Nura and her second-born baby daughter, Maha. The girls grew to womanhood in a warm and chatty household, full of guests. Aleppo was a genteel city, home to merchants and landowners, with fifteen schools scattered across it. Its population was a multiethnic collection of Arabs, Jews, Kurds, and Armenian refugees from Turkey, divided between different city quarters. Upper-middle-class Muslim and Christian boys and girls mixed freely in co-ed sports tournaments held at clubhouses. Although girls may have lived with more restriction in less affluent, more conservative, or Muslim households, Muna and Maha were encouraged to think, read foreign books, and to join in discussions with adults. Muna spent afternoons knitting with her mother and listening to the radio, and in the evening the family gathered for boisterous discussions of everything from sports to agriculture. Muna still has pictures of herself on beach vacations on the Lebanese coast, in a bikini with heeled sandals, her hair loose and soft about her face.

In the many years since, Aleppo has changed a great deal. It remains a genteel, slow-paced city, a place of night-blooming jasmine and outdoor cafés, but decidedly more conservative. Fewer women walk the tree-lined streets now, and many more of those who do are covered in the full black *abayas* common in the Persian Gulf countries. Co-ed athletics and short skirts in public are things of the past. Some childhood residents of Aleppo blame this conservatism on the infusion of the conservative Gulf culture of the 1980s, brought back by return migrants who had been forced to seek work in those countries as Syria's economy struggled through several decades of political turmoil and botched reform in the agricultural and industrial sectors. After all, migration not only transforms societies in host countries, but can alter the culture and politics of the societies left behind.

Aleppo was decidedly less political than Damascus in the 1950s, but as the Ba'ath regime gained power, consequences of political dissent could be felt in all parts of the country. It soon became apparent that Jamil and Nura had chosen the wrong side. In 1955, the leadership of their party, the SSNP, was accused of plotting to overthrow the government, and many of its key members fled the country or were convicted of conspiracy. Emerging from a series of government upheavals and a short-lived union with a dominant Egypt, Syria's Ba'ath party continued to grow less and less tolerant of dissent.

By the end of 1966, the secret police were coming for Jamil every other day. He had lost his job as a sales manager at Ford Motors after the company stopped importing cars to Syria in 1965. He had soon taken a new job, but the police came for him at work before he could even settle in. The first time he was arrested, he was shocked and humiliated that he, a loyal Syrian and veteran, could be arrested and held without charge. He was not allowed to call his wife. When he arrived home after twenty-four hours, he told her it would surely not happen again, and when he said it, he believed it. But it did happen again, and it kept on happening for months. It became impossible for him to keep a job, because he never knew when he would be taken in for questioning and held without charge. Muna describes the period as a time of intense anxiety for all of them. Finally, remembers Muna, her father stormed into the police station in anger, shouting that they should either charge him or just leave him be! It was a risky move to provoke the authorities in his position—who knew what excuse they might need to take him away for more than one night, or for longer still?

On a balmy evening in 1967, Jamil Abdelahad called his wife and his two daughters into the kitchen. He shuttered the windows and told them to sit. He began to discuss the pros and cons of leaving Syria forever versus staying on and facing the secret police. If he left, he would never be able to return, he said, but if he stayed, well, he let his voice trail off. His wife Nura's eyes were ringed with shadows. Muna, twenty-four, sat perfectly straight, her finely penciled eyebrows drawn together. Maha, fifteen, looked from her sister to her mother, fidgeting slightly. The drunken scent of night-blooming jasmine that normally fills Aleppo's evening air must have seemed inappropriately sweet outside that particular kitchen window on that particular night.

The last time the police had come for him, he had been held for only twelve hours, much less time than some of his previous detentions. But they had still not told him what he was being charged with, if anything, and he knew they would come again. And again and again, until they decided what they wanted to do with him. His life wavered precariously on someone else's fingertips. Neither his wife nor his two daughters argued with him to stay. It was agreed. In the morning, he would begin discreetly contacting people outside of Syria to find opportunities for work. And as soon as something could be found, he would leave. For the time being, Nura and the girls would have to stay here. He would try to call and send money until they could join him abroad. He eventually found opportunity in Kuwait, and fled overland to safety under cover of night.

After her father's departure, Muna took over as head of the family. Her mother, weakened by worry, was glad for her strong-willed daughter to take charge, and Muna was a natural leader. Her instinctive response to adversity was authoritative determination, and this family crisis served almost as a chrysalis for her to develop into a kind of iron-winged butterfly, a woman who was both feminine and formidable, deeply attached to family yet fiercely independent, driven by ambition, but also capable of extreme sacrifice.

It was true that Muna had grown up in a liberal household, where, as she says, "I was given the freedoms that were allowed at the time, but I always wanted more." Her parents encouraged her to study, to work, and to think for herself. She could go out with friends, and she had suitors, including an Italian playboy who took her out on dates in his red Alfa Romeo convertible. But upbringing can only go so far in explaining her strong character. Something in the core of her personality made Muna infinitely confident in herself, her abilities, and her opinions. It is easy to believe that her inner character emerged because she lived in a tolerant household in a fairly liberal city during a period of national identity formation, because of her family's commitment to progressive thinking and her particular educational opportunities. But perhaps her self-confidence, ambition, and natural leadership qualities would have emerged anyway, because a person's character doesn't form but exists. After all, the effect of external influences on personal identity is difficult to quantify. One thing was certain; Muna's characteristic self-confidence opened the door to many opportunities that many women have avoided for fear of defying certain social, cultural, or political limitations.

Her experiences indicate that the restrictive misogyny so often ascribed to predominantly Muslim societies may not be the universal or even standard experience of women who live there, and is not as rigid and insurmountable as prejudice would have us believe. Just as Western cities have a complex social fabric stitched together from the diverse experiences of their residents, each of whom has a unique family history, political belief system, and socioeconomic circumstance, so do predominantly Muslim cities. Just as Western societies include immigrant and minority communities, so do predominantly Muslim societies. We must be careful not to assume that a woman who grew up in northern Syria in the 1950s fits into a given stereotype. Muna may not represent all women of her generation who grew up in Syria, but her independence and ambition were formed because of her experiences in Syria. Early on, she sought a life of professional success, and in doing so overcame many gender and age boundaries. Crossing national boundaries would later seem easy.

After she sat for the national high school examinations in both Arabic and English curricula, Muna enrolled at the University of Aleppo, where she studied law full time, while she also worked as an instructor teaching English at the Syrian Teachers' Institute. When she graduated, she was hired at the Aleppo Chamber of Commerce, where, she recalls, no woman had ever worked before, and the person closest to her in age was a good thirty years her senior. In order to support her mother and sister, she also kept her job as an English instructor, and took on a third job translating from English to Arabic. Muna's days were long, but she was driven by a kind of nervous energy.

Since Jamil had gone, the Abdelahad household, once so hospitable and constantly full of guests, became more reclusive. There were brief, fiery fights between Muna and Nura, between Muna and Maha, but the three remained close and depended on each other a great deal. After all, missing someone is lonely business, and at times, it seemed that no one could understand them but each other. Phone connections to Kuwait were terrible and had to be booked hours, sometimes days, ahead of time with three international operators. And the few precious moments of conversation in hurried shouts could be interrupted without warning.

Muna was twenty-six when she joined her father in exile, along with her mother and younger sister. There had never been a question that the family should, above all, reunite. Their migration was follow-up migration, more of a resolution to an extended period of limbo than an independent decision to leave their country. As soon as Maha completed high school in 1969, the three women began their preparations to join Jamil in Kuwait. Although none of them discussed it, they knew they would only return to Syria as visitors. Home was, after all, where their family could live as one whole.

Much of the migration in the region at this time was motivated by political necessity, conflict, and exile. Not only had the formation of Israel destabilized its borders with all of its neighbors but those neighbor states themselves were going through at times very rocky transitions from colonial satellites to young nations, often without a viable economic or political infrastructure. Syria was not the only state in the region to struggle with recurring military coups, dictatorship, and oppressive political regimes. And the Abdelahads were not the only Arabs who sought refuge in other countries within the region. But within a period of years, as the Gulf states gained a massive windfall of wealth from the oil boom of the 1970s, the dominant character of regional migration would change from political to economic. This would change the character of the region forever, but would also reinvigorate political migrants to seek economic and therefore political reform. As Muna left her elegant and quietly noble home city behind for the commercial bustle of the Persian Gulf, she could not know how drastically the Kuwaiti expatriate community of political and economic reformers would shape her own life.

On a hill in Jerusalem stands a spacious building with large windows and broad steps leading to a grand entranceway, with high ceilings and several rooms, a building which was once the private residence of Sharif Aref Nashashibi, his wife Inaam, and his three children. To the side of the front door, a plaque states that the building was liberated by the Israeli army in 1967. Although once surrounded by a lush garden of rose bushes, jasmine vines, and orange trees, with intricate stained glass windows, it now sits on a dusty plot of land, its windows fitted with iron bars. It is now the Israeli labor court. One reason why the loss of Arab lands in the 1967 war will always hurt Muna is that this war made permanent the exile of her future husband, Hikmat Nashashibi.

For the first year following their flight from Jerusalem in April 1948, the Nashashibis believed that they would return to Palestine at the end of a brief war. The cash and jewelry, the antique pocketwatch and gemstone brooch, all that they had hastily grabbed the night of their flight, were soon sold or spent, but Sharif, Hikmat's father, could tolerate accepting charity from his wife's family as long as he knew it was temporary. Sharif was a proud man, an intellectual and a nobleman, unfamiliar with the pity and mild contempt so often bestowed upon refugees and the poor. He never prepared himself for the worst outcome of the war—permanent exile. Instead he focused his worry elsewhere, perhaps on his former colleagues and neighbors, or how much time his children were missing from school, or his house and collection of rare books. Meanwhile, as he dreamt about rebuilding his life in Jerusalem, nearly 128,000 Palestinian refugees flooded over the border into Lebanon. Unlike most of them, the Nashashibis did not have to live in flimsy tents and on intermittent food aid supplied by the International Red Cross. But when the news came that the war was over and that the new Israeli borders were closed to refugees hoping to return home, a right given to them in a UN General Assembly resolution passed in December 1948, Sharif hardly felt lucky. In fact, he was crushed. For days, he sat as still and pale as a ghost, poring over the deed to his house and his diploma from Oxford, the hastily snatched remnants of his lost life. He knew this respected diploma would do little to spirit him past the fortress of restrictions Lebanon had built around its job market against Palestinian refugees. And the carefully preserved deed and plan to his massive house would not buy him even the smallest apartment in Beirut's shabbiest quarter.

Sharif was not the only Palestinian refugee who would have to brave the severe restrictions the Lebanese government imposed in order to discourage the refugee Palestinians' integration into the Lebanese economy. Housing development was prohibited, employment of Palestinians was restricted, and martial law reigned inside the refugee camps. By 1950, the international humanitarian community acknowledged that the Palestinian refugee crisis necessitated a longer-term solution, and that year, the United Nations Relief and Works Agency for Palestinan Refugees (UNRWA) was established, with a broad mandate to address health, educational, and humanitarian needs for the residents of Lebanon's refugee camps. Unfortunately, UNRWA was rarely given the funding and political power to carry through that mandate and to address the real problems resulting from the creation of a permanent refugee population that would neither be absorbed into Lebanese society nor given a homeland of its own.

Aid workers, academics, lawyers, and policymakers have a wide array of definitions and categories for refugees, described in different ways to justify the various solutions they propose to mitigate or end each refugee crisis. Broadly defined, refugees are groups of people fleeing persecution, war, or natural disaster, and asylum seekers are individuals seeking temporary or permanent asylum in another country. The first is a negative definition, people who are leaving something behind, and calls for a humanitarian response. The second is a positive definition, and demands a policy solution that would make way for the future. Both the humanitarian and policy solutions for refugee crises are aimed at allaying the refugees' fears and providing them with a basis from which to approach the future, in either the short or long term. If refugees know they have lost much, but can rebuild their lives in a new homeland, they may begin to heal from the trauma of sudden loss and separation from home. But something changes in the psychology of those who never feel that they have control over their own life, who never feel a sense of belonging in their new life. They never feel secure, and their life becomes a singular quest for that security.

Until his sixth year, Hikmat's family had been respected, admired, and envied, leading characters in one city's pageant. Hikmat had played in long corridors and halls with great, vaulting ceilings, and had slept in his own bed. When his father spoke, other men had listened to him. His mother had met often with a group of stylish and perfumed ladies, and she had moved among them with regal poise, smiling graciously. They had gone on shopping trips to Jaffa and day trips to Jericho to swim in the Dead Sea. But now, his family was poor and anonymous, at the mercy of family members he had never known, of strangers who could refuse them food, service, or jobs, and of soldiers ringing the refugee camps. Very quickly after the end of the war, the Nashashibis had become second-class members in the household, the poor cousins who had nothing to offer, but many needs. The daily snubs fell hardest on the girls, but even Hikmat could see that they were not wanted. Now, the only educational opportunities available to Hikmat and his sisters were the UNRWA schools in the refugee camps, overcrowded makeshift classrooms without enough books to go around. Sharif suffered regularly from crushing depression, and Inaam was often short and irritable with the children. Hikmat was young enough to adapt to a poorer life, but watching his parents change so drastically was harder to get used to.

Growing up in the shadow of his father's misery, Hikmat learned at a very early age of the permanence of loss. One of the precious illusions of childhood is that nothing really bad can happen—to most children, pain is like a bruised knee, just a temporary setback, and loss is a favorite toy soon forgotten. But watching parents struggle, fade, and weaken can teach the harsh lesson that pain can fail to heal, that loss can cripple, and that things can change forever. In many ways, Sharif's wound permanently scarred Hikmat's innocence. As he grew into adulthood, Hikmat himself began to struggle with crippling bouts of suicidal depression, which would resurface each time he experienced feelings of impotence in the face of great loss.

Sharif could only stay at a job long enough for his welcome as a Palestinian to wear out, and could never earn enough for the family to amass a reasonable amount of savings. So he decided to seek work in Iraq, where society was reputed to be more hospitable to Palestinians. This migration was not a major step for the Nashashibis, who had already become exiles from home. Whether they lived on the fringes of Lebanese society or scrambled to make the most of possibilities in Iraq, they were still barred from Jerusalem. In Iraq, Sharif was able to secure a position as inspector for Arabic-language publications in Iraq, but the position only lasted until 1958, when the Iraqi monarchy surrendered to a military coup. In the midst of political tumult once again, Sharif and his family found themselves packing by night to return to Lebanon.

For Hikmat, the only way out of poverty and life on the fringes of society was education. He threw himself into his studies, and when he graduated from the UNRWA school, he won two full scholarships at one time, first to the International College, and then to study business at the American University of Beirut. He stayed with his family at night and fled to the refuge of the university during the day.

In 1961, just four months before Hikmat was to graduate from university, his father died, and Hikmat once again experienced profound loss. He spent the last of his money on the remainder of his education, pushing through his grief and the looming threat of depression in order to qualify himself for a high-paying, secure job. This was not the first time Hikmat felt the jaws of depression opening beneath him, and although he escaped it this time, he knew there would be times when it would get the better of him, just as it had broken his father in the end. Although the doctors said that he had died from heart disease, it was just as easy for Hikmat to believe that his father had died of sorrow and shame. Hikmat told himself that if he worked hard and built himself a secure life, he might be able to shield himself from this kind of gut-wrenching loss, and he might be able to stay above depression's undertow.

Hikmat buried himself in his studies, reading long papers on investment and financial institutions. He knew that Palestine must be reclaimed and rebuilt by Palestinians, if only within the remnants of the former land that still remained in Palestinian hands. He believed that through cooperation, Arabs could build their region into an economic powerhouse independent of the type of foreign intervention that kept Palestinians from their homeland and kept the Arab states dependent and weak. And only if Arabs developed strong financial and governmental institutions would they be strong enough to cooperate with one another. Since many Arab governments were sealed vaults of corruption and nepotism, Hikmat decided that the path to influence and, ultimately, to true reform lay through finance. He saw that in the post-colonial era what the Western world wielded over the rest of the world was financial power, and that the Arab world was almost entirely lacking in a suitable financial infrastructure of its own.

With some dedication, that infrastructure could be built up, and Hikmat intended to have some hand in building it. While he was still at university, he began working as an assistant to the chairman of the Lebanese Stock Broker's Association, and there he began educating himself on the key personalities, the complex relationships, and the obvious holes in the Arab investment world.

After he graduated from the American University of Beirut in 1966, a friend of his father's helped him into a job at the Kuwaiti Chamber of Commerce, where he soon became the head of its Foreign Trade Department. Kuwait was a rapidly growing commercial center in the region, and one of the region's oil producing states. Even though oil prices were still reasonably low in the early to mid-1960s, students of finance like Hikmat already believed that oil, along with the rest of the region's wealth of natural and mineral resources, would drive its development.

Hikmat had been in Kuwait less than a year when the Israeli army launched an attack and occupied lands from Egypt, Jordan, and Syria, annexing along with these the whole of his hometown, the city of Jerusalem. In Israel, the war was understood as a preemptive strike against Egypt, which had been massing troops on its border, but the occupation that followed the war was promptly declared illegal in a November UN Security Council resolution. In spite of the resolution, Hikmat nurtured no hopes that the occupation would have an easy end. At the war's end, Israel declared that Jerusalem was unified, liberated, and the eternal capital of Israel. Hikmat knew that his mother still kept the deed and keys to their family house in the city, and he knew now how futile this was.

What Hikmat couldn't know was that it was precisely this crushing defeat and the closing of the Suez Canal that would create circumstances for oil prices to explode, bringing wealth flooding into the region. Although the greatest oil wealth would not come to the Gulf states until 1973, oil prices began to rise steadily from 1967 on. When the Gulf states began to grow wealthy from oil revenues, Arab professionals and intellectuals alike flocked to the Persian Gulf to build what they hoped would be an Arab utopia, the center of a grand economic and social regeneration project that would free the Arab states from their dependence on their former colonizers. The wealth gushing out of Arab soil would be reinvested in Arab institutions and redistributed to all Arab land—that was the dream of many Arab visionaries of the time, including Hikmat Nashashibi. Ultimately, however, the oil riches would not set off the chain reaction of regional development many had hoped for. The reinvestment models the Gulf states chose would turn them into inward-looking citadels with a rich citizenry, a permanent pool of second-tier migrant laborers, and limited reinvestment into sustainable development programs.

In spite of the tragedies that had befallen Hikmat's homeland, the late 1960s was still a time of great optimism for ambitious Arab professionals like Hikmat, and he rose quickly to success. In 1969, just as Muna was moving to Kuwait, Hikmat left for a job at Paine Webber in New York City. As she struggled through her first months of exile, he learned the ways of Wall Street. The position brought with it a great deal of prestige. Hikmat was impressed with the efficiency and ambition of players in New York's financial markets, and he returned to Kuwait in 1972 with not only experience and prestige but also a clear understanding of how much the Arab region had been excluded from the world of financial decision making. When he returned, he joined a new pan-Arab economic and social development project as its investment manager. Muna Abdelahad had joined the same project just days before him.

Even for someone who believed in pan-Arabism and the dream of Arab unity, life across the different Arab states was hardly seamless. By 1969, when Muna's job at the Central Bank of Kuwait began, the oil wealth had already begun to trickle into Kuwait. As Syria had struggled to piece together one national economy from its divided agricultural and industrial, rural and urban sectors, oil drowned out all other sectors in Kuwait. In response to its windfall, Kuwait developed into what political economists call a "benevolent paternalistic state," spending its enormous wealth on exclusive incentives, services, and benefits to its citizens—in effect isolating them from other residents. Since citizenship was made all but impossible to attain, Kuwaiti citizens soon became a privileged, elite minority.

Muna lasted barely three months at the Central Bank before the obviously preferential treatment given to her Kuwaiti co-workers grew unbearable to her. Today, Kuwaiti women are often portrayed as wealthy and cosseted, married young to older men, kept at home, and leaving only veiled and accompanied to shop. In 1969, however, Kuwait was a fairly liberal society, where alcohol was not yet banned, Arab intellectuals from all over came in search of opportunity and other Arab intellectuals, and where women could be seen driving, working, and in positions of authority. Muna worked side-by-side with a Kuwaiti woman, and the two shared an even workload. Muna describes her colleague as highly educated and kind, and the two soon became friendly. But within weeks, Muna realized that her colleague was receiving three times her own salary for the same amount of work, just by virtue of her Kuwaiti citizenship.

Here we can see the resilience of the identity Muna constructed for herself. As a staunch believer in the cause of pan-Arab unity, she might have felt discouraged by her experience with discrimination in an Arab state, so soon after her father's political persecution at the hands of another Arab state. But she was also able to separate the actions of the state from her worldview, which was a staunch belief in the underlying unity of the people governed by these states. During her years in Kuwait, she developed a wide circle of friends, both Kuwaiti and non-Kuwaiti, who shared her vision, values, and sentiments about Arab unity, just as her son would one day create a diverse multiethnic and multireligious network in London in his efforts to advance human rights across the Arab region. Muna's perception of her experiences in her various Arab homes could have turned out very differently, but she looked for experiences that reinforced her own optimistic vision of Arab power and unity, and she passed on this vision to her children.

Instead of clinging to her vision and testing it with daily humiliation, Muna decided that she would feel more fulfilled looking for a job with an organization that supported her pan-Arab beliefs and gave her opportunities to grow. Although both her father and the governor of the Central Bank told her to stay on at her job, her pride told her to move on. So she found a job at a pan-Arab organization, where she felt she could sit at a table of fellow Arabs as equals. She joined the Organization of Arab Petroleum Exporting Countries (OAPEC), founded in 1968 by representatives of Kuwait, Libya, and Saudi Arabia who sought to integrate the region's petroleum industry. Muna stayed there for three years before moving on to an even newer, far-ther-reaching venture, the Arab Fund for Economic and Social Development (the Fund). She joined the Fund as its first employee in December 1972. Hikmat was its third.

By the time Muna met Hikmat, he had become something of an enigma. He was a quiet, towering man with velvety brown eyes behind his thick glasses, and a playful sense of humor. For someone with his accomplish-ments, he was approachable and friendly, and he was kind and generous with his colleagues. But behind his sweet, gentle exterior, Hikmat hid a hunger and bitterness that gnawed at him, driving him to great success, and some-times to the brink of despair. So even though Muna met a man who was full of hope for his future and for the future of the Arab world, who worked tire-lessly for the economic and financial empowerment of Arabs, the man she came to know was, at his core, deeply pessimistic. Hikmat Nashashibi was a product of tremendous personal loss and fierce ambition. Fear and hope, sorrow and affection were constantly at war inside his heart. Some part of him would always be a child refugee, drowning in despair.

Muna was, in many ways, an inversion of Hikmat. She was beautiful and glamorous, and although warm and affectionate, she was quite formidable, almost larger than life. Although she stood a full head taller than most women around her, she was utterly at ease in stiletto heels. Her hair was always perfectly styled, her makeup impeccable, and in her lilting, melodic voice she expressed strong opinions. She had a successful career of her own, had turned down many suitors in Syria. Her graceful persona hid within it a creature of iron resolve, someone with no time for weakness and self-pity. Hikmat was drawn to her strength, and she was drawn to his resilience.

Before long, Muna and Hikmat had become fast friends. They talked about politics and music, and shared stories from their childhoods. When his mother died, he turned to her for comfort in his loss, the loss of his final tie to his childhood in Jerusalem, and their friendliness grew into a sort of intimacy. Slowly, Muna began to feel her heart grow warm when she thought about him, and he quietly continued to offer her his friendship until he felt ready to offer her more. While he kept his intentions to himself, he worked to build on his career and savings. When one of them traveled for work, they exchanged letters, which both of them kept carefully.

In December 1975, Hikmat resigned the Fund to join the newly founded Kuwait International Investment Company. Muna resigned later that week, also to pursue other opportunities. And in the few weeks they had left as co-workers, a subtle change took place in their relationship. This became evident during their final business trip for the Fund, when they were both delegates on a trip to London to discuss intergovernmental cooperation opportunities. After one meeting a few days into their trip, Muna asked Hikmat if he would come with her to High Street Kensington. She had seen two lovely suits in a store window, and she wanted him to help her choose between the two. She enjoyed the thought of showing off two pretty outfits for him, and hearing him say which one made her look more attractive. They set out into the city, laughing and exploring, running the streets all day, delighting in each other. They played games and built the simple shopping trip into a great adventure. He egged her on, pretending to stop at this or that shop, and she feigned the disciplinarian, grabbing his arm and urging him to stay focused.

And then, completely spontaneously, he leaned over and gave her a kiss on the cheek. Just like that. He had never done that before, but he didn't offer any further explanations, and she didn't ask him what he meant. But with this intimate gesture, he let her know what he had been feeling for her. "It all started here," Muna says. "That was it, no further—there was just the feeling that we were special to each other."

They married in 1976. Not in a church the way Muna had always dreamt of, exchanging vows before an altar in a cloud of a dress, but in the Kuwaiti court for marriages and divorces. Because Hikmat was Muslim, their wedding had to be performed by a sheikh, and in Kuwait, non-Kuwaitis could not have a sheikh come home to marry them, but had to appear before him in a Shari'a court. It is worth noting that marriages between people of different ethnic and religious communities were not unheard of in certain Arab societies of the previous generation, but most such marriages were likely to take place among highly educated city dwellers rather than in the more conservative rural countryside, where interreligious romance could provoke harsh punishment. Whether they were both pioneers or simply products of a more tolerant environment than stereotype allows many to accept, neither Muna nor Hikmat saw religion or ethnicity as primary determining factors in a potential mate. Instead, both sought partners who shared their vision, mutual respect, and ambition.

The courthouse stood like a great dusty brick in the middle of the road. Muna tried not to think about the vivid church of her daydream wedding. Inside the courthouse, the walls were smudged and filthy, and the windowpanes were opaque with dust. From behind some of the doorways they walked past, she saw people screaming and waving their hands at each other. So this was how marriage ended, she thought, without dignity, without tears, but with vicious snarling in a small dirty room. She found out later that there had been five divorces taking place in that building on the same day she was married.

When they were called before the Shari'a court, Hikmat was asked to offer a bride price, traditionally the amount of money a man was expected to offer to his wife for her security. If he should prove unable to support her, according to the tradition, then she would have this store of money for herself. The offering of bride price was and still is widely practiced in many parts of the world, but both Muna and Hikmat were older and financially independent, and Hikmat's parents were not alive to make the formal offer. In their case, the money would be a symbolic gesture. Hikmat offered one British pound. He later joked that Muna had been both his best investment and the most successful pan-Arab project to come out of the Fund. The next morning, when the sun was bright, they set out on a two-month honeymoon through Europe, a fairytale journey to kick off the life they were building for themselves out of the fragments of exile. When they returned, they moved into a lovely bungalow with a broad verandah overlooking the street, and settled into their life together.

They had been married for two years when Muna told Hikmat that they were expecting their first child. She had thought he would react loudly, with the bois- terous joy that she felt herself, but he sat completely still, all the color drained from his face. The news could not have come at a better time. The couple had settled into an easy harmony with one another, and their prosperity had only grown. Hikmat had already risen to become general manager of the Kuwait International Investment Company, and under his leadership the company was on the verge of launching a project that would virtually create a securities trad- ing market in Kuwait. It was a bold and sweeping project that, if successful, would provide a revolutionary platform for Arab investors to generate wealth in their own region. Meanwhile, they had moved into a sun-filled villa with huge rooms and a verandah, not far from where Muna's parents and sister lived. They had developed a large circle of friends who shared their joys and their troubles with them. But Hikmat sat perfectly still, as expressions of fear, hope, pride, and sorrow chased across his face. Their life seemed perfect, but he could hear his mother's voice in the back of his mind, wistfully speaking of her perfect life and happy home in Jerusalem, a home that was gone in an instant and that she had begged him on her deathbed to reclaim for his children. Theirs was an age of war and uncertainty, and what guarantees could he give his unborn child? Muna spoke softly to him and let her optimism slowly warm him.

Shortly after she became pregnant, Muna came down with rheumatic fever. For six months she could not sleep through the night, and she would wake up choking and gasping for breath. On those long nights when Hikmat sat up with Muna all through the night, adding pillows behind her back, bringing her tea to ease her raw throat, they grew very close to each other. When she could not breathe, he held her hand, and when she was in pain, he told her little stories to keep her mind occupied. That same year, Muna would have to undergo her first of two open-heart surgeries.

At the end of it all, on March 23, 1977, Sharif Hikmat Nashashibi was born. He was in breach position; "he just had to come down on both his legs," Muna smiles. After the Caesarian section operation at a hospital, Muna went home weak but happy with her newborn boy snugly wrapped in her arms. When he looked at the baby's tiny, pink face, Hikmat saw his own father's bright blue eyes blinking out at him. And so, with Palestinian eyes and a Jordanian passport, Sharif was born in Kuwait to parents who called themselves simply Arab.

Since the great success of the Arab Company for Trading Securities, Hikmat, as its executive director, had begun to receive an increasing amount of attention and acclaim. Throughout Kuwait and the Arab world, and in financial publications of the finance capitals of the world, he was known as the man who had developed and executed the plan to bring a securities market to Kuwait. Yasser Arafat had even appointed him as a financial advisor in 1977, from which Hikmat had withdrawn after only one meeting, more because of interpersonal dynamics than any single political disagreement. By 1980, at thirty-eight years of age, he had been the subject of a handful of profiles, and his successes had been described in the *Times* of London and the *International Herald Tribune*. He sat on numerous advisory boards and committees, and by the end of 1980 he had published four books on how Arab surpluses might be reinvested into the region to promote long-range economic development. And so, because of all of these, he was able to raise $25 million in capital to launch an Arab investment banking group backed by private capital and catering to private investors. It was what he had dreamed about since his schoolboy days in the refugee camp schools.

The al-Mal Group, founded in July of 1980, was the full realization of his student vision of a pan-Arab investment group that specialized in investing private Arab wealth most profitably into Arab markets. And where better to base such a group than in the capital of the financial world? So that summer, after Muna and Hikmat had returned from their annual trip to the Arab Investors' Convention in Cannes, Muna set out on vacation with the two children, her parents, her sister, and the two nannies, and Hikmat returned to London. This time, instead of helping Muna find a nice suit, he prowled the streets to find her a suitable house.

That trip, he bought a three-story house next to a green park on a cobblestone lane, within walking distance of the same sidewalk where he'd given his wife her first kiss.

Although Muna and Hikmat were sad to leave their charming home and circle of friends in Kuwait, they were leaving as affluent, successful, highly skilled migrants to one of the most exciting and fascinating cities in the world. They were moving to a secure job and grand home in central London. They knew that they would be able to provide their two children with whatever advantages London could offer, and would be able to foster in them a firm appreciation of their Arab identity. Their migration was an indisputable move up, and they faced the prospect of migration with excitement and very little ambivalence.

Hikmat, Muna, Muna's sister Maha, Sharif, his baby sister Nura, and the two nannies moved to London in 1981. Two weeks after they arrived, their furniture joined them. As Muna unpacked in her new home, she turned on the television. That very same day, Lady Diana was blushing her way up the long, red carpet at Westminster Abbey, on her way to becoming a princess. The fairytale romance that brought a sigh from the lips of little girls all over the world also moved Muna, who had become the princess of her own fairy-tale. She looked over at Sharif, who had just turned four, and two-year-old Nura, playing among the boxes and shrieking with laughter, and looked around her at her grand, but still cozy, home. As the bride and groom kissed, she hugged her arms around herself and allowed herself to dream of the wonderful years that still lay ahead.

The migration of an exile exists in a unique category. Although many older migrants come to view their lives as having been spent in exile, migrants driven from home by war or political crisis view migration differently in old age. They experience loss as the loss of hope, and of personal agency. Their regrets are geopolitical, rather than personal, the regret that there had been no war, no coup. The generation raised in exile teaches itself to fight regret with a program of personal action and ambition.

Hikmat Nashashibi was an unequivocal success well before his fortieth birthday. He had not only achieved great professional success and material wealth but he also had a blissful and loving marriage. But he never lost his sense that his achievements were mere rope bridges over a gaping chasm, ultimately vulnerable to the harsh winds of circumstance. Muna learned early to confront the challenges of exile with hard work and ceaseless determination. She firmly believed that she could keep ahead of any crisis if she ran fast enough, and that she could rebuild anything that circumstance saw fit to destroy. For Hikmat, home and memory of home would always be loss, fear of loss, and the struggle to keep ahead of loss. But for Muna, home became whatever she could pick up from the wreckage of loss and gather close to her chest. Home was her family and the fairytale she built in defiance of loss.

CHAPTER 2

THE DOGANS' LONG
GOOD-BYE

The Dogan house is full of people, but for the moment, Mehmet Dogan and Adla, his wife of fifty-two years, are alone. It is a frosty afternoon in January 2005 in this small town just north of Hannover, Germany, and Mehmet is dressing his wife in her finest traditional Kurdish attire for their daughter Sukriye's wedding. Adla sits on the bed, her shoulders bowed under the weight of her recent stroke, shivering slightly from the icy draft gusting through the gap in the curtains to her right. Mehmet disappears into the closet and rummages noisily inside, emerging once, twice, three times with a long, crushed velvet gown, a full-length robe, and a brightly-colored shawl. He holds the hanger up to his neck, modeling the gown for his wife. Adla chuckles and then directs him to fetch a different robe, then asks him to turn on the overhead light so she can see its color. Darkness comes quickly this far north. By the time they leave for the wedding hall at four o'clock, the sky will be color of summer figs.

The long years in this foreign land have not been easy for Adla, but Mehmet is still spry and cheerful. He has spent most of his earnings helping family and friends, and has become something of a patron to the large and constantly growing Kurdish community in this town. Even without wealth, today he is happy with his life's work. In the many years since he has made this town his home, it is as if his village has grown up around him. Two of his sons live on the other floors of his house with their families, and three of his other children live within a five-mile radius. Their home is always full of family and friends, and almost every weekend, three generations of Dogans gather on colorful cloths spread on the living room floor to eat a meal of fresh flatbread and Kurdish delicacies, like parsley and tomato salad, sliced onions and mint sprigs, olives and cubes of fresh sheep's cheese, bulgur in spicy tomato paste, stuffed grape leaves, roast chicken, or lemony lentil soup. From a picture frame above the arched entranceway, Mehmet and Adla's nephew, killed by Turkish soldiers before his twentieth birthday, watches over the family meal, flanked to the left by a calligraphic engraving of Qur'anic verse and to the right by a map of Greater Kurdistan.

Mehmet helps his wife to her feet and furrows his brow in intent concentration as he helps her with first one arm of her robe, then the second. Adla frets about the time, asking if everyone has finished eating, whether the nieces have finished dressing, whether Sukriye is ready yet. Then she sighs and her chestnut-colored eyes grow moist. Her youngest daughter, married! For years she had given up hope that Sukriye, now almost thirty-three years old, would ever marry and settle down. She started trying to arrange introductions when Sukriye was in high school. Sukriye has always been her father's daughter, always so busy helping other people that she neglected herself. But last year, she finally completed her studies, the first girl in their family to receive a university degree, and now she was getting married. And they couldn't have hoped for a better match, a good Kurdish boy, known to the family, even related to the family on Adla's side, a boy who shares her passion for Kurdish history and humanitarian work, and who has an even temperament. He will be good for their restless Sukriye, the pride and joy of the Dogan family.

Mehmet cinches a belt tightly around his wife's waist and ties a silk scarf around the crown of her head, like a headband, holding in place the fine linen headscarf fringed with embroidery that frames her face. Then he drapes a long golden chain around her neck and turns her to face the mirror. He places his hands on her shoulders and looks at her reflection in the mirror, smiling broadly. "Beautiful, my wife," he murmurs.

Her thin lips lift into a small smile. She is happy today, but she is still worn out from long years of cold and illness. She has followed her husband for as long as she can remember, and she is tired of wandering in exile. Even though the

Turkish military destroyed her childhood village years ago, Adla's greatest longing is to return home. Now that her last child has been married, she still wishes
that Mehmet will take her back home where she can spend her old age in the sun.

Mehmet and Adla left their village in 1959 to look for a better life. Mehmet
was twenty-two, and at 5'8" considered tall. His nut-brown face had recently
shed most of its childhood softness and his moustache now grew thick and
full. Adla, who had just turned twenty, was considered a great beauty for her
creamy complexion and her fine, straight nose. They had already been married for eight years, and had a son and two daughters. As they set out from
home to make their fortune, they did not have much to pack, for all they
owned was a donkey, a mattress, and two blankets. But poverty was just one
of the obstacles they faced in their simple ambition to provide for their three
children. They were farmers in the impoverished countryside of a rapidly
industrializing country, and they were Kurds in Turkey.

They set out at daybreak on the dusty yellow road leading to the neighboring village Kucuka. As they walked out of their home village, Xarabe
Baba, with their backs to the sun, their shadows grew before them, reaching
deep into the valley below, where their future lay. They were used to adult
responsibilities and obligations, but somehow, as Adla thought of permanently leaving her home village and family, she found herself lagging farther
and farther behind her husband on the dusty road leading out of the village.
They were not moving far, just through the valley and over a few more hills,
but the distance from home was greater than could be measured in miles.
This was the first time anyone in either of their families had split off into a
single nuclear family. Mehmet had just returned home to the village after his
two-year-long mandatory military service, only to find that his father had
sold off his house and all of his animals while he was away. His father had
said that he had no choice but to sell what he could to fend off debt and
hunger. But Mehmet was frustrated that after so many years of hard work he
was exactly where he had been as a callow boy of fourteen, so he had declared
that he would strike out on his own and set up his own household in
Kucuka. His father, incensed that his own son would think of himself before

his duty to the rest of the family, delivered an ultimatum. Mehmet was free to go, but if he chose to leave the family, then he did so alone, with nothing from the family to help him set up his separate household.

Even if he had wanted to help, Mehmet's father did not have anything to spare. Famine and harsh land-reform policies held the entire region at the knife edge of starvation. Although today the road around them was empty, Mehmet and Adla were by no means the only people in the area that had taken to the road in search of a living. Slowly, necessity was driving Kurds from their isolated mountain villages and westward into central Turkey, first as sharecroppers for large landowners, eventually as factory workers, and finally many would travel to distant countries as temporary laborers. As the Kurds dispersed from home, the distinguishing features of Kurdish culture would be threatened—interdependence with family and independence from everyone else. The clear Kurdish majority had long been the defining feature of this part of Turkey, where the Kurdish language was heard much more often on the streets and in homes than Turkish, and had made the greatest case for Kurdish independence before the formation of the Turkish republic and in the many confrontations that followed. But as the Kurds dispersed, the physical integrity of a contiguous Kurdish majority region was compromised. Although decades later, during the brutal civil war between the Turkish military and Kurdish guerrillas, military incursions would evacuate Kurdish villages and violence would drive Kurds from the region, many Kurdish villages were first emptied out through economic strangulation.

Several histories indicate that Kurds have long seen themselves as a distinct people, even as a single nation, and at an estimated twenty million, constitute Turkey's largest minority group. In fact, the total Kurdish population, clustered primarily in the region where Turkey, Syria, Iran, and Iraq meet, has been estimated at forty million, making Kurds the Middle East's fourth largest ethnic group. Initially promised a separate Kurdistan by the victorious European powers after the First World War, northern Kurdish chieftains later found themselves included as part of a Turkey struggling to define itself as a young republic that was emerging from the ashes of the Ottoman Empire, home to at least fifty-two ethnic minorities. The republic's strategy for defining its national character was to create one Turkish identity for the many tribes that had been allied without any emotional cohesion to one another under the Ottomans.

In the new Turkey, the expression of minority pride was tantamount to threatening the national character upon which the republic had been founded. After a major Kurdish uprising in 1924 was brutally quashed, Turkey had begun to perceive all expressions of Kurdish identity as pro-independence militancy. If the Kurds should demand independence, then Turkey would not only lose the valuable water and mineral ore native to Kurdistan's mountains, but it would also lose much of its rural population, agricultural labor force, and infantry pool. Instead of incorporating the Kurds as a minority population, Turkey tried to make the Kurds into loyal Turks by criminalizing Kurdish languages, culture, and identity. In its constitution and in subsequent laws, Turkey officially denied the existence of the Kurds as a separate ethnic or linguistic minority, describing them instead as "mountain Turks," a people who had grown uncultured from their extensive isolation in the mountains they called home. Although the government's official denial of the Kurds as a minority has been reviled by many human rights activists and scholars, by far the most effective and least acknowledged weapon deployed in the Kurdish majority regions was poverty.

In southeastern Turkey, the region known to the Turks as Anatolia but to the Kurds as northern Kurdistan, poor farmers and their families more and more frequently had to contend with hostile policies that left them behind even as the rest of Turkey rocketed out of the ruins of the Ottoman Empire and into the twentieth century. While hospitals, factories, and schools sprouted all over the country's north and west, the majority Kurdish population of the southeast remained largely illiterate and underemployed, without schools, hospitals, or physical infrastructure, and with a significantly lower life expectancy than anywhere else in the country. Mehmet Dogan eventually taught himself how to write with a stick, shaping characters into the dirt during the long afternoons he spent on lonely hillsides tending flocks of sheep and goats, but his wife Adla, busy with chores from daybreak until nightfall, never learned to read or write. Mehmet did not want to leave his family behind in his own quest for work, but there was not enough arable land to go around in his home village for him to make a living through farming or animal husbandry. There had not been for some time. For the first six years of his marriage he had tried to find a compromise between his ambition for the future and the pull of his family obligations, but now that no longer seemed possible.

Mehmet had married Adla when she was twelve years old and he himself was fourteen. They were cousins and neighbors in the village of Xarabe Baba, home to seventy-five families who were all connected in one way or another, and had been promised to each other from infancy. The families had wanted them to marry later, but by Adla's twelfth birthday, her fair complexion and fine features were drawing proposals from other village families, so Mehmet had to claim her early if he wanted her. He told his sister that he didn't want Adla to be married to anyone else, and his sister relayed the message to Adla's father to plan the wedding as soon as possible. They were married in the simple, traditional way. After the fathers of the bride and groom had settled the bride price and shared a plate of nuts and raisins, which were rare delicacies, Adla was escorted around the low wall dividing the two family's homes. The very next day, the young couple joined in to carry their share of the family's workload.

At first, Mehmet shared a small plot of rocky land with his father and three brothers. Long days of coaxing a meager harvest from the unwilling soil provided one meal of watery bulgur seasoned with a single onion or tomato for all the members of the Dogan family to share. With no way to increase the size of the pie, the Dogans, like many poor, isolated villagers, were simply left to slice the pie into smaller and smaller pieces as more children were born into their household. As things were, there was barely a chance to survive from one year to the next, and no chance for Mehmet to save up enough money to buy a separate plot of land. So Mehmet, always the intrepid son of the family, asked around the neighboring villages and found that the *agha*, the landowner from Kucuka, the next village over, would hire him to cut grass and tend his herds of goats.

In 1952, when Mehmet was just fifteen years old and Adla thirteen, the young couple made their first migration from home, a sort of premigration

to Kucuka, the village they would later return to permanently. The move farther and farther away from home soil often occurs in a series of incremental
steps, in the pursuit of income, education, or peace. This first step for the
Dogans was to be a brief hop from one village to a neighboring one, simply
to supplement the larger family's food pot. But they stayed on at Kucuka for
five years, first working at odd chores, later as sharecroppers, and in the
meantime, their first three children were born. For these five years, even
from the neighboring village, they remained tied to the Dogan family in
Xarabe Baba. Every year, after the grain had been harvested, Mehmet's father
came to Kucuka to claim the family's share, leaving Mehmet and Adla with
too little to feed their own children. So after the first harvest in Kucuka had
come and gone, Mehmet began to smuggle goods over the Turkish-Syrian
border to earn extra money.

Border trade was a traditional source of income for the Kurdish chieftains
living in the buffer zones between the Ottoman and Persian empires.
Although it was now called smuggling, Kurds who lived along the Turkish,
Syrian, and Iraqi borders still moved their flocks and transported goods
freely, albeit under cover of night, and for a nominal "tribute" fee. By the
mid-1950s, smuggling was not just a source of extra pocket change but rather
a vital means of survival for many Kurds living under the burden of rural
life. For four years, Mehmet carried textiles, tea, fruits, cigarette papers, and
even animals over the borders for much-needed income. He soon grew
familiar with the best routes and developed the necessary finesse for negoti-
ation at the military checkpoints positioned along the border. To cross the
border with goods, a smuggler needed only to give the soldiers stationed
one-fifth of whatever he was carrying at crossing. But people who came from
the village on the border didn't have to pay this "customs tribute" at all, and
Mehmet soon become a familiar face. Within a few short years, he was able
to amass a handsome profit. By 1957 Mehmet had bought cows and his own
hut on a small plot of land.

Then, when he was twenty years old, he was called for mandatory military
service. For the two years he was away, Mehmet left his land, house, and cows
in his father's care. Adla returned to Xarabe Baba with her parents and the

children to stay with Mehmet's family. While she returned to her family, community, and the security of familiar faces and familiar customs, Mehmet, for the first time, ventured out into the unknown world beyond the invisible borders of Kurdistan; there it was prohibited for the many Kurdish men in his battalion to speak to each other in Kurdish, let alone acknowledge that they were Kurds. Mehmet soon learned that his military service would be much more brutal, with harder assignments and punitive repercussions, if he showed the slightest pride in his Kurdish identity. So Mehmet held his tongue, did what he was told, and learned what he could. After two years, Mehmet returned home fluent in Turkish, relieved to have his military service behind him, but also to find that much had changed.

When Mehmet learned that his father had sold off his house, herd, and land in his absence, he felt betrayed and frustrated. But his five years of steady, backbreaking service to the agha of Kucuka paid off; as soon as word of his return reached Kucuka, the agha himself made a trip to Xarabe Baba to offer Mehmet another job sharecropping his land and tending his flocks, and promised him a small hut for his family to live in and a tractor for farming. Kucuka was much smaller than Xarabe Baba, and with only twelve families, a great deal more land to spare. With the agha's help, Mehmet thought he could make a nice life for himself and his family. Mehmet's father forbade him to abandon the family to start his own household, and for the first time in his life, Mehmet opposed his father to take up the agha's offer. Mehmet was by no means an ingrate son or a rebel, he simply was a man who took calculated risks in order to reap the benefits of peace and prosperity. From his days as a hired hand for the agha of Kucuka, Mehmet had seen how much more dignity and comfort a man could give himself and his family if he owned property and his own flock, and had spent many an afternoon watching over the older man's sheep, fantasizing that they were his own. He loved and respected his father, but he wanted more for his family than the fear and insularity of the old ways could offer him. He knew that his pride as a Kurd could not be compromised by having a nuclear family household or working among Turks, and he knew that, in the long run, he could be of better service to his parents in their old age if he were his own man. Although

Adla feared for the worst when they set out for Kucuka, Mehmet never intended to turn his back on his family, and he never did.

But the day they set out to Kucuka, they set out on a path that eventually led them farther from home than Adla could have imagined. She had simply walked the few short steps next door to marry Mehmet, her cousin and neighbor. And yet the moment she had started following him in his quest for prosperity, she had kept on walking, first to a separate village, then later to a city, then later still to an entirely different country. Each migration that took her farther and farther from her home village had been the best choice for their family, but the years would find Adla retracing those steps in her mind, and regretting that they had ever left in search of work. She would lie awake at night in her old age, searching the plaster ceiling of their house in Germany, looking for an explanation of how she had ended up so far from home. How could they have made this choice, she would ask herself? Even then, on the road to Kucuka that sunny day in 1959, Adla lagged farther and farther behind her husband, halfheartedly leading their skinny donkey. The children dawdled by the roadside, and she did not raise her voice to hurry them up. Instead, she worried about her parents behind her and the uncertainty ahead of her. Suddenly, Mehmet stopped, turned, and walked back up the hill toward her, a low yellow cloud of dust rising behind him. He stopped in front of her and said, "Listen. Never tell me that my father never gave us anything. If I weren't a good husband to you, I might have squandered anything he gave us anyway. If we work hard, we can make everything ourselves." With this, he was asking her to walk beside him and to trust in his choices. After a long silence, Adla gazed squarely into her husband's eyes and slowly nodded her agreement. Then, Mehmet took the reins of the donkey, called the children, and walked beside his wife to their new home in Kucuka.

Today, we have romantic images of pastoral life as one of freedom, of shepherds and goatherds snoozing under olive trees on picturesque hills dotted with their flocks. Very much to the contrary, pastoral life in southeast Turkey was one of unremitting hardship—and a life of poverty is profoundly unfree. One of the greatest freedoms we cherish is freedom of choice. Migration theorists emphasize rational decision making as a vital component in the migration process. But free, rational decision making presupposes viable options. For poor, rural Kurdish farmers, neither staying nor leaving home was the ideal choice of a perfectly free individual. Turkey had undergone its first of many military coups in 1960, the year after Mehmet had moved his family to Kucuka, and the rural southeast, northern Kurdistan, lay under the lengthening shadow of political unrest and economic ruin. By 1966, Mehmet was no longer satisfied with what income he could squeeze out of his pastoral existence.

Since they had moved to Kucuka in 1959, the Dogans had built up a fairly comfortable life. The tiny, rickety hut the agha had first given them now had a sturdy roof and new clay walls, a wood-burning baking oven, and a stable for animals in the back. Handmade rugs covered the floor and a stack of thick mattresses stuffed with the wool from the Dogans' own sheep stood ready for the constant stream of friends and family they entertained. But Mehmet knew that his livelihood was tenuous. By the 1960s, seasonal unemployment in northern Kurdistan had reached crippling levels, leaving some 80 percent of the population with no work outside of the summer months. Luckily for Mehmet, as a seasoned smuggler living in a border village, he had been able to supplement his sporadic harvests with regular income.

He had bought his own flock from a man two villages over who was joining the throngs of Kurdish men heading west in search of work. Finally, his childhood dream of tending his own flock had come true. But his understanding of the world was changing, and his childhood dreams now seemed limited. He wanted his children to have education so that they might have better opportunities than he had had. There were two main reasons why education levels and literacy rates were so low among Turkey's Kurds; only 4 percent of all the schools in Turkey were located in northern Kurdistan, and Kurdish languages were illegal in Turkey, officially banned in all public institutions, including schools, in 1924. If he wanted his children to go to school, he would have to move to the city, which he could only manage to do if he had a large amount of money. Smuggling and sharecropping would not get him that kind of money, so he realized it was time for him to explore other opportunities.

Around this time, foreign oil companies began to invest in Turkey. One of these was an American-owned company named Aladdin Middle East, which launched oil exploration and drilling activities in southeastern Turkey as early as 1962. Although the engineers, managers, and planners for the firm were all Americans, the company needed unskilled laborers. Its recruiters canvassed the region, going from village to village to enlist workers to work at its factories in the city of Diyarbakir. Each village was requested to provide at least one supervisor and as many laborers as could be spared. When the recruiters came to Kucuka, the choice for Mehmet was obvious. He signed a three-year contract with the American company.

He joined a group of men from the village and went to work in Diyarbakir, leaving his wife and children several miles away in Kucuka. He came home on leave ten days out of every month, spending the rest of his time in the workers' barracks in Diyarbakir. Called Ahmed in the northern Kurdish dialect Kurmanci, Diyarbakir is known to many Kurds as the capital city of Greater Kurdistan. Although most Kurds have lived and still do live in small, dispersed villages, by 1970 Diyarbakir's population had exploded to 140,000 from just 30,000 in thirty years, making it the most populous and thriving Kurdish-majority city in the Middle East. Mehmet built up a network of friends, but he focused all of his energies on steadfastly saving every penny he could spare to bring home to Kucuka. But even though the pay was steady and much greater than what he had ever earned before, he still found himself indebted at the end of his contract. One of his daughters had taken seriously ill during the second year of his contract, and he'd had to save her life instead of money. As the end of his time in Diyarbakir approached, he mulled his choices. It was always the same dilemma; if his daughter had been able to have access to proper medical care before infection had set in, she wouldn't have had to battle death for two full years. And he might have been able to save up enough money to buy a house in the city. But life in Kurdistan was full of such frustrations. He couldn't worry about how things might have been. He could only worry about what to do next.

And then a friend from Kucuka told him of an opportunity that would change his life and propel him as a migrant to Europe, far away in the cold, wealthy West. The mayor of Mardin, the closest city to Kucuka, was collecting names of young men from its surrounding villages. These names would go into a lottery, and each year a random drawing would send a certain number of men to Germany as guest workers. The work terms would vary from six months to two years, and guest workers would be stationed in factories throughout Germany, rebuilding the industrial base that had been destroyed during the Second World War.

As he traveled to Mardin to register his name on the mayor's list, Mehmet hardly thought that he was making a drastic decision. After all, he had spent his entire working life following the thread of most secure income, and that thread had led him farther and farther from home, which lay in the agricultural fringe of a modernizing world. As industrial centers sucked in labor and resources, rural areas throughout the world were left with limited opportunities to offer young men and women, who drained out of villages in search of work. As villagers flooded the cities, opportunities there also grew scarce, and these same internal migrants began looking for opportunities overseas. In our perspective, there is nothing farther from a pastoral village in the isolated mountains of Kurdistan than a German factory, but for Mehmet, the incremental migration that took him there was logical. When there were no options in his home village, he had gone to Kucuka. When sharecropping promised no secure future, he went to work on the border. When the border tightened up, he found work in a city more than a day's travel away from home. When he learned of the chance to work in Europe for more money than he'd ever heard of, he took it. He had learned of this opportunity the same way he had learned of all the others that came before it, by word of mouth, in conversation with young men like himself, Kurds with families to support from villages with no means.

As he sat in front of the lottery registration officer in a stuffy building in Mardin, his only thought was to say whatever was necessary to get the job. The officer asked Mehmet, in Turkish, if he could read and write, and, his mind flashing briefly back to those few months he'd spent shaping letters in the dirt while the goats grazed, Mehmet answered "Yes." The officer said that he would have to return with a certificate proving that he had completed five years of elementary school, and Mehmet quickly replied that he'd only had four years of schooling. He had never seen the inside of a school building.

"Well, then, write something," said the officer, sliding a blank piece of paper across the desk.

Mehmet, who had learned to write with a stick, gingerly took the pen. "What should I write?"

"Write 'I want to go to Germany,'" suggested the officer. Mehmet slowly bent over the paper and wrote, in his uneven hand, the closest approximation of those words that he could sound out.

"I don't know whether what I wrote was right or wrong," he said, laughing. "At any rate, they took me!" Two years went by before his name was drawn in 1972.

In the same year her father left Kurdistan for Germany, Sukriye was born on the holiest night of the year. "You were born the night after the month of fasting had ended," her mother later told her. "It was February, and the weather was fine." The political climate, on the other hand, was far from fine. Violent confrontations between the Turkish military and leftist militant groups, including members of a budding Kurdish nationalist movement, had escalated until the army seized control of the government in March of 1971 and introduced martial law in twelve of the country's sixty-seven provinces, including the province that held Kucuka. Thousands of Kurds were rounded up and detained in prisons. In a speech, the minister of the interior said that the Kurdish movement was the main reason for martial law, making Kurds enemies of the state, even as the state continued to deny the very existence of Kurds.

In spite of the fear and violence sweeping the region, the roadblocks and checkpoints cropping up on the dusty, empty roads, the military bases appearing on the mountaintops, high above where the villagers tended their sheep and goats, life in Kucuka somehow went on as usual. During Ramadan in 1972, the tension of life under martial law gave way to the excitement of holiday visits and preparations. The sacrificial goat had been killed and cured with salt. Inside a bag made from the goat's skin, the village women took turns shaking yogurt to make butter for the feast to mark the end of the month-long fast. They baked in shifts at great communal clay ovens, piling up stacks of fresh hot *nane*. Finally, on the festival night, everyone retreated into their houses to prepare tea and snacks for the rounds of visiting.

In the mountains of Kurdistan, the breeze picks up in the evenings, carrying the pungent scent of wild herbs into the village houses. Tonight, as Mehmet paid visits to family and friends to wish them an auspicious and happy year, he would have enjoyed its fragrance mingling with the aromas of fresh black tea, homemade sweets, and the special treats only made on this night each year. While he made the rounds from house to house, Adla prepared to wash the children for the evening feast. She had cleared one stall in the stable behind the house, where she was preparing the girls' baths. She was at the tail end of her seventh pregnancy. Her loose, soft robes billowed around her swollen body as she moved. She had just returned from fetching water and had lifted the large wooden canisters from the donkey's sweaty back. The country's ambitious irrigation projects had never reached the Kurdish hinterlands, so villagers here still relied on the natural water supply. The Dogans used two creeks; the one for bath water and for the animals was a half a kilometer away, but the one with drinking water was more than three kilometers away. Every few days, Adla went to the drinking water creek with her four girlfriends, who had accompanied her through her chores from girlhood into womanhood. There was little leisure time, so the women wove leisure into their long work days, and in sharing their daily struggles they created a place where they could share their deeper troubles. Life lived together was life worked together.

Adla wiped the frothy sweat off of the donkey's flanks and began to build the fire to heat the water. The house was full of guests, and she knew she should be entertaining. But she sat on a pile of dry grasses to rest her throbbing feet and stole a moment of solitude. Suddenly, slow waves of pain radiated out from her pelvis to her thighs, rippling up her spine. The baby, she thought. It's time. She sat on the floor, her breath rasping in low, windy moans. She called out to her eldest daughter, Ramziye, and told her to fetch her mother.

Like all women in the region, Adla brought her children into the world without doctors, prenatal or postnatal care programs, without hospitals or ultrasounds or epidurals. The nearest hospital was many miles away, and Adla had never heard of a doctor specializing in childbirth and women's reproductive health. During her first pregnancy, she was thirteen years old, and hadn't even realized she was pregnant until she went into labor, which she had mistaken for a bad case of indigestion. Armed with nothing more than instinct and the personal experience of her previous childbirths, Adla felt that something was going horribly wrong this time.

She swallowed hard, trying to calm the violent nausea rising in her throat. With a deep breath, she began to push. She pushed and gasped, her face red and sweaty, and the baby began to emerge into the world. But it came feet first. Adla's mother drew back and cried out that she couldn't have anything to do with such bad luck. She left her daughter alone in the animal stable, where she sat panting in the dung and straw and blood. Adla cried out roughly to her second daughter, Fauziye, to run for the old lady in the village everyone called for births and deaths.

Soon, Fauziye returned, leading the old lady, who led Adla's anxious mother behind her. The old lady knelt beside Adla and placed a rough hand on her lower abdomen, kneading it with her knobby, calloused fingers. She quickly drew her hand back and reached around her back for her braid, which she thrust into Adla's gaping mouth and into her throat. Adla's body convulsed with a deep gag, and the baby slid out into Adla's mother's waiting arms. She was a little girl, and would be named Hasbiye. Then, just as the old lady was gathering her skirts to leave, Adla's mother told her to wait, that there was another baby.

After one more gag, out slid the second daughter. She would be called Sukriye, meaning "gratitude," a second child to be grateful to Allah for. Adla sank back with her two black-haired daughters at her side, exhausted but calm. She hadn't known she was carrying twins; no one in her family had borne twins before. She lay with her daughters in the bloody hay, stroking their small heads, asking herself how she would raise them into healthy women. Mehmet was out of work and the village was under martial law, but Allah would provide a way. And so Hasbiye and Sukriye were born in a stable, on the holiest night of the year, in a country that could not be born.

Although the older women in the family were dismayed that Adla had "tossed out" two more girls, when the family desperately needed more boys to work and earn, when he returned home that evening, Mehmet praised Allah for giving him Hasbiye and Sukriye. Girls did not go to school in Kurdistan, and could not leave home in search of work, but Mehmet had a different vision for his daughters. He would encourage them to study, travel, and learn how to help other people. Never mind that five of his eight children were now girls, he wanted them all to be strong, resilient humanitarians and proud Kurds. Although all of his children were bright and caring, it was Sukriye who would come to embody all of his personal hopes and dreams. Many years later, Adla vigilantly shielded her from the temptations of German society, but Mehmet encouraged her to engage with and learn from it, and she would become a scholar and a humanitarian. Allah did indeed provide a way, in the blessing and curse of a life in a foreign land, far from home but with opportunities never dreamed of at home.

For the first six months of her life, Sukriye lived in a shadowy land of near-death. Adla, suffering from acute malnourishment, could not produce any milk for the newborns, so they were fed a mixture of cow's milk and water. Hasbiye fed and slept contentedly, but Sukriye could not hold any food. No sooner had she eaten than she had soiled her cloth diaper and was screaming with hunger again. The family exhausted all of its options—three wet nurses, cow's milk, sheep's milk, even formula powder bought at exorbitant prices from Mardin, a full day's journey away. Ramziye stayed up all night rocking her miserable baby sister in a homemade wooden cradle, and Adla even tried feeding her sleeping pills a neighbor brought from town. The older ladies of the village told Adla that Sukriye was a spirit changeling. So she tried everything the village elders knew to convince the spirits to bring back her human child in return for their own, from placing her in a freshly dug grave to holding her over flames. With no proper health care, they had only hope, rituals, and prayer to fall back on.

Sukriye had just begun to sleep through the night when Mehmet called his father, his mother, and his wife together and told them he had some big news. He looked at each of their faces and swallowed. They looked tired, too tired to show much curiosity for what he had to say. His parents had lived through a period of great violence and poverty, and had grown old. His wife looked weak and listless from the strain of caring for her sick infant. He took a deep breath and told them, "My name has been drawn to work in Germany."

"They all cried," he says, "They all said, 'Don't go.'" Mehmet had never before seen his father cry. His mother was most worried about his spiritual health; no one from their family had ever gone to live among nonbelievers. Adla simply did not have the emotional fortitude to be left behind with two infants and no help. She wept and wept for him to stay. He told her he would only go for six months, just long enough to save money to make the Hajj, the pilgrimage to Mecca mandated for all Muslims. It would be no different from when he worked in Diyarbakir. Only six months, he promised.

Mehmet never made the pilgrimage to Mecca. And Adla never forgave herself for allowing her children's father to go live among strangers. From her earliest childhood until now, her life had been a grinding struggle. If she wanted food for her children, she had to harvest it, and if she wanted heat, she had to gather the wood to build a fire. But still, later in her life, she would sit next to the heater on the second floor of her three-story house, and look beyond her fully stocked refrigerator into the snow swirling outside her window. There, she would look into the past and see the village of her childhood. She wouldn't see hardship and suffering, but instead saw herself walking beneath the limitless blue Mediterranean sky, on the road to her mother's house, carrying a basket full of freshly harvested figs with her children skipping around her. Memory is a strange mirror, and in it we see ourselves as we are, reflected alongside what we want to be. More than anything, in her old age Adla wished to be home.

Conventional wisdom claims that people have no power to change the past, and that actions taken now can determine only the future. A single person can change the course of his life. But the past is constantly changing as well, refracted through the lens of how a person views his own life in the present. Adla speaks of longing for home, and yet when she describes her youth and early married life, she describes a life of only poverty and work. The day Mehmet left for Istanbul, and from there for Germany, he pressed his wife's hand and told her again that he would just be gone for six months. She was weeping so hard that she couldn't even see his face. Mehmet did stay for six months. But then he stayed on after six months, until six months became a year, then another, and another. By the time Adla was finally reunited with her husband, they had lived apart for eight full years.

When Mehmet traveled to Istanbul for processing later that week, it was the farthest he had ever traveled and the deepest he had ever gone into Turkey proper. For ten days he stayed in Istanbul, where he and each of the other would-be guest workers underwent a thorough physical examination. Mehmet, who had never had a physical examination before, was weighed, measured, tested, and asked to give blood, urine, and saliva samples. The doctors were not just assessing his health or testing for communicable diseases but were also checking to see what each man's capacity for work would be. Mehmet had not even assessed the physical capacity of his goats and donkeys this well.

Then he was asked for information that would determine his pay scale. Germany had been reconstructed as a social welfare state, with universal health care and a variety of other benefits available to its citizens. One of these benefits was "Kindergeld," or a monthly allowance provided to a family for each of its children. Guest workers with children were also eligible for a child allowance, at half the rate of what every German citizen was entitled to receive. But it would not have been profitable for Germany to pay child allowances to every child in larger families, so it was decided that only applicants with five or fewer children would be eligible to work. Mehmet had eight children, but he needed the income desperately. So he simply did not register Hasbiye and Sukriye, and wrote that his sixth child, his son Abdul Karim, had died in infancy. Hasbiye and Sukriye never found out what their date of birth was, and years later, Sukriye would simply celebrate her birthday on May 1, International Labor Day, as leftists and anarchists demonstrated on the streets of Berlin, which often ended in violent confrontations with police squadrons. Since she was born with the Kurdish national movement, she saw it fitting to celebrate on a day of protest.

In March 1972, Mehmet flew from Istanbul to Munich with the rest of his batch of new guest workers. They stepped off the airplane, some of them bewildered, some of them swaggering, for most their first steps on foreign soil. That year, according to German government estimates, some 500,000 guest workers recruited through the central registry in Istanbul arrived in Munich for distribution throughout the country. Mehmet and his co-recruits were ushered onto trains leaving from Munich to all different parts of the Federal Republic of Germany. Mehmet boarded a train to Hannover, and watched the countryside slide smoothly by through his tired, aching eyes, and wondered at the speed and silence of the train. Slowly, rolling hills gave way to flat farmlands, veined with thick, black highways. Everything looked so smooth and somehow fake. Mehmet could not quite comprehend that this strange place was real, let alone that it was now where he lived. When he arrived in Hannover, Mehmet's new supervisor met him at the train station and drove him to the factory for registration. Then he offered Mehmet one week off before beginning work, but Mehmet replied to his translator and new colleague in Turkish, "I've come here to work. In fact, I could start working right now." When the sun rose over Hannover the next morning, it fell on Mehmet, hard at work on his first day as a guest worker.

The months stretched into years and the distance between Mehmet and his family remained. He saved up just enough money to return home once each year. It is difficult to capture the constant limbo in which a divided family lives. Those years were little more than long, dull patches of loneliness broken by letters and the yearly visits. The greater frustration of absence overshadowed daily frustrations, and the greater joy of seeing one another after the long absences eclipsed daily joys. Mehmet filled his days with work, long shifts at a large automatic saw, cutting and stacking lumber. Adla filled her days with caring for her children.

Every week, Mehmet sent tapes telling the children stories of his life in Germany, and he sent money to his wife. He lived on the 720 DM monthly child allowance he received, and sent all of his salary, some 12,000 DM a year, to his family. He told them about parts of his life, but many things he left out. He told them of cars and trains and of the people he met. He did not tell them about the narrow room he shared with three other men, in an isolated, plain barracks building. When he was moved from the lumber mill to a motor manufacturer, he did not tell them about the strenuous work of welding, the injuries he received, and the strain on his eyes. His family and friends gathered around the small tape recorder that he had brought back from Germany to listen to his voice. No one in the village had seen such a thing before, and at first Mehmet's mother thought that her son had somehow crawled inside the metal box. When they made their own tapes to send to him, the children's voices spilled over one another. "Papa, we greet you! We miss you! When are you coming? Bring red shoes when you come, ok? We kiss your hands!"

For the first four years Mehmet worked in Germany, Adla and the children lived with her parents in Xarabe Baba. Since there were no schools, all the village children who were too young to work spent their days playing in the sloping fields, riding donkeys, picking grapes and figs. Their house stood at the top of a hill, surrounded by sky. Sukriye often stood on her tiptoes at the window, looking out at the valley below. It was a golden basin, full of light. She looked at the hills stretching out as far as she could see, and this is what she remembers—the many hills of one Kurdistan, unbroken by the invisible borders dividing it.

For Sukriye, those memories of her childhood in Kurdistan constitute a mythological memory of home and history. "They are sort of fragments. But they are also pictures that I always carry within me. That is my yearning, what I always seek when I travel to Kurdistan, to somehow relive those pictures of my childhood." She was proud of her father, who was working at a prestigious job overseas and sending money to the family. Just as memory's mirror made her mother's impoverished childhood beautiful, Sukriye's patchwork picture of childhood became whole and meaningful through the lens of future events. War ravaged the Kurdish countryside and Xarabe Baba was eventually reduced to rubble. Kurds sought temporary refuge in the cities then later permanent asylum abroad, and as a social worker in Germany, Sukriye would dedicate her life to helping Kurdish and other refugees from war navigate the rocky pathways of recovery and immigration. She fueled her future with these happy memories of home.

But for Adla, Mehmet's departure to Germany marked the beginning of the darkest phase of her life. As a woman alone, she often felt crushed by her own vulnerability. She fell into a deep depression each time Mehmet extended his trip by yet another six months. She had never eaten much, but now her appetite vanished completely. She grew weak and thin, and began having fainting spells. Mehmet's mother worried that her son had grown impure, living among Christians. When she saw that his hair had begun to gray, she said "See, his hair has gone white from living among the whites!" As Adla's illness became worse, and her fainting spells more frequent, it was decided that she would be better off living with her brother's family in the city of Nusaybin, where there were doctors. So, four years after Mehmet had left his home country, Adla left her home village, never to return.

With the money Mehmet continued to send, they were able to purchase a two-story house on the edge of town, with a large courtyard for animals and a sizable garden, where Adla moved with the children. In front of their house was a wide street leading out into the countryside, and beyond the street were empty fields, where the Dogan girls and their many cousins sometimes wandered, collecting herbs and grasses for salads, teas, and home remedies. To one side of their house, the ancient Silk Route intersected the street, and on the other side ran the Baghdad-bound railroad tracks for the Orient Express, laid by Prussian kings in the nineteenth century. Just beyond the Baghdad rail line, in Syria, lay Qamishli, Nusaybin's sister city. Under Ottoman rule, the two had been one city, and families which had been separated by the international border often sneaked over the border with smuggled goods and gifts for visits during the Ramadan festivals. Over time, Arab nationalist resettlement policies in Qamishli and Turkish military rule in Nusaybin changed the characters of these cities, but the native Kurdish residents of the region would always see the cities as one, and as their own. It seemed that Sukriye, who later settled in Berlin, was destined to live in a city divided by geopolitical boundaries.

Some days, Sukriye learned to read the Qur'an from the local mullah's wife, but most days she was left to play in the streets with the other children. Although Mehmet might have pushed for his daughters' education, Adla, living without her husband, was not prepared to face further scrutiny from her neighbors. Sukriye remembers knowing only one girl who went to school with the boys, an orphan girl her neighbors were raising who would have to provide for herself. Sukriye was content to organize games in the street, but Hasbiye began getting into fights with her cousin-brother over her father.

Tensions were rising outside of the family sphere as well. Throughout the countryside, the Turkish military fought Islamist militias on the right and on the left, communist rebels with whom a growing Kurdish nationalist movement had aligned itself. In addition to political crisis, the country also faced economic crisis, one cause of which was attributed to Germany's decision in 1973 to officially end guest worker recruitment. For nearly fifteen years, remittances by the veritable army of workers like Mehmet Dogan had provided a major source of consumer wealth and public income to Turkey. Two years after the end of Germany's guest worker recruitment program, in 1975, Turkey experienced a massive economic meltdown. Facing growing economic and political instability, the government once again imposed martial law, first on thirteen, then on nineteen of its provinces, most of which were in northern Kurdistan. Villagers fled military oppression and flooded into the nearest cities. Although it is difficult to find official accounts of what transpired in the villages at this time, many historians and economists note that the period saw a sharp increase in mass migrations of unskilled, impoverished farmers from rural areas into cities all over the countryside. The sheer numbers of these migrations suggest more than economic migration alone, and many Kurds from the region speak of a collective flight tantamount to a refugee crisis. Sukriye remembers that their home in Nusaybin became shelter to several families from the surrounding villages.

It was a period of great fear, but also of anticipation. Nearly fifty years after the birth of the Turkish republic, the economic and political isolation characteristic of the Kurdish experience was brewing into a kind of sweeping, collective discontent, and a small group of Kurdish nationalists had begun intermittent activities they hoped to translate into a broader nationalist movement. The decades of legal and military efforts to eradicate Kurdish national pride, coupled with the extreme poverty under which most Kurds had been forced to live, had led several younger Kurds to believe that

independence was the only way to ensure the economic, political, and cultural freedom of their people. Since the 1924 uprisings by Kurdish chieftains,
and in light of ongoing Kurdish independence efforts in neighboring Iran
and Iraq, the Turkish government had perceived Kurds as a national security
threat instead of a minority community. The historically hostile relationship
between the Turkish government and any expression of Kurdishness translated into a policy of zero tolerance toward the embryonic Kurdish independence movement. The small, relatively weak independence movement
was met with disproportionate government vigilance and military strength,
which, in turn, fed the nationalist sentiment spreading through Kurdish
villages.

Around the same time that the nationalist movement began to smolder
and military presence increased across the countryside, two students came to
live at the Dogans' house in Nusaybin. Although the house had always been
full of guests, somehow these two young men seemed like particularly honored guests. When they spoke, everyone fell silent and listened. Sukriye's
older brother spent long hours sipping tea and discussing hush-hush things
with these two gaunt-faced young men in khaki jackets behind closed doors.
Sometimes, the three of them disappeared for many days at a time. She later
learned that the three were politically involved with a group that was organizing and preparing to free their people from the Turkish military. The
Kurdistan Worker's Party (PKK) was officially founded in October of 1978,
and soon afterward it issued a formal statement for the independence of
Kurdistan and launched a series of attacks on right-wing and state bodies.
Within months, the country looked as if it was careening toward civil war.
One young boy who had come to live with the Dogans to escape his abusive
father joined the movement, and the family later learned that he had been
shot and killed in the mountains. Sukriye's childhood thus coincided with
the infancy of the Kurdish national awakening, and what she saw around her
now became her image of what a proud, successful Kurd should be. The students were respected and honored not just as political activists but also as
students who were applying their education in service of the Kurdish people,
which made a lasting impression on her.

The steady stream of refugees from the villages grew. Although many Kurds lived in the big cities in the region, like Nusaybin, Mardin, and of course, Diyarbakir, the mountain villages were the traditional Kurdish homeland. The villages were also where the PKK was most actively organizing to raise awareness about the movement, reinvigorate the sense of Kurdish nationhood, and recruit new members. And the villages were where the Turkish military focused its efforts to rout the young movement. The disappearances of suspected PKK members and intermittent military checkpoints in the villages were foreshadows of what was to come. But it was not the refugees in his house in Nusaybin, the roughness of the soldiers who patrolled his childhood village roads, or the other impending signs of war that made Mehmet a loyal supporter of the PKK's cause. He had always been comfortable in his Kurdish identity, and his children had all grown up singing songs of praise for Mulla Mustafa Barzani, an Iraqi Kurd who had led a series of revolts against the various Iraqi governments over the decades, and whom many Kurds hoped would become the liberator of Kurdistan. What made him believe in the need for a Kurdish nationalist movement was his conviction that the Turkish majority never intended to accept the Kurds as equals, or to give them equal opportunities to prosper in their state.

Although this thought had been floating around in his mind since the days of his military service as a young man, it was truly driven home in 1976, when he returned from Turkey on a visit from Germany, and happened to drive through a town called Kaiseri, near where he had been stationed many years before. The last time he had seen it, some twenty years previously, the town was a lot like Kucuka, small and rural and forgotten. But while Kucuka had remained much the same in the twenty intervening years, 150 new factory buildings had been built in and around Kaiseri, along with a bus station and a bustling city center. "It was then, for the first time, that it became clear to me, that I really understood that there were differences in our country," he remembers. "I asked myself, what is the difference between us? Why is there military, soldiers, poverty, no schools in our village but not here? I told myself then and there, I can say a thousand times that I am a Turk, but they will never see me the same as them. After all, they have created the difference between us."

Amid violence in the countryside, tragedy struck at home as well. Just after Mehmet arrived for his annual visit in 1978, his twelve-year-old son, Abdul Karim, was killed in a truck accident. Mehmet, who did not often let superstition get the better of him, could not help but remember that, those six long years before, he had written in block letters next to Abdul Karim's name "deceased." To win a spot as a guest worker in Germany, he had foretold his own son's death.

After he had buried his son, Mehmet returned to Germany with a heavy heart. But before he left, he told Adla that he thought it was time for her to join him in Germany. Life at home was deteriorating, and, with war in the air, he did not think it was wise for him to leave a paying job to come back now. Since the end of the guest worker recruitment program, the only way into Germany for divided family like the Dogans' was through family reunification, and he didn't know how long that window would be open. In fact, the German government had already begun promoting return migration for former guest workers. Mehmet told Adla that she should bring their four youngest children, who were still unmarried, and come to wait out the war with him in Germany. Adla, weary of grief and separation, agreed to join him in 1979.

The night before Adla and her four youngest children left Kurdistan behind, their neighbors threw a grand party. The whole neighborhood stayed up late, eating, singing, laughing, dancing, eating some more, then, finally, crying. No one knew what Germany was really like, but the children whispered collected bits of information to each other. Those staying behind urged those leaving to eat, eat, eat more stuffed grape leaves, you might never eat them again! Adla felt as if her own body was being torn, leaving four of her children behind and a fifth buried in her home soil, and taking her youngest ones far away to be with their father. Sukriye's stomach hurt from sadness and from too many stuffed grape leaves. In the morning, they set out with the family of another guest worker Mehmet worked with in Germany, and a thick knot of family, friends, neighbors, and curious children threw water at the departing car, for good luck.

Before she knew it, Sukriye sat in an airplane miles above Kurdistan, fingers curled into her palms, contemplating the plastic tray full of food her mother had warned her against eating, for it was certainly *haram*. Her youngest brother had taken the window seat, and now he curled against it, fast asleep. Hasbiye, her twin sister, leaned against their older sister Celile, also asleep. Adla sat stiffly, repeating soft prayers over and over to herself. Soon afterwards, Adla, Celile, the twins, and Abdel Selam stepped off of the airplane, coming home in a foreign land. Before them, beyond a blur of snow and frosty air, stood Mehmet. Many miles behind them lay home, drenched in sun and blood, with the staleness of their longings and the grief of their losses buried in its rocky soil. They walked toward him, too tired and hungry to think about the future, but happy, at last, to be together.

Most immigrants never fully leave home until years after they have lived in a new country. Physically, they board an airplane, boat, train, or car, but with the intention of saving and returning, waiting out the hard times, waiting until the war ends, waiting until the time is right. But years pass and then there are a thousand smaller negotiations between home and abroad, the old ways and new, the past and the future. Finally in old age, when the children are grown and settled, when home is no longer as it was, the immigrant realizes that home has been left behind. And then begins the return migration of memory.

Mehmet had the confidence that comes from personal agency, knowing that at each junction in his life he had taken the greatest opportunity available to him for the benefit of his family. After he had retired from his years of underpaid labor in Germany, he took pleasure in the fact that he had been able to take advantage of both his German present and his Kurdish past to give his children choices and to recreate some semblance of his lost mountain village in the middle of the northern plains. His memories of home were fond and proud, for the past had its place and he still honored it. Adla would always regret the decision to leave home, which, to some extent, was a decision made for her. She was grateful for the health of her family and the happiness of her children, but she always felt that life outside of the homeland was life in exile, and that life in exile was no life at all. She had survived the loss of a child, the loss of her home, and, much later, survived a stroke, but she had tired of surviving. Her memories of home were full of longing, for she had never chosen to leave.

Mehmet followed opportunity to Germany and returns home every time he sits down to tea with someone from his home village. Adla followed Mehmet, and returns home every time she closes her eyes to sleep, to dream.

CHAPTER 3

THE ISLAMS' LAST RESORT

Rafiqul Islam sits in his apartment in Queens, New York, on a frayed couch in the late afternoon sun one fine summer day in 2004, his left arm flung behind his head. His right hand fingers the edge of the grayed, stained sheet covering the couch. The sheet bunches under his thighs. To his right, the Disney channel blares from the television on a tall shelf against the wall, but neither he nor his four-year-old granddaughter Ayesha pays any attention to it. She chatters plaintively, begging him to play with her. His grandson Rasha, not yet two years old, crawls over Rafiqul's thighs and plops down beside him. Rafiqul has always been a quiet man, but his quietness is more contemplative these days. In the eight years since he arrived in New York, with the dream of somehow navigating his way into permanent residence here, nothing has gone as he had hoped. Even though their struggles have had more to do with chance and politics than with him, he still blames himself for the hardships he and his daughter Nishat have had to face.

Mounted on the living room wall are several small, intricate sculptures Rafiqul carved from balsa and plywood. Delicate swan-shaped napkin holders, miniature chairs, and reclining ladies, all resting on individual plywood platforms, have transformed this somewhat dingy living room into a dreamy gallery. But a quick glance around the rest of the apartment reveals signs of wear and tear, of new things now fading, broken things unrepaired, old clothes unreplaced. When he and Nishat first moved into this apartment, on her wedding day, they were planning for a full future here. Now, they have begun neglecting the apartment, because neither of them believes that they have long left in the United States.

The couch he sits on was brand new when his son-in-law Mohammad bought it as a part of Nishat's wedding trousseau—a pastel-colored living room set and a white lacquer bedroom set, a new bed and arts table for Rafiqul. But barely three years after the wedding, his son-in-law was taken into custody and detained for immigration violations. Mohammad, like Rafiqul and Nishat, was an undocumented immigrant in the United States. Although he was imprisoned in New Jersey, he might as well have been sent to another country, for neither Rafiqul nor Nishat could visit him without papers.

Rafiqul had hoped to enroll Nishat, his third and cleverest daughter, in a college here in the United States and to put his engineering degree to good use. But instead they both find themselves stagnating, with fewer and fewer options to earn a solid living. The average under-the-counter clerical job in Queens would bring in an hourly wage of $3.00, and a babysitter would cost Nishat at least $10.00 an hour, so she had not been able to work at a full-time job since the birth of her second child. And Rafiqul, who could not return to his factory job after his heart attack five years before, now makes his living painting watercolors for tourists in Central Park. On a good day, at the height of summer, he might earn as much as $200. But winter is coming, and he is at a loss for what to do when the snow and ice keep him from this little income. The limits of their lives have grown narrower and narrower, with nothing more for them to do than get from one day to the next.

Nishat prepares the evening meal in the kitchen, sautéing turmeric and cumin powder with red chilies for a chicken curry. A sharp fragrance wafts into the living room, where Rafiqul still sits, lost in reverie. He would have been content to remain in his childhood village in Bangladesh, where he would have spent his days casting fishing nets and his evenings sitting on the broad porch swing. He is a simple man who craves a simple life. But he knows that the many paths that have led him away from home into the dis-illusionment and decay of this life cannot be retraced. Any return home would be a humiliation, the admission of defeat, and the abandonment of his daughter in a hostile, foreign land. He would like to dream of home, and tell stories of his youth. But he cannot entertain those thoughts now. He draws in a deep breath and pulls his grandson to him. He plants a kiss on his drool-soaked cheek and checks to see if his diaper needs changing.

When Rafiqul Islam was three years old, his family fled their village near Kishoreganj in 1945 in search of food. For several days and nights, they journeyed by foot and boat to the capital of their colonial province, the teeming city of Dhaka. His province, Bengal, was then a part of India, the jewel in the crown of the British Raj, and Bengal was starving. For nearly seven years, Bengal had been in the clutches of one of the worst famines in its history, one brought about almost entirely by British wartime policies of crop blockades and forced expulsions. By the time Rafiqul's father decided to take his family to Dhaka, more than five million people had starved to death and millions more had fled the desiccated countryside in search of refuge in the cities. Rafiqul's family joined the throngs of starving refugees headed for Dhaka, only to find displaced villagers dying on the city pavements. It was soon evident to Rafiqul's father that, without relatives or work in the city, his own family would be forced to live in the slums choking the city's periphery. They stayed barely two years before they joined the stream of people fleeing the cities back to the countryside, this time running from a disaster far more terrifying than the famine—the worst communal bloodbath in the history of the South Asian subcontinent.

In August of 1945, the British Empire withdrew from the subcontinent after some three hundred years of rule, precipitating one of the greatest mass migrations and bloodiest border riots ever known, in which twelve million people left their homes and some two million people lost their lives. As we have seen in the previous chapters, the boundaries drawn by Western colonial interests were often haphazard and profoundly destabilizing in regions with contending national interests. The new state of Pakistan was formed from the former Raj provinces with Muslim majorities. East and West Pakistan were divided by a 1,000-mile-wide arrowhead of Indian territory, and had nothing but their faith in common. In the minds of its people, East Pakistan, or eastern Bengal, simply remained a colony to a foreign power, and had in addition become a nation divided. West Bengal, the Hindu-majority part of the province, became a state in the new India. After partition, the British administrators and Hindu landlords in East Pakistan were simply replaced by West Pakistani governors. Now, instead of English, Rafiqul had to learn Urdu in school. Instead of learning British history and poetry, he read Urdu poetry and learned the history of the rulers of Pakistan. Although East Pakistan was rich with natural resources and generated most of the new country's export wealth, it remained largely left behind by the rapid economic development programs introduced by the West Pakistani government. Educational institutions in the countryside remained limited, and so Rafiqul found himself returning to the city as a youth, this time to attend college.

Rafiqul's father, his father, and his father before him, and as far back before him as anyone could tell, had lived in the same village. They had harvested fish and rice from their generous natural environment and lived peacefully. For many generations, fishing had been enough to keep the Islam family reasonably prosperous. With the money they earned fishing and trading at the city markets, Rafiqul's family had managed to build a three-story stone house on a nice plot of land, with a broad verandah shaded by tall neem and tamarind trees. Although the Islam family wasn't the most powerful in the village hierarchy, they were generally known to be comfortable, and were well respected in village society. Rafiqul's father was a man who believed in investing in his family's future, in laying the foundation for a steady rise into the middle class. But after so many years of colonial rule, it now looked as if Bengal was no closer to autonomy, but rather belonged to another nation of distant rulers who had little to gain by developing its countryside. Rafiqul's father had no wish for his sons to be exploited along with the countryside, and so he encouraged all of them to educate themselves and find a way out of the country. Although the family kept its village home, and one of Rafiqul's brothers remained there to raise his own family, one of his brothers became a teacher in Dhaka, East Pakistan's provincial capital, and another, like Rafiqul, set out on a path of migration that would eventually take him overseas to the United States. But that story lay far in the future. For the time being, Rafiqul and his brothers only hoped to leave the village for salaried jobs in town.

Although the ocean stretched its fingers across the entirety of Bengal's body, and although the land itself was vulnerable to cyclones and floods, the villagers often said there hadn't been droughts and famines until the British came. Colonial land use policies set the stage for a cycle of flood and famine that continues to strangle the countryside in modern-day Bangladesh. By the final years of British rule, regular waves of refugees fleeing disaster flooded to the province's main cities, Dhaka in the east and Calcutta in the west. Even as Bengali nationalist poets praised the beauty of their voluptuous natural countryside, even as Bengali artists depicted romantic fishermen and women in rope sculptures, even as Bengali engineers dreamed of rebuilding the rural infrastructure, Bengalis were forced to seek opportunities for higher learning, professional growth, and artistic expression in the cities. Rafiqul had always exhibited an artistic streak, but he also excelled in his studies in the village school. Rafiqul's father knew that if his son had a hope of a life less beholden to the temperamental weather and a chance at highly paid West Pakistani jobs, then he must become an engineer. So after completing his high school studies with honors in the village and town schools, Rafiqul set out to study a course of engineering at Dhaka, returning home during holidays and between school sessions, to fish with his brothers and fill notebooks with sketches.

As we have seen, regional migration may result from conflict, economic strangulation, or political persecution, often taking migrants in incremental steps farther and farther from home. But scholars have shown that rural migrants fleeing natural disasters in the Bengali countryside often returned to their villages after a short stay in the cities. Rafiqul's family was just one of thousands trapped in a cycle of flight and return migration between the country's villages and cities, which made up the dominant migration trend of the region. This is partly because many of these migrants were of a lower skill group and could not be absorbed into the permanent economy of the cities where they sought refuge, and partly because the resource-rich Bengali countryside continued to offer work, if only seasonal, to fisherman and farmers. For skilled professionals such as Rafiqul eventually became, the main reason to return to or to keep his family in the villages was that for the first twenty-five years of its existence, East Pakistan's cities were almost constantly paralyzed by political demonstrations, strikes, riots, and martial law.

As early as 1956, East Pakistan's dominant political party, led by the volatile Sheikh Mujibur Rahman, began agitating for an independent Bangladesh, and the civil and ethnic strife that spread across the country culminated in the West Pakistani president's declaration of martial law. Most of the riots and demonstrations in Dhaka centered around the old Hindu quarter of town, so Rafiqul, who was not by nature an agitator, avoided the troubled sections of town and focused on his studies. He proved to be a star student and, upon completing his course of study in 1962, won a highly coveted university spot in Karachi, in the West Pakistani province of Sindh, to study polytechnic engineering. The spring before he arrived in Karachi, the government drew up a new constitution that essentially institutionalized martial law, and Karachi exploded with prodemocracy demonstrations. The day Rafiqul arrived in Karachi, he saw tanks on the streets. He resolved to keep his head down and nose in the books and return to his Bengal in one piece.

He had just turned twenty years old when he boarded an airplane for the first time in his life to travel over 1,000 miles to the first capital of his country, the hometown of its founding father Muhammad Ali Jinnah. When he landed and felt a hot, dry wind so unlike the lush humidity of home against his face for the first time, he realized that although he was still among his countrymen, he was, for the first time in his life, among foreigners. Karachi was the commercial capital of the country, and the only city with no regional ethnic majority population. In Dhaka, apart from the West Pakistani administrators and businessmen, everyone was Bengali, and everyone spoke Bangla. Here, the city was a quilt of separated neighborhoods for Pathan craftsmen, Baluchi laborers, Punjabi businessmen and civil servants, and Sindhis, whose provincial capital this was. But the city's largest population consisted of the Urdu-speaking *muhajirs*, Muslim refugees from the Indian states, who had arrived during Partition. A large part of Dhaka's culture came from its traditionalism, its connection to its land and its history; most of Dhaka's people still maintained deep ties with their home villages, and so with the slow-paced, ancient soil of the countryside. As Pakistan's main port city, on the other hand, Karachi was packed with businessmen making and taking opportunities. Refugees have no ties to the land, and money has no past. And so, to Rafiqul, Karachi felt rootless and hard-edged.

The vendors he saw on the streets of Karachi were Muslim, like him, Sunni, like him, and yet so much about them was unlike anything he had seen in his own eastern province of Pakistan—from the cut of their clothes, to the smells rising from the foods at the roadside buffets, to, of course, Urdu, the strange language on everyone's lips. In this country, his country, he was supposed to find safe haven among his fellow Muslim brothers, in this outpost to the *ummah* that had been separated from India just for him.

In his three years in Karachi, Rafiqul was never able to feel at home. Even after he had learned to speak Urdu fluently, and could navigate the streets of Karachi with his eyes closed, he still felt that the people were inherently different. Where West Pakistan struggled to manage the political and economic tensions between its strikingly different provinces, home to different ethnic, linguistic, and cultural groups, East Pakistani people still saw themselves as one people, with their own homogenous and marginalized Bengal. "Pakistani people are very arrogant and violent," he says. "Bangla people are calm, very humble and quiet." This belief, born of his sense of alienation in his country's capital city, which was home to only a very small slice of the country's teeming population, would only be cemented during the years of violence leading, finally, to Bangladesh's independence from Pakistan.

In 1965, Rafiqul returned to his home village. He had come to Karachi to learn, and nothing more. He returned home with an education, a fierce distrust of West Pakistanis, and a desire to marry.

His family had arranged a marriage for him with a petite girl from a village nearby his own, a girl named Kamal Nahar but called Jorna, which means "fountain." Jorna had finished the tenth grade before her wedding. Her father, a high school headmaster, had insisted that his daughter be educated before she was sent away to another family. So, on the day of her wedding, when the priest and official witness came to ask her to sign the formal registration of her marriage, she could proudly write her own name instead of a simple X.

As she sat beside him under their wedding canopy, Jorna would only have been able to acquaint herself with her future husband's face by sneaking sidelong glances at him from beneath her red bridal veil. But she would have found his appearance reassuring; his eyes were warm and round, his nose dove down in a long, straight line to his thin mouth, where it hooked slightly at the end, and his complexion was the creamy color of weak tea. She herself was all triangles, with high cheekbones and a sharp, petite nose, and, under the yellow turmeric she'd been decorated with, her skin color was a nuttier brown. He had traveled and studied, and he was nearly ten years older than she was. But she came from a cultured family. Her father had a master's degree in English literature, and was one of the few Bengali Muslims to pursue advanced, Western education under British rule. It was a good match.

Shortly after the wedding, Rafiqul went to work in the city, where demonstrations and riots for autonomy increased with every passing month. This was an unsafe environment for Rafiqul's fifteen-year-old new bride, so Jorna stayed behind in the village with Rafiqul's parents, two brothers, and their wives. At least once each month Rafiqul returned home to the village, where he felt happiest. As was the tradition, male and female society operated separately, each concerned either with the procurement or preparation of food. Even when Rafiqul came to visit, he was rarely left alone with his wife. Jorna, still a young woman, was busy learning the trade of wifehood from her sisters-in-law while Rafiqul was assigned to seek the family's livelihood. In the village, Rafiqul's three brothers and his parents shared a home with a wide verandah, where, on the rainy nights, after a day spent hard at work under the sun or above the wood-burning stove, the family gathered to listen to the rain and share news. Rafiqul hoped, within a few years, to save up enough money to bring his wife to join him in Dhaka, where they would be safe from the floods and droughts that periodically crippled village life. But as the country careened toward civil war, riots crippled city life, and Rafiqul decided that Jorna was safer, for the time being, in the village.

The peaceful life of the village erupted into violence in 1971, during a bloody and brutal civil war that finally led to the creation of Bangladesh. Dhaka, where Rafiqul spent most of his time, had been plagued by fits of nationalist violence since 1966, when the nationalist leader Sheikh Mujibur Rahman, known affectionately as Mujib, was released from a seven-year-long imprisonment and announced a program for East Pakistani autonomy. In the pro-autonomy strike that followed, Mujib was once again arrested, and the violence escalated. By 1970, the entire country had fallen into a state of near anarchy as protests, strikes, and riots broke out in every major city in all of Pakistan, until a new West Pakistani leader placed the country once more under martial law. Movement to and from the villages became more and more difficult, and Jorna often huddled around the radio with her sisters-in-law and worried about her husband as news from Dhaka grew worse and worse.

Ultimately, the catalyst for war was another natural disaster, a cyclone that in November of 1970 destroyed vast sections of Bengal's coastal lowlands, killing hundreds of thousands of villagers. Within weeks, the death toll had risen to over 500,000, as the Brahmaputra River swallowed towns and villages whole. In the villages near Kishoreganj, which also lay under the Brahmaputra, water rose up to meet the mists. The lower countryside was littered with bodies, drowned along with the province's grain supplies. Rafiqul's parents, two of his brothers, their families, and his wife, struggled to fend off starvation and fever. No one could make it past the mud and waters to Kishoreganj for supplies, and even if they could, there were no supplies to be had. East Pakistan hovered on the brink of famine and plague, and several days after the cyclone had hit, still no aid had arrived from West Pakistan.

Fury at West Pakistan's neglect delivered an indisputable victory to the pro-independence East Pakistani party during the national election less than a month later. Mujib, who was set to become the prime minister of Pakistan, was jailed instead, and as a rash of mass civil disobedience broke out in East Pakistan, the Mukhti Bahini (Bangladesh Freedom Fighters) seized a radio station in Chittagong, declared Bengali independence, and called upon all Bengalis to resist the Pakistani army. As negotiations continued in West Pakistan, Dhaka shut down. Rafiqul came home to the village to sit out the showdown.

At first, life in the village bore no visible traces of the tension paralyzing the country. Certainly, more men were without work, milling here and there on verandahs in the balmy summer afternoons, sucking on tamarind and sipping tea, calling to each other through mouths stuffed with *paan*. But soon, the young men of the village, some of them barely more than boys, began to gather by night to organize into militias. In the evenings, when the families sat on their verandahs to listen to Mukthi Bahini radio announcements as they digested their meals, and the children played games in the streets, the younger men quietly withdrew from the circle of gossip and chatter and crept off to gatherings in the fields and among the trees, wearing scarves around their heads. On the verandahs, mothers followed their young sons with worried eyes but said nothing. A civil war was coming, and Bengal was preparing to fight.

On March 25, 1971, the 60,000 West Pakistani troops that had been stationed on the streets of Dhaka launched a wholesale slaughter to shut down a massive, pro-independence demonstration, and the war had begun. Soldiers marched into the Hindu areas of town, bearing lists of Mujib supporters to be killed. Tanks fired into the halls of the University of Dhaka. Intellectuals, businessmen, and suspected subversives were hauled outside of the city and shot in mass executions. It was reported that three battalions of troops—one armored, one artillery, and one infantry—attacked the undefended city. By March 28, some 15,000 Bengali men had been killed.

By June, the countryside had retaliated with a full guerrilla war, as more and more men joined the Mukhti Bahini to fight the occupying Pakistani army. Throughout the summer, monsoon, autumn, and misty seasons the bloodshed continued. During the monsoons, when the fields separating villages were flooded, boats carrying refugees from one village to the next steered gingerly past bloating corpses. All summer long, clouds of vultures hung in the hazy sky above the villages, casting thick shadows on the hot earth. No one came out onto the verandahs. Rafiqul's village emptied out as its residents retreated farther into the countryside to the homes of relatives whose villages had not been blockaded by soldiers or freedom fighters. The villagers kept their preparations for flight secret from one another, for

Mukhti Bahini fighters were blocking villagers from retreating in the face of the Pakistani army. As the conflict shifted into the countryside, and the neighboring villages became battlegrounds, Rafiqul and his brothers went into hiding and the women stayed still and vigilant, until word came that the Pakistani soldiers were coming.

When the Pakistani soldiers came to Kishoreganj, Jorna was pregnant with her first child. They came at night with torches, and Jorna took to the fields with her sisters-in-law. The fields had been left muddy and exposed when the monsoon waters had retreated, and were covered with stubby dead stalks. The women crouched close to the ground, with nothing but mist and darkness to hide them. Jorna had no idea how many soldiers had entered the village, but she watched for their torches and listened for the crack of their gunshots through the mist. No one spoke of what had been going on, but everyone knew that the soldiers would not respect children, women, and the elderly. Since the war had broken out, the Western Pakistani soldiers had been tearing through the countryside beyond the capital, on the hunt for young men to kill and women to rape. By December 1971, when the war eventually ended, it is estimated that Pakistani troops had killed between 1 and 2 million Bengalis and raped some 200,000 Bengali women and girls.

For several months, well into the eighth month of her pregnancy, Jorna and her sisters-in-law lived as wandering refugees. Sometimes they stopped in one village for a night, sometimes a week, before moving on to the next village. Some nights, they slept under the foul-smelling nets in fishing boats, and some nights they huddled together in fields just outside of villages. Somehow, they always managed to stay just out of the soldiers' way. It was a period of terrible fear and constant exhaustion. Jorna never knew where the father of her unborn child might be, or whether he was even alive. When their first daughter was born, just after the war's end, Rafiqul and Jorna were delighted that, although she was incubated in fear, the baby was a happy and healthy little girl.

In December, after tense negotiations between the Indian government and the pro-independence leadership, the Indian army crossed into East Pakistan and began its march on Dhaka. Within days, the Pakistani army was encircled by the Indian army on its west, the Mukhti Bahini to the north and east, and was being eaten away by pro-independence civilian militias from within. Pakistan surrendered on December 16, and Sheikh Mujib, released from prison, entered Dhaka as its new leader. Everyone in the Islam household had survived, but with indelible fear and hatred of Pakistan woven into their collective memory.

On the heels of the destruction wrought once by the Pakistani military, and many times over by the cyclones that repeatedly spun off of its southern coast, Bangladesh's countryside had become an economic dead zone by the time the country had gained its independence. People left the villages in droves, most of them with no promise of work. Many would live in impoverished slum settlements on the outskirts of the cities, taking jobs as temporary construction workers, textile workers, or domestic servants. The steady push of rural-urban migration continues today, leaving the nation to deal with an underdeveloped countryside and a demographic crisis in the cities. Studies estimate that in the twenty years following independence, Bangladesh had an urban growth rate of 6.5 percent each year. Since independence, Bangladesh's cities have struggled with a glutted unskilled labor market, slums, disease, and an overburdened physical infrastructure. And still, the cities represent greater opportunity for most villagers than the rural countryside.

But when Rafiqul left the village for good in 1975 with his wife and two toddler daughters, he left with a guaranteed job, a solid education, and the promise of a successful, middle-class life in the new capital city, Dhaka. Even though his newborn country was devastated, teeming with hundreds of thousands of freshly impoverished refugees, Rafiqul had faith that his academic and professional background would serve as a solid foundation and scaffolding for him to build upon. He believed, as he had been taught to believe, that the way out of insecurity and the threat of poverty was through education and through strict adherence to a personal moral code of honor. He was doing things the right way, and felt certain that he could shield himself and his family from the vagaries of political turmoil.

The decision to move his family from the village to the city had been easy, obvious. But the journey that lay before them was arduous. Long before first light, Rafiqul and Jorna set out on foot with their two small daughters, Farhat Jahan, whom they called Lipi, and Nighat Jahan, called Shilpi. After a long walk, they settled into a boat, which would take them to a ship, which would take them to a train, which would take them to Dhaka, where they would have to hire two rickshaws to take them to their new home. Rafiqul's job with the central government was a tremendous opportunity to earn real money, to send their daughters to good schools, and to move toward a more secure life. Jorna, who came from an educated family, could think of nothing better than this move. Village life was oppressive and unchanging, full of monotony and shortages—in food, electricity, medical care, and respite from work. She knew she would not venture out of the house often in Dhaka, that the boundaries of her world would remain her home's walls, but her family's world would most certainly expand.

After the long muddy tramp from the village to the stream, the family was quiet. Rafiqul and Jorna slouched down into the boat's lap with their two daughters, Farhat Jahan, whom they called Lipi, and Nighat Jahan, called Shilpi. Paddy fields hugged the slender stream on both sides, crowding towards the small boat slithering down the stream. The boat hissed and sighed as it slid forward. The girls drowsed while their parents looked across the fields, thinking their separate thoughts, letting the boat carry them forward. Dragonflies the same green as the paddy hovered here and there along the sides of the stream, like tiny trembling arrows pointing the way out of the country and into the city.

Jorna squinted as she glanced around her, watching the fields sway with the tilt of the boat carrying her downstream, away from the village. By now, Kishoreganj would be coming to life with the slow resurrection every sunrise brought to its near-dead streets. Shopkeepers would be kicking the street dogs out of the way to make room for their wares, and the farmers from the neighboring villages would be spreading their mottled produce on sheets of burlap. Jorna was almost glad that the last time she had laid eyes on it, the weary little town that was the closest approximation to a city near their village had been fast asleep under the still-dark sky.

They first moved into a three-room flat in Dhaka, overlooking a narrow alleyway cluttered with slum huts and tiny shops. They had a small balcony, and the children would soon be enrolled in a good school. On the rooftop, where the neighbors congregated as the villagers had on their verandahs back home, Jorna planted a potted garden with tomato plants, lemon trees, and jasmine. While she gardened, she could see the whole city spread out at her feet.

As Jorna and the girls settled into their new life, Rafiqul was sent throughout the country on assignments. He came and went, came and went, but was a steadier presence in his daughters' lives than many men of his generation were to their children. He was an affectionate and loving father, leaving Jorna to play the role of disciplinarian. Soon, they were able to appoint three servants—one nanny to help tend to the girls, one boy to run errands to the market, and one woman to help with the housework. Jorna established the rules and always prepared the meals. As they grew, Jorna refused to let her daughters work in the kitchen for fear that the heat from the stove would darken their complexions and ruin their prospects for marriage. Nishat Jahan was born one year after they had moved to Dhaka, the first city-born child in their family, and they called her "Happy." Her parents believed that she would have an auspicious life, for she was a clever and energetic baby, with her mother's fire and her father's thoughtfulness. Theirs was a proud, middle-class household.

Good enough is never good enough to a young professional in an impoverished country. Although his life was pleasant and reasonably stable, Rafiqul was aware that his densely populated country, with its predominantly agricultural economy, could not offer him the best opportunities his engineering degree could command. Rafiqul, for his part, was content with the luck he had received so far, but Jorna often pushed him to look for more and better opportunities. By 1981, they had four children—three daughters and an infant son—to support. Once he had succeeded in a government job, the only place he could go to earn more and better would be abroad. In the mid-1970s, the beginnings of the global transmigrant labor market was emerging. Newly independent nations, struggling with the complex problems of building and diversifying their own economies, found themselves with too many unskilled laborers and not enough opportunities for their highly skilled workers. A generation of trained professionals, familiar with the languages and industrial cultures of their former colonial rulers, began to look to the industrializing world for work.

Just then, the explosion of oil prices filled the coffers of the oil-rich Persian Gulf countries, and since their own labor markets could not meet the spike in demand for all levels of labor, first private companies and eventually governments themselves made arrangements for the recruitment of temporary workers. Although the first wave of foreign workers in the Gulf were recruited from other Arab states, by the early 1980s, the majority of foreign workers in the Gulf states were South- and Southeast Asian. Scholars argue that official estimates are likely to underestimate actual numbers of workers, but some estimates suggest that roughly 2 million Indians, 1.5 million Pakistanis, and 200,000 Bangladeshis were working in the Gulf states by the late 1980s.

In 1981, Rafiqul joined the vast armies of South Asian laborers heading toward the Gulf, taking a job in Oman through the Bangladeshi government. In great part, the flows of migration, return migration, and earnings remittances took place with little official coordination between the sending and receiving countries, but Rafiqul, who was cautious, would only migrate with a firm opportunity in hand. Most of the South Asian laborers seeking or renewing working permits in the Gulf states worked in the less prestigious construction or service industries, but Rafiqul took a position as an engineer on a petroleum pump. Unlike many of his compatriots, who lived in cramped, spare barracks, often several to a room in trailers, Rafiqul worked in a well-paying job with spacious, clean quarters. Since his was a government job, he also enjoyed generous vacation benefits, coming home for a full month each year.

Separation was nothing new for Jorna, whose entire married life had been built on distance punctuated with brief visits from her husband. Because Jorna and her young daughters could not stay alone, and the only male in the house was still an infant, Rafiqul's brother, a teacher in Dhaka, moved into their flat. For both Rafiqul and Jorna, distance brought with it opportunity, which lessened the pain of distance somehow. Rafiqul's work was prestigious, and it gave his family standing in Dhaka. Within a year, Jorna gave birth to her fifth child, another daughter, and she was busy caring for all her children. When Rafiqul returned on vacation, he brought suitcases crammed full with dolls, toys, new clothes, nail polish, and chocolates. For the duration of his visit, they would gather in the evenings and play Monopoly together, just the family.

Looking back over the years, Nishat remembers the comparative wealth of this period more than the absence of her father. "That time, we was so rich," she reminisces now. "My God, we was so rich. We had plenty of money. We had everything." She watched her mother and learned then that it is not such a terrible fate for a woman to sacrifice her present family cohesion for the future financial gain of her children. Happiness was fleeting, but money and social status held. This life lesson instinctively guided her to survive, even in a measure to thrive, many years later when her own husband was imprisoned without any promise of release. In actuality, much of her nostalgia for the past grows out of the irony of her current struggles. She remembers that in the past, her family had wealth and status, none of which she has now in America, the land of opportunity. But Nishat's memories of the past are also largely a construct of her present troubles. Even in the past, her family's wealth and status was not what she remembers it to be, and that wealth and status proved as fleeting as the shared family time sacrificed in order to achieve it. Now, she says that her happiest childhood memories took place when her father was working overseas. But her mother must have struggled with the separation, and her struggles may not have been as silent as Nishat remembers. Jorna was loving and affectionate with her children, and Nishat remembers napping with her head on her mother's stomach even after she had graduated high school. In her husband's absence, Jorna grew deeply attached to her daughters. Nishat thrived under her mother's love and attention, which itself, she allows, grew partly out of her mother's loneliness.

It was during this time that Nishat learned what she saw as a valuable life lesson about love, attention, and success. When she was in the first grade, Nishat and one other boy in her class received the highest cumulative scores in their class. Since there could only be one class captain, the school's teachers drew up a tiebreaker exam, and Nishat scored higher than her opponent.

Her uncle, who was living with them as a sort of acting father for the children, was a teacher at a prestigious school, and when he learned of Nishat's academic success, he enrolled her in a school where she could study until the twelfth grade. Nishat remembers that her teachers organized a grand party for her, and that her headmistress wept to lose Nishat, whom she called "the hope of her school." On that day, Nishat learned that intelligence leads one to success, and that success opens the door to love, pride, and more success. This lesson not only shaped her worldview but it also served to deepen her disappointments later in her life.

But the chain of events that followed teach another lesson altogether—that opportunities may come, but they don't always open the way to success. Rafiqul worked in Oman for five years, and by all accounts he should have been able to save a neat bundle to bring home. But Rafiqul was always soft-hearted, and his compassion for his countrymen got the better of him. By the time he returned home, he had given much of his savings away to one person or another, fellow Bangladeshis in worse situations than his own. Jorna, who was much more practical, wrung her hands in dismay every time he returned home with just enough to pay for their basic housing and food costs. But Rafiqul smiled softly as he listened to her sharp words, for he believed in the value of his education and his honor. He never for a moment doubted that these qualities would give him luck and would lead him to more and better opportunities.

In 1986, Rafiqul received word that his youngest brother, just twenty-five years old, had died. The distance between his work and his home suddenly seemed oppressive and unbearable, and he returned home.

Back in Bangladesh, Rafiqul once more set out to make his fortune, only now with five children and a wife to support. This time, he tried his hand at entrepreneurship. Within a year, Rafiqul was the owner of a grocery store. Within a year after that, he had opened a lucrative dairy farm with thirty-two Australian dairy cows. He believed that he had made it, set up a successful enterprise in industries that would always be in demand, and set about to fulfill the immigrant dreams of his friends and relatives from his childhood village. Soon, he had hired a handful of cousins and childhood friends, to whom he entrusted several management and accounting roles. For all intents and purposes, the family's life appeared settled. Jorna had begun the girls' Qur'anic studies with a group of women who came to the house, and their son Kamrul was now attending school. With what they earned from the grocery store and dairy, they could afford to send their children to good schools. For five full years, they lived a happy, stable middle-class existence.

Then, all at once, they suffered a major crisis of their own. After five years of entrusting his accounts to others, Rafiqul was shocked to find that his business was operating at a tremendous loss. He spent several nights poring over his long-neglected accounts before he told Jorna the terrible truth— their middle-class life had been an illusion. All along, it seemed, his many cousins and family friends had been skimming a little here, a little there for themselves, and his own family had been living on the verge of poverty. In 1991, just as Nishat entered the ninth grade, Rafiqul went bankrupt. Within a few months, he had to sell the store, and then the dairy. They were ruined.

Rafiqul's decision to go to the United States was an act of desperation, a decision he never would have taken in better times. His was the rational choice migration theorists speak of, but a choice made among less than ideal options. Five years after his complete financial collapse, he was still out of work, and his family was overwhelmed with debts it owed creditors and moneylenders all over town. Rafiqul had been corresponding with his brother, who had moved to Chicago some years before, and once again decided that his way back into the middle class was through work overseas. Since he was making a desperate choice, compelled by the need to make as much money as quickly as possible, this time he did not proceed deliberately with security on his side. He knew that work visas to the United States were nearly impossible to come by, and even when they could be obtained, took years to process. So he made his calculations and decided to enter the United States as a tourist and to overstay his tourist visa illegally. He planned to take a job he was sure to be overqualified to fill, then to save as much money in as short a time as possible until he could pay off his debts and return home. In 1996, he left Bangladesh for the third time in his life, only this time with no promise of a job or a position in school, but with all the hope that he would return home soon to his happy, middle-class life again.

When her father's businesses collapsed right as she was beginning secondary school, Nishat was faced with a great hurdle. Although public universities cost little, secondary schools were very expensive, and Nishat now had to find a way to pay for her own education. She had never been as diligent a student as her oldest sister, but she was bright and could score very well with less study than her sisters. As her father's wealth dwindled, she approached the elementary school a few buildings down from her home and offered her services as a tutor. She tutored in every elementary subject, from science and math to English, until she had paid her way through the twelfth grade, completing her Intermediate degree in accounting. When she graduated from the twelfth grade, she placed in the First Division, among the top twenty students in her graduating class. Unlike her fellow First Division classmates, Nishat had received her rank without attending after-school coaching centers or employing a private tutor. Her uncle quietly took her to one of Dhaka's finest clothing stores and bought her a grand salwar kameez, hand-embroidered with tiny green and white beads. It was clear to everyone that she had become the hope of the family, because she was resourceful, independent, and capable of succeeding under pressure.

Nishat had just completed one year of her honors program in management at Dhaka University when her father informed her that she would be accompanying him to the United States. They would travel to New York City on tourist visas, where they would first stay with a family friend living there. Once there, Rafiqul would look for work and Nishat would join a college program. When she was settled into her classes, she would find a part-time job as well. By the time she completed her studies, according to the plan, Rafiqul would have saved up enough to go back home a comfortable man. Nishat would have a degree from an American college, and would go back home on the fast track for success. Jorna secretly hoped that Nishat might marry an American citizen and settle into a life of luxury, with a car and air conditioning in every room.

America was the great familiar unknown, and it was the universal solution for desperate people. It was the hardest but the best answer to their troubles. America was oceans away, and still farther away than its physical distance, but it was, after all, the proverbial land of opportunity. They did not have food shortages and electricity grid failures in America. If someone cheated you, you could take them to court in America. A rickshaw driver in America could earn more than an engineer in Dhaka. Jorna feared she might never see her daughter again, this bright-eyed, sharp-witted daughter who was most like her, but she did not begrudge her this chance at true happiness. After all, wealth was the true freedom, and if freedom couldn't bring happiness, then what could?

On August 18, 1996, the day Rafiqul and Nishat left, Jorna prepared a huge meal with Nishat's favorite dishes. But she was too sick to enjoy any of it, for she had come down with a bad case of food poisoning after a celebratory dinner out with friends. She had been sick for nearly two weeks. Already, their departure had been delayed twice, but now it was time to go. Nishat closed her eyes and leaned against her mother, who wept silently and stroked her daughter's brow. At six o'clock in the evening, one of Nishat's uncles arrived in a microbus from the private bus company he managed. Nishat, her father, her mother, two of her uncles, and her little brother climbed in and pulled the door shut behind them. They had packed lightly, because they did not want to arouse suspicion that they were anything but tourists, so there was not much baggage. Nishat kept her eyes closed. In fact, she kept her eyes closed for almost the entire twenty-two-hour journey to New York City. When all the other passengers were straining to catch a glimpse of the Statue of Liberty, of the gleaming island of Manhattan over the Boeing-747's massive wings, her eyes were still closed. It had been her first flight.

Rafiqul Islam had never been a determined migrant. He moved in search of work almost because economic migration was the dominant paradigm of his world. He grew to manhood in a society that valued higher education and proficiency in English, the language of world domination, but a society with no institutions of higher learning. So he had to migrate to pursue what was desirable. As someone who could have happily spent his life as a fisherman in a village, an education might not seem like a necessity. But where he grew up, personal happiness was less valuable than prestige and living out the hopes and dreams of one's father. Once he had successfully educated and qualified himself, he had no choice but to set himself on a course of migration. Professional jobs are in cities, so he had to leave his village behind. Government appointments as officers on Persian Gulf petroleum pumps were as prestigious as they were lucrative. After he had completed his term of service in the Persian Gulf, Rafiqul felt that his era of migrations was over. He had pursued prestige and fortune where it had taken him, and had found happiness in keeping a simple business in his homeland, where he could watch his children grow.

But crisis overturned his choices and his belief system. He found that his pursuit of prestige had left him with nothing, and his pursuit of happiness had left him with less than nothing. He had always believed that education and a code of personal honor would serve him in the end, but every morning in his daughter's apartment in Queens, he pulled the cord for the light bulb over the bathroom sink and, and contemplated the lines disappointment had drawn onto his face. But he found his principles hard to relinquish. Even when he had nothing left, he still gave what little he earned as a factory worker, later as a street painter, to fellow Bangladeshis stranded, like himself, in undocumented America. He hid this fact from his daughter, who, he knew, would disapprove just as her mother would have. What he also hid from her was that these gifts were more than just his code of honor, his softheartedness, or his inability to say no. These gifts were his way of justifying the terrible guilt he felt for sinking his family into poverty and for driving his daughter into exile.

PART II

INTEGRATION AND IDENTITY

CHAPTER 4

RECLAIMING THE
DISTANT HOMELAND

From the very beginning of their life in London, both Hikmat and Muna Nashashibi were engaged in making things better in their homelands. Because of their relative wealth, they had little interest in focusing on gaining access to British social services and institutions. While Hikmat worked to expand the horizons and opportunities for Arab investors and Muna sought out opportunities for political activism that would have been impossible in Kuwait or Syria, Britain's largest immigrant communities were struggling with entrenched economic and social disenfranchisement. Even as Arabs from northern Africa settled into working-class neighborhoods in and around London, most of the Arabs Muna and Hikmat knew were well-off professionals, more moved by injustice at home than by inequality in Britain.

As soon as the children were settled in school, Muna jumped into action. First, she began monitoring the British media for the Arab League, where she would summarize reports carried in the major broadsheets into reports that she submitted to all Arab embassies in London and to the foreign ministries of all Arab countries. Then she and a group of women founded the Arab Women's Association, originally intended to act as a political lobbying organization. But none of the women had British citizenship, and so when the group drafted its first letter on the eve of Israel's 1982 invasion of Lebanon, many of the women were afraid to sign and risk upsetting their home governments, particularly Jordan, which had expelled the PLO after a bloody civil war in 1970. The group decided to change itself into a charitable organization, and Muna, disappointed, disengaged from the group's leadership. Although she had no intention of putting her activist interests aside, Muna realized that she was dealing with both a community that was unwilling to take action and a country that was somewhat impervious to her community's concerns.

There are many reasons why Britain's Arabs were relatively slow in engaging directly in British politics or organizing lobbying structures, including lack of citizenship and their experience with repressive political regimes. Unlike the country's largest immigrant groups, South Asians, British Arabs were not citizens of Commonwealth nations, and, as such, were not automatically British citizens. This in part explains why, when they did engage in political activism, British Arabs largely worked on foreign policy issues. But the reason also lies in the nature of the social contract Britain has traditionally offered its immigrants and ethnic minorities, a subject that has been hotly debated in recent years. Unlike other Western European countries, the United Kingdom did not recruit temporary foreign labor, but the majority of its new citizens were former colonial subjects of the vast and powerful British Empire. Britain did not set itself up as an immigrant destination; in fact, it had a negative migration balance well into the 1970s. Until 1961, the British census did not inquire into the ethnic or national makeup of its populace. Immigrants were assumed either to have been absorbed as British, whose political interests would therefore reflect those of the mainstream population, or to constitute a percentage of the population too small to form a sizeable interest group. As such, British politicians did not effectively court immigrants or minorities, and up to the present day, immigrant communities remain greatly underrepresented in Parliament. As early as the 1980s, scholars and researchers began developing a body of literature on race-based and minority political identity in Britain, but the political parties themselves were slow to incorporate these groups through an actual minority outreach strategy.

Eventually, it would be political crises that would bring immigrants to engage with the British political system and begin organizing interest groups. Domestic political crises would move South Asian immigrants to organize around the advancement of Muslim or Asian social interests in Britain, but British Arabs would continue to focus on the British response to crises in their homelands for many years to come. They would organize into a small but vocal lobby, and one of the loudest voices for change would be Hikmat and Muna's son, Sharif Hikmat Nashashibi.

In a manila envelope with frayed corners, the Nashashibis keep a collection of documents, evidence of what they have lost. There is a floor plan and lay-out of the Nashashibi home in Jerusalem, along with a picture of Sharif, barely twenty years old, standing at an empty intersection across the street from their home, squinting at the sun, without a smile on his face. Behind them stands a building once filled with family memories and keepsakes, which has not belonged to them in nearly sixty years. Sharif did not learn of the presence of this house until his adolescence, and when he did, his parents had already made their home in the United Kingdom. But the documents, kept safely in the manila envelope, wrapped inside a plastic bag, and stacked on a shelf with other papers and bills and clippings, is a reminder of what they have lost, what might have been, and what they have little hope of ever reclaiming. Since he learned of that lost home, Sharif has spent his life think-ing about ways of reclaiming—neither the home itself nor the simple return of his family to their homeland—but as much of the lost homeland as can be reclaimed for the millions of Palestinians who still remain homeless.

Sharif Nashashibi, the eldest of Muna and Hikmat's three children, learned that he was Palestinian just before he turned eleven years old. Until then he believed that he was, as his and his father's passport stated, a Jordanian. The day he found out he was Palestinian, he also learned that the Palestinians had been homeless for forty years, so just as he gained a nationality he lost his country. It was a profound realization for a young boy at the verge of adoles-cence, at the moment where a person begins to realize his individuality and develop an identity. Learning about his Palestinian background was an epiphany for Sharif and, although he was also Syrian, Iraqi, and Lebanese, Palestine would become his personal obsession, his passion, and his calling, as well as his heritage in the coming years. In fact, it might be seen as the moment that Sharif became who he would be for the rest of his life.

It was December, 1987, and Sharif remembers that reporters on television said that the people of Palestine had started an uprising they called an *intifada*, or a "shaking off," which was spreading through the Gaza Strip and West Bank. Spontaneous demonstrations had broken out on December 8 in a Palestinian refugee camp in the Gaza Strip when its residents, protesting an attack on two vans carrying Arab day laborers, took to the streets and set tires ablaze. Within a matter of days, waves of demonstrations, protests, and strikes had spread across the length and breadth of the Palestinian territories as pent-up resentment burst out against Israel's twenty-year-long occupation of the West Bank and Gaza Strip. Outrage against expanding Israeli settlements in the West Bank and Gaza Strip, the destruction of Palestinian homes, the checkpoints, identity cards, arrests, and disappearances evolved into outrage among Palestinians everywhere against the general decline in Palestinian economic and cultural well-being since the beginning of the occupation. Crowds of young men and boys hurled stones and Molotov cocktails at Israeli soldiers, who often employed harsh repressive measures. The demonstrations continued and groups organized to sustain what seemed to have become an organic revolutionary movement.

The media coverage of the Intifada brought the distant and convoluted conflict into the living rooms of the West. Its images were symbolic and iconographic, forming a clear visual discourse that was easy for people unfamiliar with the conflict to interpret. Since the late 1960s, the era of antiwar demonstrations in the United States and massive student protests throughout Europe, the media's role in conveying and contextualizing remote conflicts had changed. Now, Western media consumers often expected media outlets to place conflicts into a clear oppressor-victim dialectic. Images of the powerful and well-equipped Israeli military arresting young stone throwers cast the conflict as a Palestinian David taking on an Israeli Goliath. These images repeated over and over would become a part of the long-term media lexicon in portraying Arab youth, Muslim youth, and conflicts in the Middle East. The repeated portrayal of Arab or Muslim youth as angry, volatile, and primitive would be criticized as dehumanizing by scholars and media critics less than twenty years after the Intifada, when exactly these kinds of images had gone far to humanize the Palestinian struggle to media consumers in the West. Muna described the Intifada as a turning point in Britain's sympathy for the Palestinians, which was also a turning point for the British Arab population's sense of belonging in Britain.

The Intifada was also a crucial moment for Sharif. From the first day of the demonstrations, his parents were virtually glued to the television set and read newspaper reports aloud to one another. They made long, tense phone calls and held involved political discussions in Arabic that Sharif only partially understood. One evening early on in the Intifada, the family gathered to watch a documentary on the Israeli army's suppression of the uprising. One particular scene showed two Israeli soldiers holding a Palestinian protester's arm while a third soldier hit it over and over again until it broke. This documentary was eye-opening for all of the Nashashibi children, but it was the beginning of a life journey for Sharif. He was both disgusted and fascinated by the images of people throwing stones and being shot dead by soldiers with guns and tanks. Keeping his eyes riveted to the screen, he asked his parents who these people were. Who are these people, he asked? Where are they from? Who are they fighting? Muna and Hikmat together began explaining the history of the Palestinian people, the 1948 war, the 1967 war, the occupation and settlement of Palestinian lands. And then they told him that he was Palestinian, and that his father was born in Jerusalem. He was first shocked but then outraged. How could they have not told him who he was?

Muna still says she was surprised that Sharif did not know that he was Palestinian. "We didn't try to hide it, but we didn't try to emphasize it. We didn't want to make it an issue for him. He had been born in Kuwait and loved Kuwait, he was carrying a Jordanian passport, but he was Palestinian. For a young boy, it was bound to be confusing—you live here, but you're from here—and unless you want to explain to him about the whole Nakba and the attack . . . we didn't want to overburden him." Sharif's parents had made a decision to protect their child from information that he might have difficulty processing, and from possible confrontations with a British populace that they had on several occasions found to be much more sympathetic to the Israeli point of view than the Palestinian one. Since they both felt a strong allegiance to the principles of pan-Arabism, Hikmat and Muna chose instead to foster pride in their children as Arabs, not as belonging to any particular nationality, which they believed had been imposed upon their native region by Western colonial powers anyway. They saw no benefit to politicizing him so young.

Yet Sharif would view their parental decision to shield him from the trauma of his father's past as a betrayal, and he experienced a certain sense of psychological displacement when he learned of it. He coped with this displacement by educating himself. Instead of turning to his father, a primary source on Palestinian history, he turned to books. He never learned how his father came to have a Jordanian passport, and he never asked his father what his childhood in Jerusalem had been like. Partly, this was because Hikmat traveled for work a great deal, and so the family's time together was often spent cutting up and playing practical jokes, raiding the refrigerator in the middle of the night, and going out on fun day trips and to fancy restaurants, not in serious conversation about the past. But partly, it was because Sharif felt strongly about developing his own views on Palestine by educating himself through books and documentaries.

While Sharif was absorbed in his struggle with his newfound identity, his parents were engaged in a struggle of their own. In fact, his father had just returned home from a two-month-long stay in a treatment center for victims of suicidal depression when the Intifada broke out. It was a fitting symbolic moment that Hikmat emerged from his illness just as his homeland rose to reclaim its national identity and free itself.

Just two months before, on October 19, 1987, "Black Monday," the New York Stock Exchange experienced the largest single-day drop in its history, sucking the international financial market, along with all of Hikmat's life savings, into the vortex with it. In 1985, Hikmat had left the Arab investments firm he headed to buy an American securities firm, hoping to expand Arab investor's horizons beyond Europe and into the global investments market. He had assembled a group of investors to put up the $12 million needed to acquire a controlling stake in a struggling Boston-based brokerage house, and he himself had personally invested everything he owned in the project, from his home to his children's future tuition money, and had taken out a loan against the company's share price. Under Hikmat's guidance, the firm had increased in value by 284 percent. But when the market crashed, the firm collapsed, and Hikmat Nashashibi was ruined. The day of the crash, after all of his colleagues had gone home, Hikmat had dragged himself from his desk and driven straight to Charter House, a hospice specializing in depression. He checked himself in for treatment and that night was put on suicide watch.

That night, when Muna went to the hospice to visit her husband, she found him miserable and distraught, lying with his face to the wall in a small room with a shuttered window, unable to discuss any solutions to their problems. Muna was used to her husband's dark spells, but she herself was not a person who crumbled in times of crisis, nor was she a person who easily indulged in self-destructive thinking in the face of a daunting task. She took easily to being in charge, so she decided that, just as she had taken over as head of her father's household when he was exiled from Syria, she would do the same with her husband's household here in London, until he was back on his feet. She dropped her activist work immediately and set about building a catering business, which could generate a lot of money with limited start-up costs. With her sister Maha's help, with less than three hours' sleep each night, and with significantly less time to spend with her children, Muna saved her family from bankruptcy. She wanted to support her husband through this difficult time, but after fighting to raise a business from the ground all day, she found that she had little energy to hear her husband out as he spoke of his feelings of hopelessness and longing for death. So, after that first visit to the hospice, she brought a Walkman and tapes of the great German operas and Russian ballets, and for the duration of her visits, she would lie in silence beside her husband on his narrow hospital bed, each of them listening to the strong chords and lofty musical flights out of one earpiece, healing together instead of dwelling on their difficulties.

In less than two months' time, Hikmat had recovered and Muna had managed to keep up with the loan payments and keep the household running. As the Intifada raged on, Hikmat returned to the world of high finance, this time with the Arab Banking Corporation. His work frequently took him away from home for five days a week, and in the meantime, Muna's catering business continued to expand, keeping her away from the house much more often than she had ever been before. Sharif was often left to his own devices, and left in charge of Nura and Omar. In this way, the family's dynamic began to shift just as Sharif began to grow into his Palestinian identity, mirroring the change in the dynamic of the Israeli-Palestinian conflict as Palestine began to grow into its own nationalist struggle.

Sharif's remembers his adolescence as turbulent, filled with personal loss and political conflict. As he informed himself about his nationality and began to form his identity as a Palestinian, he found this new identity brought him into conflict with some of his fellow students and, later on in high school, with some of his teachers.

Just after the Intifada began, he experienced death within the family for the first time. Muna's father died that year, followed by her mother almost exactly six months later. Sharif had been very close to these grandparents, who had co-parented him in Kuwait. Shortly after his grandmother's death, Sharif sat for the common entrance exam, which would be graded by a city-wide central committee. On the basis of his score on the exam and the results of interviews, he would be invited to apply for admission to certain secondary schools. Sharif had always been an excellent student, so his parents had little doubt that he would do well. But the day he completed the exam, his teacher returned the essay section with a note in its corner addressed to his mother, asking her to read the essay and then come for a meeting at the school the next day. Muna read the essay with some apprehension, but found her son's prose beautiful, and his story poignant. He had described a fight he'd had with a Jewish classmate over the Intifada, and had written that the incident only reminded him that he had lost not only his grandmother but his country as well. Muna assumed that the teacher would take issue with the essay as pro-Palestinian, and stayed awake all night preparing for a fight.

But the next day, Sharif's teacher greeted Hikmat and Muna with a warm smile and said, "Wasn't that a beautiful essay?" She carefully went on to say that she didn't know who would be reading the essay, and that she was afraid that the political sensitivity of Sharif's essay topic might jeopardize his chance for admission at some schools. She said that she was requesting permission for Sharif to sit for the exam a second time and resubmit his essay. While Hikmat and Muna thought it a shame that the political climate was such that Sharif would not be able to submit an essay that spoke honestly of his background and his feelings about his country of origin, they agreed that it was not worthwhile for him to compromise his future prospects just to express his identity in the common entrance exam. This incident foreshadowed the basic conflict that would define much of Sharif's early adulthood. Should he keep his political opinions separate from his career goals, or should he express what most occupied his thoughts and force others—teachers, admissions officers, and bosses—to contend with their own prejudices? Was there a time and place for being opinionated? He resubmitted his essay for the common entrance exam, but as he grew into adulthood, he would repeatedly choose to voice his opinions rather than keep his politics personal and focus on professional success.

After the results of the exam were in, he was invited to apply to St. Paul's School, a top boys' preparatory school in England, where he had been invited for a preliminary interview when he was eight years old. Muna remembers that while Sharif was giving his preliminary interview, she and Hikmat met with the school's headmaster. Muna recalls that the headmaster asked Hikmat if, as a Nashashibi from Jerusalem, it might be a problem for him to send his son to a school with a large Jewish presence. Hikmat replied that he had several close Jewish friends, lived and worked closely with Jewish colleagues and neighbors, and had never encountered difficulties in his personal relationships because of the Israeli-Palestinian conflict. Muna describes this meeting as though the headmaster were warning them, as Palestinians, that they would not fit in at the school. But academic success at St. Paul's would be sure to guarantee Sharif admission at a good university, and so when the time came for him to choose a secondary school, he decided to attend St. Paul's.

But he found his time at St. Paul's to be challenging, in no small part because of the school's social atmosphere. He describes the school as "elitist, and in a lot of ways racist." There were eleven Arab students in his class, and "there was quite a lot of racism directed toward us," he says. Although most of what he felt he describes as hidden racism, Sharif remembers the months surrounding the Persian Gulf War as a time when covert anti-Arab feeling exploded into open confrontation with his classmates. Iraq's invasion of Kuwait on August 2, 1990, came as a great shock to Arabs everywhere. For Sharif, who was himself part Iraqi and had been born in Kuwait, the tragedy of one Arab country invading another was not only a personal tragedy but a political tragedy as well. "The occupation and run-up to the war and the aftermath, in terms of divisions and divisiveness in the Arab world, that was just the depth. . . . I obviously wanted the liberation of Kuwait because the occupation was wrong, but then we were under no illusions that Iraq wasn't being bombed to oblivion, and the sanctions afterwards. The price that the Iraqis paid was horrific."

After refusing to comply with a UN order to withdraw from Kuwait on January 15, 1991, Iraq launched missile attacks on Tel Aviv, and Yasser Arafat publicly declared PLO support for Saddam Hussein. Anger and outrage in London's Jewish community collided with the shock and sadness in the Arab community, escalating Jewish-Arab tensions around the city. Although international pressure kept Israel from retaliating against Iraq, the perception of the war was recast as a Jewish-Arab conflict among the student body of St. Paul's. A confrontation between Jewish and Arab students on the day Iraq surrendered sticks out as particularly emblematic of the mood of the time in Sharif's memory. He describes sitting in a row with some other Arab students who were his friends, waiting for an early-morning biology class to begin, when a line of Jewish students filed into the room and stood in front of them, shouting "We won the war! We won the war!" He remembers that they leaned close, thrusting their fingers into his and the other Arab students' faces. Sharif doesn't remember how long the taunting went on or what compelled the students to stop, but he says that there were teachers present who did nothing to end the confrontation or stand up for the Arab students. This fairly short incident became one of his most vivid memories from his secondary school years. Through Sharif's memory of this confrontation, we gain insight into the process by which Sharif came to see himself as an out-sider in a system that protected the rights and privileges of another people at the expense of his own people, and excused aggressive behavior of that peo-ple against both his people and himself.

Sharif's resentment of Israel's policies would bring him into confronta-tion with his fellow students again and again. During an art class two years later, a teacher trying to motivate Sharif's imagination asked him what he didn't like. He remembers answering with a knee-jerk reply, "Zionism," and says that word quickly spread through the school that he had made an anti-Semitic remark. He recalls being called a "Nazi." There was talk of a fight after school, and Sharif remembers going home surrounded by a protective group of his friends that day. Through this memory, we see how Sharif came to believe that criticism of Zionist policies and even of Israel's policies could lead him to be cast as an antipathetic figure, unwilling to play by the normal rules of social conduct.

The process through which Sharif constructed his identity as one of oppo-sition contributed a great deal to his eventual activism. But another con-tributing factor was the era in which Sharif came of age, a period of sweeping global change in which existing social and political modalities were called into question. Within a period of about five years, the Cold War ended and the world broke into a tumult of economic transition and regional conflict. Two of the defining conflicts of the Middle East at this time—the Palestinian Intifada and the Persian Gulf War— represented not only moments of con-flict and growth in Sharif's personal life but also the two opposing faces of the new post-Cold War order, as described by some leading theorists of the time: neonationalist violence and multilateral collective security. The Intifada appeared to be the first in a wave of nationalist movements defined along reli-gious, ethnic, or linguistic lines that broke over the world as the Cold War ended, prompting renewed intellectual discourse on postcolonial discontent and reviving a cultural modality of protest, alienation, and solidarity among minorities in the major cities of the West. The Persian Gulf War, which took place four years later, was seen by many international relations scholars as a uniquely multilateral war to punish a violation of international law. It was described as surgical and pragmatic, and prompted much policy discussion on the role of the Western states in intervening collectively in conflicts overseas in the interests of preserving the international system as a whole.

Of course, nationalist movements and ethnic conflict existed long before the end of the Cold War, and many have questioned the motives and consequences of the Persian Gulf War. But the discourses resulting from this dichotomy shaped many young activists in the West, including Sharif, who looked to certain accepted principles of international law as the compass for moral outrage and as the basis for political action. Some have suggested that a "new Left" was born after the end of the Cold War, consisting of activists who pursued often vastly different goals—nationalist, humanitarian, environmental, labor, and dictated by gender and sexual orientation—in the interests of establishing a post-Cold War order that would correct the imbalance between the powerful and the powerless. As Sharif grew into the activist he became as an adult, he drew from a wealth of sources—personal experiences of racism, the history of Palestine, and international law that supported Palestine's right to a state of its own and the end of Israeli occupation of Palestinian territory— to form the basis of his own action. He read a great deal of theoretical analysis and watched several documentaries on the Palestinian struggle to inform his opinions, and he believed that international humanitarian principals and solidarity-based activism would eventually be the key to his people's liberation.

As Sharif began to take an interest in political activism, British Arabs began to awaken to their own ability to engage in British politics on behalf of their homelands. As we have noted, the Palestinian Intifada galvanized the scattered and invisible Palestinian expatriate population worldwide, often into political, social, and cultural action. Although Palestinian organizations had existed even before the occupation of the Palestinian territories began in 1967, the years after the Intifada saw a proliferation of various organizations in Europe and the United States that focused on development and relief, research and education, media production, or advocacy and solidarity in Palestine. As the Palestinian cause was taken up by Palestinians and non-Palestinians alike in activist and advocacy movements in the West, a new generation of British Arabs began to enter into adulthood, young men and women who had grown up with democratic political institutions. But even as the Intifada raised British sympathy toward the Palestinian independence movement, many British Arabs continued to perceive the British government as inaccessible and unresponsive to their interests. The Persian Gulf War and the harsh sanctions imposed on Iraq in its aftermath outraged many British Arabs, who felt that the British government had looked the other way as Israel broke international law even as they punished the Iraqi people for the transgressions of their dictator.

British Arabs were a relatively young and divided minority community in Britain, and many of them, coming from politically repressive countries, were reluctant to involve themselves in British politics. Although Arabs had been migrating to the United Kingdom since early in the nineteenth century, when Yemeni seamen working on British ships began settling around the ports where they docked, large-scale Arab immigration did not begin until the middle of the twentieth century. First Palestinians, then Iraqis, Egyptians, Sudanese, Algerians, Somalis, and Gulf Arabs fleeing political crises in their home countries began arriving in waves and settling primarily in and around London. They formed pocket communities in London's many neighborhoods, often founding cultural associations but staying away from political activism. As late as 1999, there were no Arab parliamentarians or local councillors in Britain. Arabs were not given a separate census category, and as such, were split between several ethnic, religious, and even racial categories in the British government's records. But by the end of the twentieth century, a combination of factors led the British Arab community to coalesce and begin engaging in lobbying. Although most British Arab lobbying would continue to focus on issues in the homeland, a few leading individuals would begin to urge British Arabs to come together as a community to lobby on behalf of domestic issues, such as census categorization and race relations legislation. In many ways, the Intifada, in generating British sympathy for the most powerful and unifying cause among Arabs, and in leading the British Arab population to begin organizing as a political community to influence foreign policy issues affecting their homelands, helped to create an atmosphere of belonging and engagement in the British Arab community.

For many years to come, however, British Arab political engagement would center on British foreign policy decisions. Just as the loss of Palestine served as one of the greatest symbolic unifiers among Arabs and even all Muslims, ongoing Western policies affecting the Palestinian quest for independence and for statehood would serve as a litmus test against which to assess the sympathies and true intentions of Western governments. In the long run, disappointment with British government policies first toward Palestine and later toward Iraq generated an ongoing feeling of frustration and alienation among many British Arabs.

But these frustrations were still to come. Five years after the Intifada began, the Oslo Accords seemed to lay out the path to peace and statehood for Palestine. The PLO and Israel entered into a mutual recognition agreement, and the Palestinian Authority was formed. It seemed to be a time of cautious but nonetheless real optimism among Arabs worldwide.

Late at night on Sunday, January 30, 1994, Hikmat called his wife, as he did every night he was away on his travels. He had been away for nearly a month, and Muna was looking forward to his return. She worried about his health, because he never watched what he ate, how hard he worked, or how much pressure he put on himself to succeed, and she looked forward to having him at home for a little while. But to her chagrin, he told her that he would have to travel to Beirut almost as soon as he had arrived back home. His sister's husband had been diagnosed with a terminal case of cancer and she believed that he was now on his death bed. On the phone with his wife, Hikmat fretted that he was tired and could not keep taking time off of work. He had already spent two weeks with his sister that month. Muna tried to dissuade him from going, saying, as the Arabic expression went, the living do not wait for the living to die. But Hikmat felt bound by duty to go. He had taken over as head of the family after his father had died, and had seen to both of his sisters' marriages. He felt responsible for his sister's happiness and her sorrows alike. He was arriving at home on Wednesday, and he asked Muna if she would go with him to Beirut that Friday.

The next day, Muna scheduled in some extra time to go shopping for a new black suit jacket to take to Beirut, just in case her brother-in-law passed away during their visit. Early Tuesday morning, she traveled to her sister's house in Wimbledon, on the outskirts of London, where she had headquartered her catering business, and stayed working so late that she missed Hikmat's call to remind her of his arrival time and other minor details. She crawled into bed late, long after everyone else was asleep. Although she was exhausted, her head whirled planning for a major event she was catering, Hikmat's arrival, and their upcoming trip to Beirut. After a good deal of tossing, she fell into a troubled sleep.

In the middle of the night, Muna woke with a gasp and sat straight up in her bed. A singular sensation had woken her, as if something vital and powerful was draining from her womb, almost as if some life force was being sucked from her body by vacuum. She reached out into the darkness and clutched at the damp, hot sheets. Her whole body trembled. Breathing slowly in and out she willed her heart down from her throat and back into her chest. She had a deep, sudden longing to have Hikmat at her side. She turned on the light and squinted at the clock at the side of her bed. He would be there in just a few more hours. She tried to calm herself; she needed the rest. She had had an open-heart surgery the previous October, the second in her life, and her doctors kept telling her that she needed to sleep well at night.

She must have fallen back asleep, because the alarm clock woke her, as it did every morning, at 3:30 a.m. Her muscles felt tired and sore, as if she had been lifting heavy boxes instead of sleeping. She stretched and sat up, then got up with a sigh. She knew she should start packing. She did not look forward to the trip; it was sure to be a sad and exhausting one. In the very worst case, there would be hurried funeral arrangements to make. Hikmat's relatives, as Muslims, would need to be buried on the same day of their deaths.

After she had finished some paperwork and read the newspaper, Muna went downstairs into the kitchen. It was almost February, and the tiles were so cold that they hurt her ankles. She wrapped a plastic bag around her hair, to keep the smell of oil from it, and pulled on her cooking sweatshirt. Since Hikmat would be coming home today, she had planned to make one of his favorite dishes. While she was in the middle of cooking, the front doorbell rang. She quickly snatched the plastic bag off her head and went to the door. One of Hikmat's colleagues stood before her.

Hikmat had been in an accident, he said, hurriedly adding that he had broken his leg and been taken to the hospital. Muna thought to herself, how strange, why isn't Hikmat speaking to me himself? She turned and strode over to the telephone, asking over her shoulder for the name of the hospital. The colleague said confusedly that he didn't have the number for the hospital. Muna began to feel irritated, and impatiently asked if there was anyone she could call, someone at the office perhaps?

Suddenly, Muna's sister Maha appeared behind the colleague. She stepped around him and came close to Muna. She looked worried, like she had been crying. Muna, still impatiently, asked Maha why she was crying. The colleague blurted out that, actually, Hikmat had had a heart attack, but he was fine, and was in intensive care at a hospital in Bahrain. Muna replaced the telephone receiver and said that, in that case, she needed to go to him right away. The colleague argued that she would need a visa. Muna said it didn't matter, she had a British passport.

And then the colleague told her that her husband was dead. He was fifty-one years old.

Muna's memories of this, perhaps the greatest trauma in her life, form a disjointed narrative. Her love for the dramatic made her an elaborate story-teller, and with great attention to detail, she was able to deliver a full account of her life's experiences, intertwining political and personal history. How she learned of her husband's death, however, would always remain fractured in her memory and difficult for her to narrate. Although trauma often causes distortions in the clarity and chronology of memory, in Muna's case, the narrative is also fragmented because Hikmat's colleague had been trying to break the news of her husband's death slowly in the futile hope of sparing her from shock. Since she was a heart patient, he worried how she might react to the news. So he had consulted first with Maha and brought a doctor along in the car.

When Sharif arrived home from school that afternoon, he saw his mother and aunt in the family room. Both of them were crying. They called to him to come in and sit with them. He remembers feeling a deep sense of dread that held his feet to the ground just outside of the family room, a physical resistance to going in to join them. Suddenly, a single thought came into his head, and his worst fear manifested itself as a kind of premonition: "My father died."

That night, Sharif broke the news to his ten-year-old brother Omar, who most closely resembled their father in both looks and temperament, and with whom Hikmat had always been the most playful. Sharif took Omar up to his bedroom on the third floor and closed the door. He sat beside his brother on the bed, and then very quietly told him what had happened. Omar jumped up as if startled by a loud noise. Sharif pulled his younger brother down onto his lap, and held him as they both cried together. It was the first and also the last time Sharif and his brother ever discussed their father's death, and it was the last time he would ever cry in front of his brother. From that moment onward, Sharif began to see his younger brother and sister as more than just his siblings, and assumed a protective and dominant posture with them. Just as Hikmat had taken on the responsibility of looking after his younger sisters and brothers when his father had died, and just as Muna had taken on the responsibility of caring for her younger sister when her father was exiled, the cycle continued and Sharif, who had not yet turned sixteen, became the man of the house.

Although he instinctively took on this role, he was overwhelmed by his sudden grief and unprepared to face the responsibility right away. As a very private person, he would have preferred to spend the first weeks of mourning alone with his family, but, as was the Arab custom, for forty days after his father's death the Nashashibis entertained guests who came to pay their respects. As the man of the house, Sharif was expected to greet the guests, serve coffee, and accept condolences for his family's loss. He recalls that almost every guest he entertained took the opportunity to remind him that he was now the man of the house and had to be responsible, and over time, he began to feel oppressed by the general expectation that he should be strong and stoic, that he should be a man well before reaching actual manhood. One close family friend told him not to listen to the other guests, but to take his time and be however he felt like being. But he remembers feeling put off and alienated from the other guests, many who were long-term friends of his parents. He returned to school the day after his father's death, just to avoid the public mourning, which he steeled himself to face. He did not wish to cry in front of strangers, so he remembers stuffing his emotions and grief deep inside and keeping his face like an expressionless mask, only for his grief to resurface months and months later.

Hikmat had died during the holy month of Ramadan, which according to Islamic belief meant that he would ascend directly to heaven. In keeping with Islamic law, Hikmat should have been buried on the day of his death, but it took nearly four days to arrange for him to be brought from Bahrain. Sharif's four closest friends, a Lebanese boy, an Indian boy, an Iraqi Kurdish boy, and a Jewish boy, stood by his side during the funeral, and the Indian boy, a Hindu, even joined in with the Muslims during their fasting for the holy month, out of solidarity. Sharif and his other Arab friends had been fasting during Ramadan for four nearly years, since they had turned twelve, the age when a Muslim is expected to begin fasting. He never saw it as an active attempt at claiming his Arab identity, just as a sort of festive thing he and his friends did together. He remembers waiting with his friends for the appointed hour, watching the clock until they could dive into the feast waiting for them. Then they would start with the soup, dates, and apricot juice and keep on eating until they were bursting. Sharif started fasting as a way to lose weight, and after his father's death, he incorporated fasting into a broader health regime. Suddenly, watching his health had become a top priority to him. In a way, he says that he felt let down by his father's death, because his father had never done anything to combat his poor health. "I don't want to say that my dad failed us, but I want to live as long as possible for my family. . . . Just live long for the people you love. And I learned that from him."

Losing his father at this critical time in his life fundamentally changed Sharif. Not only did it teach him to value his family above all else but it also changed the composition of his personality. "Losing a parent when you're young, it just changes you in so many ways," he says. "In some ways it makes you stronger, in some ways it gives you lots of insecurities." This experience of loss transformed Sharif into a person with a profound sense of responsibility and obligation, and this transformation was the cornerstone in Sharif's life of activism. "I feel like I should be responsible, not just to my family but to my people," he says. In assuming personal responsibility both for his family and for a nation, he also gave himself the burden of constantly feeling as if he was not doing enough. Throughout his life, Sharif would suffer from bouts of crippling anxiety, often crashing into deep depression. This would be the terrible second face of the sense of purpose and responsibility that drove Sharif's life, and eventually, his career.

On September 17, 2000, Sharif looked around him at the more than 2,000 people who had gathered on Trafalgar Square to rally for the right of Palestinian refugees to return to their homes in Israel and the Occupied Territories, and he thought to himself, "This is the beginning of a movement." As he surveyed the crowd, Sharif saw children and elderly, students and professionals, Arabs and non-Arabs alike, gathered under the overcast sky. Although the rally was relatively small compared to later peace demonstrations Sharif would join and even help organize, it was the first of its kind in Britain, and it was the first such event Sharif had been involved in organizing. It was some three months after peace negotiations between Israel and the PLO had broken down at Camp David. A full thirteen years after the Intifada had begun, still no progress had been made toward the creation of an independent Palestinian state, and frustration was the prevailing sentiment among Arabs everywhere.

But now a younger generation of Arabs was emerging in Britain, a group of young people who felt confident enough to speak out against what they saw as an entrenched media and policy bias in Britain against the Palestinian perspective. The September 17 rally was the culmination of months of work and weeks of sleepless nights by a small group of students and activists who, with no money or experience, had arranged both a pre-rally event and a full program of international speakers for the rally itself. Sharif had joined the young group spearheading the rally, al-Awda, the Palestinian Right to Return Coalition, as a rally organizer early in the year. As he listened to Azmi Bishara, a prominent Arab Israeli member of the Knesset, Israel's parliament, who had in 1999 been the first Arab Israeli to run for prime minister of

Israel, and heard the roaring of the crowd around him, Sharif was moved nearly to tears. He was proud of the rally's success, thrilled that so many Londoners had turned out to support this cause, and empowered with the discovery that if he spoke out, others would join him and still others would listen. For the first time in his life, it occurred to Sharif that he could actually do something with his knowledge to help right what he had always thought was an irrevocable, entrenched wrong against his people. It was after this rally that Sharif decided to found his own activist organization. "I'd spent my teenage years reading and studying, and I basically felt confident now to speak out and be a spokesman," he says.

Sharif had spent his high school years learning all he could about the Israeli-Palestinian conflict. But when it came time for him to choose a course of study for college, his mother refused to let him study international relations. With a degree in international relations, he would only be good for cocktail party conversations, and would never be able to find a job, she maintained. He exerted himself to score highly in the business course his mother insisted upon, but only so that he would be able to choose his own master's program. By the time he was ready to apply, he had spent so many years reading about international relations and international law that he decided to pursue a degree that would give him the vocational skills to apply his knowledge. He chose journalism.

He showed a natural knack for journalism, winning one of only four spots reserved for British students at the prestigious school of journalism at London's City College, and was the single student of his class selected for a winter internship at Reuters. Since he knew he wanted to write about issues in the Arab region, upon graduation Sharif decided to enroll in a six-week-long intensive Arabic course in a small town just north of Beirut, on Lebanon's northwest coast. It was during this stay that Sharif, with the help of his aunt who still lived in Beirut, paid his first visit to a Palestinian refugee camp. His aunt arranged for a camp resident to meet with Sharif, his cousin, and his roommate in the program, and to accompany them past the guards and around the camp.

Then they entered what could only be described as an enclosed shantytown, with sewage running on the streets and heaps of garbage piled everywhere. The camp had not expanded or developed in the forty years since its inception, even as its population multiplied well into the third generation of the refugees who had originally fled here. With no permission to work, travel, or expand, the camp residents were forced to live in a state of paralysis and poverty. What struck Sharif as more deplorable than the conditions themselves was that these conditions were purely the result of a political impasse between governments unwilling to allow Palestinian refugees to realize their potential, contribute to society, take care of themselves, and feel at home where they were. The visitors met an older man who insisted on inviting the three of them to lunch with him and his family in their small house, which Sharif describes as a shack. They ate a delicious meal in the single-room dwelling that was home to a family of eleven, under a prominently displayed picture of Yasser Arafat, one of hundreds they had seen throughout the camp. The sight of this much hospitality amid this much hopelessness moved Sharif, and the sight of so many pictures of Arafat angered him. He asked himself how the camp residents could so naively continue to support a leader who he felt had forgotten them. This visit opened Sharif's eyes to what he saw as the greatest tragedy of contemporary Palestinian life, the condition of its refugees living as permanent outcasts in the neighboring Arab countries. After the visit, he became a passionate advocate of the right of Palestinian refugees to return to their homes in Israel, the West Bank, and the Gaza Strip, a right guaranteed under international law since 1949, yet hotly debated and rejected by many in Israel because the influx of some two million Palestinian Arabs would make Jews a minority in Israel, essentially putting an end to Israel's character as a Jewish state.

Sharif thought he would never see a worse picture of Palestinian suffering than this, but after he had completed a second internship, this time at the Middle East Economic Survey in Cyprus, his mother suggested that it was time for his first visit to Palestine, his father's homeland, before he returned to London to look for a job. The two-week-long visit to various relatives of his father's in the Gaza Strip, West Bank, and parts of Israel brought Sharif into direct confrontation with his family's losses and with the harsh realities of occupation. Sharif and his mother started their trip with a visit to relatives in the Gaza Strip and then crossed over into the West Bank, eventually visiting some cities in Israel proper, including Nazareth and Tiberias. Although economic conditions in the West Bank were much better than in the refugee camp Sharif had seen in Lebanon, and better even than the standard of living in Gaza, he found the inequalities and injustices of the occupation to be more evident in the West Bank. "You'd see a lot more [Israeli] settlements next to Arab slums," he says, adding that the proximity of the communities only highlighted for him the discrepancy in wealth and status between the two peoples. He was shocked by small economic realities, like hearing Palestinians in the West Bank speaking Hebrew or seeing Arab shop owners selling "I ♥ Israel" T-shirts and Israeli flags. In Jerusalem, he stayed at a hotel owned by his father's cousin, right outside of the Damascus Gate to Jerusalem's Old City. They went to visit Hikmat's childhood home, but were not allowed inside. It was then that Sharif and his mother learned that his grandfather's mansion, their family home, had been "liberated" by the Israeli military and had been turned into an Israeli courthouse. "For a long time beforehand I didn't want to go because I was worried I'd get upset," says Sharif. "I was very upset, but I don't regret going. It made me see."

Although his travels opened his eyes, Sharif never considered moving abroad, let alone to Palestine. This was largely because he found the circumstances in Palestine itself to be stifling, and felt better prepared to serve his people with the resources and opportunities available to him in Great Britain. But it was also because he couldn't think of leaving his family and move away from his full life in London. The loss of Hikmat had brought Muna, Maha, and the three children very close to each other. The closeness is very clear when the family is together, in the way they pile on top of each other on the couch, and in the little nicknames and silly jokes they share. After Hikmat's death, Muna closed the catering business to spend all of her time with the children. For many months after his death, she struggled to manage the household and take care of three children without a breadwinner, and she struggled with her own feelings of overwhelming loss and confusion. She never returned to work, but did return to activism, joining the boards of nearly a dozen different Palestinian rights and Arab activist groups.

In some ways, it seems as though Hikmat's death, in shattering the traditional family order, blurred the lines between family roles—parent and child,
relative and friend. Well into adulthood, all three children still lived happily
at home. Muna may have been strict about things like education and grades,
but in some ways she was very tolerant, particularly of the boys' social lives.
Throughout high school and college, Sharif was a house music deejay, often
spending late nights in clubs, and even winning some high-profile competi-
tions. Muna never questioned his comings and goings and teased him about
his success with women. For his eighteenth birthday, Muna baked Sharif a
cake shaped like a pair of woman's bare breasts, with red gumdrops for nip-
ples and a heart-shaped pendant dangling in the frosted cleavage. She welcomed his girlfriends into the house; in fact, one of his girlfriends, a Swiss
woman, lived in their house for two years. Although Muna headed the
household and relied on her sister for much of the help she needed, Sharif
was still the man of the house and as such, had a particular status in the
household. Even though they often clashed, Muna and Sharif were not only
mother and son but were also the closest of friends, and her influence on
how he approached politics and which causes he chose was great. Certainly,
Sharif's political beliefs were entirely his own, but he had absorbed his
mother's belief that political activism was a natural expression of cultural
pride for Arabs. As time passed, and Muna returned to her own activism
after many years in the workforce, Sharif joined her at demonstrations and
lectures. It was from his mother that he first learned of the group al-Awda,
and under her guidance that he became involved in British Arab activism.

The al-Awda rally was the pivotal moment in Sharif's progression toward
a life of activism. Through his involvement with the rally, he garnered a great
many practical skills and plugged himself into a network of people who
cared about what he cared about. More important, he saw that he had the
qualities of a leader, the capacity to organize, and a vision of his own.

Then, within two weeks of the rally, news of the second Intifada, known
as the al-Aqsa Intifada, burst into the headlines. Sharif read these headlines
and felt that the major British newspapers repeatedly neglected to put the
uprising and the failed Camp David meetings in the proper historical

context. Media reports often stated that the meetings had ended with Arafat's rejection of an Israeli peace offer without further explaining that the peace offer had not incorporated previously discussed statements regarding the halting or dismantling of Israeli settlements on land designated for Palestinian residential and agricultural use in the West Bank and Gaza. Within days of the outbreak of violence, Sharif began to recognize the pattern of bias and incomplete reporting. It seemed that most news coverage of the conflict excluded significant details on the history of the conflict, the illegality of settlements and occupation under international law, and how military presence and occupation policy restricted Palestinian life. He felt that articles, timelines, and chronologies of suicide bombing attacks on Israeli civilians should be offset by similar descriptions of Palestinian homes demolished to make room for settlements, Palestinian civilians killed during Israeli military actions in the Occupied Territories, and Palestinian rights under international law. He felt outraged but, for once, not resigned. He knew what he wanted to do to serve his people: his activism, as a journalist, would be to monitor the British media and hold it accountable for whatever instances of inaccurate, biased, and lazy journalism he could clearly identify. Wasting no time, Sharif formed a Yahoo! e-mail group called Arab Media Watch, which he described as "an independent, non-partisan media monitoring coalition" with membership spanning the religious, political, and ethnic spectrum.

Although it was the British media that first opened Sharif's eyes to the existence and struggles of Palestinians living under occupation, the same media now became the target of Sharif's activism. In the United States, it is often suggested that the British media is more balanced, and even occasionally more sympathetic to the Arab perspective in its coverage of the Israeli-Palestinian conflict. But Arab Media Watch has conducted widely published studies showing that, from the locations of British news bureaus on the ground, to the ethnicity of expert and witness sources quoted in articles, to the historic context of articles, British media from tabloids to broadsheets to broadcast were demonstrably biased toward presenting the Israeli perspective, despite an appearance of objectivity and neutrality.

Slowly, as the group grew in membership and in scope, Sharif found that his activism made it difficult for him to pursue a career in journalism. Older friends and acquaintances of Muna's had often criticized her for taking her teenaged son with her to political rallies and demonstrations, saying that his future prospects would be ruined; but to the contrary, Sharif had never found that his political beliefs or his Arab background hindered his ability to find a good job. In fact, he landed the very first job he had applied for when he had returned from Palestine, an editorial job on the energy and commodities desk at Dow Jones. Within a few months, he was even brought on to edit copy from the general news desk. Many of the editors he encountered edited newswire copy from all over the world and, since they were not experts on any particular region of the world, were not likely to be sensitive to biased or incomplete information dispatched from a particular bureau. It was here that Sharif really began to feel that his political activism and mainstream editorial practices would not mix. As his work with Arab Media Watch heightened his sensitivity to the frequency of media misconceptions regarding the Israeli-Palestinian conflict, he found it harder and harder to tolerate lack of expertise in the general news editorial staff processing reports on the conflict for public consumption. Contrary to what he might have expected, his activism and his background did not make it hard for him to be hired, it just limited the number of organizations whose editorial standards lined up with his own.

Sharif describes one particular incident as a pivotal illustration of how mainstream editorial practices diverged from his own values. He recalls that one day, the head of the general news department, an American woman named Gabriella Stern, addressed the editorial staff on how to standardize language for reporting on the Intifada. He remembers that she said that all suicide bombings and attacks by Palestinian militants in Israel should be referred to as "terrorist" incidents, to which he remembers insisting that, since "terrorism" is a subjective term with no accurate definition, the word "terrorist" should either be used to describe acts of violence committed by both sides in the conflict or not at all. He remembers Stern responding that Israeli settlers just sought a peaceful life and that the Israeli army did not target innocent civilians and children, to which he remembers citing wire reports in which the Israeli military had indeed targeted children and Palestinian homes had been destroyed to make room for settlements. He describes the incident as a confrontation between himself and the head of news, in which he openly stood up to and challenged the big boss in front of a large room full of his stunned colleagues. Finally, as he recalls, several of the other editors chimed in on his side, agreeing that describing only one side of a conflict as "terrorist" would be unfair. Stern recalls that there were many editorial discussions on the use of the word "terrorism" in news organizations throughout the world at the time, but she does not recall any particular confrontation with Sharif or her own editorial staff. She recalls that while some news organizations, like the British Broadcasting Corporation (BBC), chose to institute what some have called an "informal ban" on the use of the word "terrorist," Dow Jones did not.

In Sharif's memory of the incident we once again see a reinforcement of his self-image as one of opposition, standing up to powerful institutional forces on behalf of his underrepresented and misrepresented people. Shortly afterward, Sharif left Dow Jones for a position at the *Middle East Times*, hoping to be able to grow his career with a news organization more open to his political beliefs and perspectives. Unfortunately, the organization was struggling with financial and management issues, and so Sharif decided that his best bet was to focus solely on developing Arab Media Watch into a full-fledged organization. Meantime, a series of talks had been unable to stop the cycle of violence in Israel and the Palestinian Territories, and following a suicide bombing in April of 2002, Israel reoccupied many parts of the West Bank, placing Arafat's compound under siege. During the violent clashes accompanying the reoccupation, Israeli military actions inflicted a great deal of suffering on Palestinians even as the suffering of Israeli civilians targeted by suicide bombing attacks prompted widespread media coverage and outrage in the West, and Sharif felt that Arab Media Watch should seek to fill what he saw as a critical reporting gap in presenting the impact of the reoccupation on Palestinian civilians. When he made the decision to focus on his organization, he had neither a secure, permanent source of financing nor a full-time, committed staff. But he felt that if he wanted to make his organization work, and realize what he had been building toward since he first learned that he was Palestinian, he would have to take the risk and dedicate himself to making Arab Media Watch succeed.

As a second-generation immigrant, Sharif drew on several resources to construct his identity, to define his place in society, and to give himself a purpose and a role. His parents were iconoclastic, independent, and strong-willed people who felt a strong sense of national pride and personal determinism, and had overcome great political and financial adversity in order to maintain a certain standard of living for their children, and to make personal contributions toward the advancement of their political beliefs. Sharif discovered his father's nationality during a particularly dramatic media spectacle, and spent many years independently searching for the truth, learning a history of which most of his classmates were ignorant, and in the process discovering a passion for investigating and exposing the "other" side of a conflict story. He identified himself with this "other" side, and in doing so, developed a strong sense of otherness. The loss of his father led Sharif to develop broader feelings of duty and social obligation, which he would channel into an interest in activism. Even though he would always identify himself as both British and Palestinian, his life and work would reflect an ongoing process of shifting group identification. Nonetheless, Sharif's identity as a Palestinian would largely define many of his life and career choices as an adult.

But in the years after the al-Aqsa Intifada began, a new discourse would emerge in the production of media, culture, and policy, the so-called "clash of civilizations" discourse. The concept of a fundamental conflict between Islam and the West proved to be virulent and titillating to certain vocal elements on both sides of the supposed divide, and contributed to a dramatic reframing of long-standing racial and social tensions in Britain. In the summer of 2001 some of Britain's worst race riots broke out in the north, bringing into living rooms across Britain images of predominantly Muslim South Asian youth attacking English businesses with Molotov cocktails. The riots prompted far-reaching discussions on the nature of segregation, disaffection, and exclusion in Britain's social and political institutions, and launched a national debate on how to elevate British citizenship from a simple legal status into something that carried an intrinsic sense of value, belonging, and loyalty. In the coming years, several events would occur that would focus national scrutiny on disaffected Muslim youth in British society. And in many instances, the occupation of Palestine and eventually of Iraq would be cited as sources of Muslim outrage, the primary symbol of alienation and irreconcilable differences between Muslim and Western societies.

For Sharif, pushing for Palestinian civil and human rights was an essentially secular cause that should appeal to all thinking and feeling people. In fact, both he and Muna emphasized that Sharif served as a uniquely accessible spokesman for the Palestinian cause, one who undermined common prejudices toward Arabs and Palestinians. With his fair complexion and blue eyes, his British accent and eloquent style of speech, his youth and secularism, and his nonpartisan, multiethnic, multifaith coalition of volunteers, he hoped to reach a broader audience. Indeed, he rarely interacted with British Muslim activist organizations, and over time, made an effort to distinguish Arab Media Watch from organizations and networks that were predominantly religious or ethnic in character. With his work, he hoped to break down the effects of "clash of civilizations" thinking that threatened to invade even the most stalwart of media organizations. But time and time again, his feelings of otherness and outrage would make it difficult for him to take a position defined as moderate in the Western political debate surrounding Palestine and Arab countries. In the coming years, both internal and external pressures would challenge his vision of and commitment to media activism. As he struggled to negotiate his role and his place in British society, he would have to face his personal fear of failure, overcome his feelings of political and social alienation, earn a living in a society that was unwilling to fund and advance a pro-Arab organization, and make his voice heard in a cultural environment that had less and less room for bipartisan thinking. And as Arab Media Watch struggled for funding and legitimacy, Sharif would begin to think that a Britain that had no place for his professional voice had no place for his personal voice either.

CHAPTER 5

RECREATING THE
LOST VILLAGE

Mehmet Dogan came to Germany for one purpose only: to make money and then, at the end of his contract, go back home. He had a whole life waiting for him there, and no intention of building a new one anywhere else. But he waited too long, extended his contract too many times, and when he finally did decide to take a look around him and figure out what he wanted from a life in Germany, his village was under siege and his homeland was too dangerous for him to return. Almost instinctively, he began to recreate his lost village, in the process integrating and empowering an entire generation of Kurds in his small West German town. Adla respected the logic of her husband's decision to settle in Germany, and she was tired of living without a husband. But she never sought anything from German society, so she never felt that she stood to gain anything from her life in Germany other than the advantage of living with her husband.

While Mehmet worked, Adla spent her first days in Germany alone with the children in a single-room basement sublet that was their temporary home, until the renovations on the apartment Mehmet had rented could be completed. Two weeks after their arrival, the landlady turned off their heat and electricity after finding Adla making flatbread to comfort her children. When Mehmet came home several hours later to find his wife and children shivering under a thin blanket in the icy basement, he confronted the landlady, and after a bitter fight, was thrown out of the house with his wife and children. They moved that night into the unfinished apartment, without proper boots or any moving equipment, and used empty grocery bags as pillows. The landlady may have had a good explanation for her actions, but since she was unable to communicate in a shared language, she made a decision that the family could only understand as punitive. Adla found this incident profoundly dislocating. The repercussions of living in a foreign culture where the simple and obvious task of making bread for her children could offend someone struck her as too great. She realized that without language or community, a misunderstanding could quickly devolve into an untenable situation, and if some private citizen or government official decided to abuse her, she lacked the basic equipment to explain herself, protect herself, or fight back.

When Adla arrived, Germany was in the midst of a nativist moment, in a state of political denial that its immigrants, who had begun arriving twenty years before, were there to stay. Germany never intended to become home to a permanent immigrant population. In fact, until 2000, German citizenship was primarily passed on through blood inheritance, not by birth on German soil. After the Second World War, West Germany found itself in dire need of a labor force to rebuild its devastated infrastructure and industrial base, so it began to recruit foreign labor through treaty arrangements with several Mediterranean and North African countries. Guest workers' contracts were to last just two years, but German companies found it easier to renew their contracts than hire and train new recruits, and as more and more factories opened up, more and more positions needed to be filled. And so the guest worker population multiplied. Guest workers were housed in fenced-off barracks, and since they worked too many hours to form a visible presence in the cities where they lived, they were tolerated by German society. But as recession struck in the 1970s and unemployment rose, German public opinion toward the large foreign work force took a nosedive. By then, many of the guest workers had settled down, and many had begun bringing their families from home. When guest worker recruitment officially ended in 1973, the non-German population continued to grow through family reunification visas, which was how Mehmet brought his family to join him. Although the German government started talking about developing an "integration concept" in the late 1970s, it would continue to pass laws designed to restrict immigration, curtail immigrants' civil and political rights, limit immigrants' opportunities and movement, and encourage and even pay them to go back home. In fact, the German government would not officially draft an "immigration policy" until 2000; all laws dealing with immigrants instead fell under the country's "foreigner law."

By the end of the twentieth century, immigration had altered the country's demographic makeup so irrevocably that German society would have no choice but to acknowledge that the German state did not belong solely to the German nation, and the German government would have to develop a system for incorporating a population that had been forced to remain foreign well into the third immigrant generation. Of the eight countries that signed guest worker recruitment treaties with Germany, Turkey sent by far the largest and most persistent stream of foreign workers. Many scholars and activists have suggested that the main reason for Germany's long trepidation against integrating or even accepting its immigrants was that its largest immigrant population was non-European and Muslim.

Organizations and lobbying groups founded by children of Turkish guest workers began to develop political and social networks to protest the longstanding policies that had kept their parents and many of their peers economically, socially, and culturally excluded from German society. But even as the Turkish community grew in visibility and influence, the Kurds who had migrated from Turkey would remain largely ignored as a group with its own identity and concerns separate from the Turkish community. They were invisible in the eyes of the German government, and disregarded or in some cases despised by the same Turkish immigrants who were leading the push for minority rights in Germany. As a Turkish lobby formed and began advocating on a wide array of domestic issues, the Kurdish community remained fractured and underrepresented, many of its most recent arrivals coping with the collective trauma of war. The Dogans' youngest daughter, Sukriye, would dedicate her life to helping Kurdish refugees navigate their way through the minefield of psychological trauma and German bureaucracy.

On her kitchen wall, in her apartment on a tree-lined Berlin street, Sukriye keeps a picture of the hillside where her childhood home once stood.

Beneath a startling blue sky, Sukriye, a young woman in blue corduroys with a sash twined around her hair, sits on a rock with her head in her hands, amid the flattened ruins of the village where her parents were born and married. The picture is emblematic of her existence; a whole person in a destroyed village, a constant reminder of both her loss and her survival, and that she is still standing where so much has been reduced to rubble.

Sukriye left Kurdistan before war broke out, and when the war officially ended twenty years later, the homeland she had left behind was no longer the same, but irrevocably scarred. Her home village, Xarabe Baba, was among the thousands forcibly evacuated and razed during the war; between 3,500 and 4,000 villages are estimated to have been destroyed and some 380,000 people displaced between 1984 and 1999. Sukriye's experience of personal growth during a period of collective loss shaped her consciousness and became the basis upon which she founded her political identity. She entered into adolescence in a setting that gave her greater opportunities for personal growth than she might have had in a homeland strangled by elements of racism, misogyny, and poverty. But as Kurdistan suffered from destruction, military occupation, and depopulation, her personal memories of an idealized childhood combined with her dreams of a lost and mythic homeland. It became her life's work to serve her homeland's memory and hope for liberation through her own personal development, cultural celebration, and political activism.

As much as Adla may have worried that she was making a moral compromise by bringing her daughters to the licentious and godless West, Sukriye thrived on the freedoms and opportunities in Germany. She had her father's ambition and adaptability, and he fostered in her a progressive outlook and belief in community service. In Kurdistan, she would have been expected to learn the craft of keeping a house and raising a family; virtuous girls from good families did not go to school but were carefully preserved and groomed for marriage. In fact, schooling for girls was considered *haram* in Kurdistan, forbidden under that society's interpretation of the Islamic moral code, and while Mehmet had wanted his daughters in school, Adla had not wanted to risk public shaming while he was out of the country. In Germany, where schooling was mandatory, the twins finally had the opportunity Mehmet had always wanted for all of his girls. Adla insisted on keeping their fourteen-year-old sister, Celile, at home for company and help in running the household. Celile, who like Sukriye always craved an education, would eventually teach herself to read and write German, Turkish, and Kurmanci, the northern and most widely spoken Kurdish dialect, but she would be married at nineteen and a mother by twenty-one, without the time or formal education needed to pursue a career. In a large family, there is often a sort of progressive liberalization. By the time they arrived in Germany, Celile was already set on a course that left little room for personal ambition, but Sukriye, who was just five years younger, essentially had the opportunities of a generation younger than her sister's.

Even before she moved to Germany, Sukriye had begun to see education as a path to both her personal liberation and to the liberation of Kurdistan. Indeed, many leading development theorists and practitioners have stated time and again that poor, agrarian societies develop much faster if women are given power over decision making and the opportunity to educate themselves. Both within her family and in her later work with the community, Sukriye repeatedly saw how misogynistic conservatism disguised as religious morality or as honor drastically restricted the opportunities and freedoms of women in Kurdistan. "Thank God school was mandatory here," she says. Although she respected and loved her mother and older sisters, she saw how lack of education left them with no choices other than to run a household with whatever limited means they happened to receive from their husbands, and to live their lives by the dictates of their men. "I never wanted to become a housewife the way my mother was, I wanted to have a career. I defined my freedom as a woman as not wanting to marry. I thought to myself, I can only free myself from these [sexist] structures if I have an education."

Their first year of school was not easy. The twins were nine years old when they were enrolled, and since they had never had any formal schooling, they were placed in the first grade. On their first day at school, Sukriye and Hasbiye huddled together in one corner of the classroom, afraid to speak. Their younger classmates had attended preschool and kindergarten, and were familiar with the concept and format of school, but Sukriye and Hasbiye were overcome with diffidence, only able to giggle nervously when the teacher addressed them directly. Both girls were moved back from the first grade to preschool for the remaining half of the school year, where they spent their first four months in Germany playing and coloring, and more importantly, learning how to interact in a school setting. They were put back in the first grade just in time for the summer session, and through plays and competitive sports, Sukriye blossomed. A girl who had been just one more daughter in a large family, another child roaming the neighborhood, she now became one of the most popular kids at school, full of confidence in herself and her abilities. She took up gymnastics and began to compete regionally, specializing in advanced floor program. Although her mother forbade Sukriye from pursuing gymnastics after middle school for fear that she might damage her chastity, her father took a progressive attitude in encouraging her to pursue whatever activities would help her develop into a strong, motivated person who could become a leader for her people.

In the early years of her life in Germany, she remembers feeling that her people and her identity were somehow invisible rather than hated or looked down upon, and this freed her to build up her own self-worth, to educate others about the beauty of her culture, and quietly celebrate her own pride. "In those days, Kurds did not exist as a familiar concept. Even adults would ask what that was when you said you were Kurdish. Well-read people might say, ah, Karl Mai, *Through the Wilds of Kurdistan*." Sukriye remembers that Kurds or Kurdistan were never mentioned in the press, even as a bloody civil war raged in Turkey, but were in essence an invisible people in the mainstream German consciousness. This could have been a challenging experience for someone from a culture that had long contended with threats of forced assimilation, historically underacknowledged and underrecognized, but Sukriye saw it as a clean slate, an opportunity to build up knowledge and love of her culture where there had been no comprehension before.

She later learned that her cultural pride was unique among the children of Kurdish guest workers in Germany. Throughout her schooling, when classmates branded her with anti-Turkish racial or ethnic slurs, she simply replied that she wasn't Turkish, and felt somehow impervious to prejudice. Her close-knit, proud family certainly played a major role in the development of her cultural pride. But perhaps the one major difference between her own childhood and the general experience of Kurdish children in Germany was that she grew up in a small town without a large Turkish population. In Barsinghausen, a small town just north of Hannover, the largest employer of guest workers was the Bahlsen cookie factory, which had recruited from the earliest pools of guest workers, primarily from Spain and Italy. Sukriye and Hasbiye were the first children in their class to arrive from Turkey. In the major cities of West Germany, guest workers were recruited to metals and electronics factories, to lumber mills and heavy construction during the peak of the recruitment era, when most of the guest workers were arriving from Turkey. The majority of these guest workers originated from the rural southeast, which politically conscious Kurds describe as northern Kurdistan, suggesting that a significant percentage of Germany's Turkish guest worker population may actually have been Kurdish.

But those Kurds arriving among the guest workers recruited from Turkey were registered by a Turkish government whose official policy was to deny the existence of Kurds. In fact, until 1991, the Kurdish language was illegal in Turkey; speaking, writing, or reading Kurdish was a punishable offense. In diasporic Turkish and Kurdish communities, these policies had simply been translated into ethnic intolerance. Sukriye later learned that many Kurds of her generation, raised and even born in Germany, were passing as Turks within a large and visible Turkish community for fear of hostility from Turkish peers. By lumping Turks and Kurds together as compatriots, Germany inadvertently set up institutional frameworks in which Kurds often found themselves reliving troubles they believed they had left behind in Turkey. The instances where German institutions led to the further negation of Kurdish identity, to some extent continuing the program of forced assimilation imposed on Turkey's Kurds, were countless. Kurdish names were illegal in Turkey, and when the German government issued a list of acceptable children's names provided by the Turkish government, it now became illegal for Kurds in Germany to give their children Kurdish names.

Kurdish businesses were vandalized with Turkish slogans, which were not seen as ethnic hate crimes but rather as individual conflicts within a single community. In setting up obstacles for non-Germans to receive citizenship, Germany required Kurds to renew their passports with sometimes hostile Turkish consular officials. In later efforts to right past wrongs and reach out to an increasingly organized Turkish community, German government and news organizations celebrated the anniversary of the Lausanne Treaty, which had created the Turkish Republic and reneged on an earlier treaty guaranteeing Kurdish statehood, unconsciously legitimizing the event that represents the greatest political tragedy of the modern Kurdish nation.

In perhaps the most insidious of German government initiatives that negated the expression of Kurdish identity, Germany set up what were known as *Ausländerregelklassen*, segregated classes for foreign-born children who spoke no German. Since the majority of non-German guest workers had migrated from Turkey, these classes were often taught by teachers recruited by the Turkish government. It was widely believed in Kurdish circles that Turkish classes in Germany were taught by people on the Turkish government's payroll to collect the names of children who expressed pride in their Kurdish heritage. Starting in the fourth grade, when Sukriye and Hasbiye were eleven, they were enrolled in a class offered for Turkish children two afternoons each week, taught by a Turkish woman who received her honorarium from the Turkish government. Although the Dogan children, as Kurds, spoke Kurmanci at home, Mehmet thought it would not be a bad idea for the girls to learn Turkish in order to protect themselves from potential trouble with Turkish authorities. The year they joined the class, in 1984, the ongoing tensions and violence in southeastern Turkey exploded into a full-fledged civil war between the PKK (Kurdistan Workers' Party) and the Turkish military. Kurds traveling to and within Kurdistan who were suspected of allegiance with the militant movement risked detention and even torture, and in those days, it was rare to meet a Kurd who did not support the PKK, including the Dogans. Every other year, Mehmet, Adla, and the four children traveled by car to Kurdistan, and Sukriye remembers facing the border crossing at Turkey and the checkpoints set up throughout Kurdistan with silent terror, afraid of speaking Kurmanci in front of soldiers, and even more afraid of being questioned in Turkish and unable to answer.

On the first day of class, Sukriye and Hasbiye found themselves in conflict with the teacher, who could not comprehend that anyone who grew up in Turkey could not speak Turkish. The girls had grown up in a region where everyone had spoken Kurmanci, and so they explained that they were Kurds. Sukriye remembers that the teacher tensed up immediately, replying "What do you mean? We're all Turks here." She then went on to say that, given that there was a "certain past history," she didn't want any talk of the "Kurdish problem" to be spread in the classroom. Although Sukriye describes her childhood as a period in which she was secure enough in her Kurdish identity to feel unthreatened by expressions of Turkish nationalism, later encounters with Turkish professionals in German institutional settings who denied the existence of Kurds would only fortify this memory as her first experience with the perpetuation of official Turkish policy toward the Kurds in Germany. But the class seemed to proceed for some time without incident. The girls learned the Turkish language and studied Islam, learning the religion's central teachings and how to pray. One day, however, the class began to center on Turkish national education, and the children were asked to memorize the Turkish national anthem, nationalistic poems, and chants, historic interpretations that Sukriye describes as propaganda about the father of the Turkish nation, Mustafa Kemal Ataturk, and how to draw the Turkish flag.

In an example of how integration founders not at the borders but within institutional frameworks set up by host governments themselves, the German government, by instituting Turkish-government sponsored curricula, had created a program in which children educated in Germany received nationalistic training and indoctrination meant to develop the national character and cohesion of a different country. Not only did this educational program foster a displaced sense of national loyalty to Turkey instead of to the country in which the children were growing up, it also replicated the forced assimilation program of the Turkish government toward the Kurds. Sukriye, who had lived under martial law, seen a constant worsening of the Turkish-Kurdish conflict each time she had returned home, and had family members arrested, interrogated, searched, or otherwise hassled, remembers telling the teacher they were not in Turkey, and even in Germany they were not required to learn the national anthem. The girls decided not to return for the next class, and soon afterward, Mehmet began pushing for the creation of Kurdish-language classes through Kurdish organizations. Since the Turkish course was optional, unlike formal Auslaenderregelklassen in cities like Berlin, Sukriye and Hasbiye were able to forgo it and continue with the normal German educational program. State-funded foreign-language schooling would eventually become a hotly debated side of the integration debate. Certainly, her comfort with the German language had aided Sukriye in integrating into German society and accessing opportunities, but it was her fluency in Kurmanci that most strongly cemented her sense of self.

Eventually, the presence of a large and active network of Kurdish community and solidarity organizations in the Hannover area allowed for Hannover's Kurdish community to achieve strides in both political organization and in Kurdish-language schooling unparalleled in other cities in Germany. Hannover would be the first and, as of 2006, only city in Germany to offer formal Kurdish-language instruction. Sukriye, who had graduated long before Kurdish-language classes were available in school, learned how to read and write Kurmanci through informal private instruction from a Kurdish poet and good friend in Hannover when she was in high school. By the time she left home to attend university, Sukriye was completely fluent in both spoken and written Kurmanci, and her fluency gave her a good deal of the cultural proprietorship that she later found to be largely absent in many of her Kurdish friends and acquaintances in Berlin. A common language is one of various ways cultural anthropologists define collective identity, taking their cues from the ways in which groups define or delimit themselves from others. Although the history of Kurdish nationhood has been described in a number of ways by historians, novelists, poets, and politicians, all with their own perspective, to Sukriye the greatest external expression of Kurdishness, the clearest signifier of Kurdish national pride, and the strongest link for a Kurdish nation divided and weakened by politics was the continued use of the Kurdish language.

Long before she became fluent in formal, written Kurmanci, Sukriye had
begun developing another concrete anchor in her cultural identity, and that
was through acts of service to members of her community who were in need.
It is often believed that the recipient of service, in gratitude, feels the greater
kinship to the giver, but often the giver of service develops a strong bond to
the people she serves, not just singly but also collectively. Through community service, Sukriye developed a deep sympathy for the struggles of her people and for the vulnerability of their traditions. During their hasty flights
from home and long exile among non-Kurdish populations, many of the
families Sukriye met and worked with had lost mementos and cultural signifiers, and had in some cases abandoned the traditions that distinguished
them as Kurds for fear of drawing attention to themselves and risking further persecution. This taught her at an early age to prize those traditions,
allowing her to avoid the cultural ambivalence experienced by much of the
world's immigrant youth.

Sukriye began serving her community as a natural extension of a role she
had played in her family since her earliest youth. By her tenth birthday, Sukriye
had become the official interpreter, translator, and social worker for her family. She translated letters, legal forms, and bills, and accompanied every member of her family to doctors' offices and government ministries. Like most
guest workers, her father had lived in a barracks building with three roommates, and had had neither the time nor opportunity to learn German. As one
of the first Kurds to settle in Barsinghausen, Mehmet had taken a special interest in seeking out and welcoming newly arrived immigrants, economic immigrant or refugee alike, into the community. Just as he had invited every person
he met to their home in Kucuka, Mehmet invited every non-German colleague
and new arrival to his new home. From the earliest days of the civil war in
Kurdistan, Mehmet and Adla opened their home to countless families in need
of a meal, place to stay, or a feeling of community, just as their children would
continue the tradition and open their own homes over the years. Mehmet's
social outreach work was not motivated by pity or any desire to be a powerful
figure; he simply took pleasure in belonging to a large, energetic, and interde-
pendent community. Since he housed so many people over the years, looked

out for so many children who had lost parents in the war, mentored so many young men who had lost their faith and pride, and helped so many young couples settle into life in Germany, he became a sort of patron to a growing community of Kurds. Almost as soon as Sukriye arrived, she naturally fell into role of cultural intermediary for her family, and Mehmet set about grooming her to become his right hand in his community service efforts.

By the late 1980s, a second wave of Kurdish immigrants had begun arriving, and in contrast to the first wave of Kurdish guest workers, who had largely been content to keep their Kurdish identities and politics quiet, this time many were openly political, refugees who had been imprisoned and tortured for their involvement with or support of the Kurdish nationalist movement. Forced evacuations, violent confrontations between villagers and so-called village guards, and widespread disappearances were prompting a massive exodus of Kurdish refugees from Turkey into Europe. Germany floundered to devise a legal and physical infrastructure to make room for these new arrivals. Until 1993, Germany had no single law addressing the asylum process, instead relying on a body of international human rights conventions, its constitution, and its Auslaendergesetz or "foreigner law," the basic German law dealing with foreign nationals living, working, or studying in Germany. Following reunification and the Balkan crisis, Germany would have to devise a clear asylum process, but for the time being, most asylum was granted on a case-by-case basis. This caused delays in the asylum application process that often left people, some of whom were leaving behind dead or wounded family members or demolished home villages, unsettled and rootless for years on end.

The Kurdish refugee crisis hit home when one of Sukriye's older sisters fled Turkey for Germany with her husband and two sons and, after a harrowing and circuitous trip to Egypt, then to East Berlin, tried to cross into West Germany on the city's East-West subway line. When they arrived at passport control, they were taken into custody and locked up in a detention center on the outskirts of East Berlin, where they were held for three days with nothing to eat but mandarin oranges. Mehmet arranged for her and her family to stay in a "safe house" in a church basement near Barsinghausen until she and her family could officially apply for asylum and move into a nearby government-run asylum home, a giant, fenced-in building, the first of many they would live in for nearly five years until their asylum process could be completed. Refugees from all over the world crammed into over-crowded rooms—one room per family—lining a long hallway bookended with communal toilets and showers, a marked departure from the traditional separation of men from women in Kurdish societies. Adla and the girls spent entire days cooking and grocery shopping, then packed the car full to over-flowing and took the food, along with other items like hotplates and clothes, to be distributed among as many families as possible at the asylum home.

Over the years, not only did Sukriye's sister and her family spend a great deal of time in asylum homes but her uncle's family and later her older brother's family became refugees in Germany as well. Every weekend, Mehmet drove to the various homes and collected all of his family members, bringing back all three families to spend the weekends in his four-room apartment. There was not much room, but the family was happy to be together, and everyone accommodated everyone. The girls all slept in one room, on thick Kurdish mattresses laid side-by-side on the floor, and the boys slept in another, just as they would have in Kurdistan. In the mornings, they all gathered for elaborate breakfasts with homemade bread Adla had learned to cook with German flour, and precious food items hoarded from the latest trips to Turkey. Adla remembers that in her early days in Germany, she could not find the eggplants, zucchini, and green peppers she had always cooked, and was forced to make do with canned tomatoes more often than fresh tomatoes. But her house was always full, and Adla was resourceful. Sukriye formed many vital components of her own social and political identity at home with her parents, who taught that the comfort of others can be much more rewarding than one's own comfort. The personal was political for Sukriye; although she would spend her adult life engaging in social work and political activism, the way that she affirmed her Kurdish identity and cele-brated her national pride was to recreate the experiences of her childhood by filling her home with guests, serving traditional Kurdish delicacies, and play-ing Kurdish love songs, metaphors of longing for home, on her stereo.

As she began to accompany her father to the asylum homes more and more often, Sukriye began to see herself as a champion and spokeswoman for Kurdish asylum seekers in Germany, many of whom spent years and years bouncing from home to home, unable to settle. She saw children born to parents who had not been granted asylum or any other permanent migration status, who were now effectively born stateless in Germany. Contrary to the common misconception that asylum seekers stood to gain a wealth of social and civil rights by tapping into the extensive German welfare system, most of the asylum seekers Sukriye saw lived for years in protracted states of emotional and physical paralysis, waiting for German officials to review or process their files. They lived four, five, six people to a room in underheated, undercleaned group homes, never in one place for more than a few months at a time, unable to work or buy their own food and clothing. "There was a certain period of time where almost every [Kurdish family] had relatives, acquaintances, or loved ones who had come as refugees. That is to say that all of us as a community were confronted with the problems concerning the Kurds," she says. "Of course, there were those who said, 'We work and the asylum seekers get everything for free here, we would never give them our daughters to marry,' but I never felt that way." In the major cities, Kurds who had for thirty years been hidden within Turkish communities began organizing and emerging in support of the Kurdish nationalist movement.

Eager to involve himself with a formal social outreach program for Kurdish refugees, Mehmet began to set up meetings with representatives from governmental and nongovernmental organizations, such as Amnesty International and the mayor's office in Barsinghausen, to learn what he could do to help. He built up a long list of contacts in the process, but could find no programs that specifically addressed the needs of Kurdish asylum seekers in Germany. One day, he learned of a pastor who had been providing support and counseling for Kurdish students in Goettingen, and who was moving to Barsinghausen. After an initial meeting at the pastor's new church, Mehmet invited the pastor, his wife, and his three children home for dinner, and the German family gathered on the floor with the Kurdish family for traditional Kurdish fare. Two weeks later, the Kurdish family joined the German family for dinner around a table carefully set with chicken and beef, but no pork dishes, out of respect for Muslim observances. With this beginning, the two men founded an organization they called "*Die Bruecke*," or "The Bridge," launching one of the most successful, wholly grassroots, bicultural support and friendship groups in the area. They provided weekly office hours for legal and bureaucratic counseling, collected food and clothing for humanitarian crises like the Anfal poison gas attacks on Kurdish villagers in Iraq, mediated with regional authorities to secure the right of the children of refugees to attend school, and set up a community center. The entire Dogan family got involved in organizing events for the community center, including Newroz festivals to celebrate the Kurdish New Year, readings, and Amnesty International events. They built a clay oven in the center, there in the church basement, where once a week a group of Muslim women led by Adla met to bake fresh flatbread in the traditional Kurdish style.

In this way, by encouraging dialogue and intercultural education between the German and Kurdish populations, by fostering Kurdish national pride and appreciation of German opportunities in his children, by holding his family together with warmth, tenacity, and tirelessness, Mehmet Dogan worked to recreate what he loved most about his Kurdish village in Germany.

It has become fashionable for German journalists and politicians to discuss what they call a parallel society of Muslims living among them. After five years of an often self-effacing discussion on Germany's failure to offer its large and long-standing non-German population citizenship, equal opportunity, or even the status as "immigrants" rather than "foreigners," the mainstream German press enthusiastically embraced Holland's public outrage following the murder by Muslim extremists of a controversial filmmaker in 2004. But Germany's historic rejection of its immigrants as permanent members of its society differentiates it significantly from Holland, which has for many years had an active integration policy. Nonetheless, even highly respected and thoughtful German publications put out extensive analyses stating that Muslims, in their unwillingness to conform to Western values of secularism and gender equality had, in effect, exploited Germany's tolerance and democratic institutions to create a so-called Islamic parallel society. All talk of the country's long history of national, regional, and local policymaking aimed at restricting and discouraging immigrants' integration into German society suddenly seemed to disappear from the public debate. Although immigrants have, within recent memory, been banned from moving to certain city districts in several German cities, prohibited from forming political parties or voting in local elections, enrolled in "foreigner schools," criminalized for allowing bartering in their shops, and tracked to remedial vocational schools, several German journalists held Islamic fundamentalism solely responsible for the creation of this so-called parallel society. Commentators have bolstered this claim by reporting that, under the protections of German religious freedom statutes, mosques propagate anti-Western sentiments, that Muslim girls are held hostage by their families, and that there has been a purported rise in forced marriage and honor killings in German cities in recent years. Such reports, published not only in Germany but in media outlets in the rest of Europe and in the United States as well, often include statements of outrage by the commentators themselves.

Yet for every mosque in German cities there are dozens of secular, community-development organizations representing Turkish and Kurdish immigrants who clamor for equal rights and protections. And although it is true that since 2000 there has been a rise in honor killings brought to the public's attention, the roots behind this practice are complex, not merely attributable to a rise in Islamic identification among Europe's urban youth. After several years of research and experience with Kurdish victims of sexual violence, Sukriye has suggested that the practice of honor killing in Kurdish society may result from psychological and interpersonal dysfunction common in collectively traumatized societies rather than from religious dictates. Some have even questioned whether there has indeed been an increase in these practices themselves, or simply an increased public awareness of them because of strenuous efforts by women's rights groups to bring these concerns to light. Instead of examining the complex backdrops to these issues, some of Germany's leading publications have conflated religiosity with fanaticism, traditionalism with ignorance, conservatism with violence, and Islam with deep misogyny. Racist stereotypes of "ignorant Anatolian farmers" abound in the media, as does the misguided interpretation of the personal decision to wear a head scarf as a sign of oppression. Sukriye embodies a contradiction of these public misconceptions. Raised by very religious and conservative parents, Sukriye is nonetheless an empowered and individualistic woman who moves with ease between German and Kurdish society.

Sukriye's upbringing was a delicate balance between traditionalism and liberation. Rather than restricting her opportunities, her traditional home life gave her a grounding and confidence in her heritage, sparing her the need for open rebellion. She spent the better part of her teen years pushing to widen her sphere of movement, but only in the advancement of her personal principles and her professional aspirations. Her father supported her desire to expand her horizons, hoping that she might carry the work they had started together to the highest levels of political power in Germany, and eventually work to liberate her people. Her mother, concerned for her moral well-being, was more likely to set limitations. As part of a traditional Muslim upbringing, the Dogan girls were not allowed to wear makeup or skirts (unless they were wearing pants underneath), and it never even occurred to them that they might date, go to dance clubs, or drink. But at the same time, Adla acknowledged that Sukriye's desperately needed social work, translation and interpretation services, and assistance would take her all over the network of outlying cities and exurbs around Hannover. The value of her services trumped the demands of modesty time and again and, as a teenager, she began accompanying Kurdish women, including her own sister, into gynecologists' offices and hospital delivery rooms. Sukriye was so busy working that she did not have the time or even the interest to rebel over makeup or clothing. She just tied her hair back into braids, wore pants instead of skirts, and saved her energy for the larger battles.

Later, when she was in high school, her father's standing in the community invited many inquiries from distant cousins or family friends after her hand in marriage. She made it a point to tell her parents unequivocally that she had no desire to marry before she had completed her education. While her mother would have been pleased for her to marry, both she and Mehmet felt strongly that the key to Kurdish uplift was education. Adla had no argument if Sukriye wanted to put off marriage, but what she did not know was that Sukriye had begun to see marriage as an institution that would limit her freedom of movement and personal development.

Freedom was the one thing that she hungered for more than anything, both for herself and for Kurdistan. She knew she could do little for Kurdistan from where she was, so she focused on her studies to free herself. In 1990, when she was eighteen years old, Sukriye became the first person in her family to be admitted to *Gymnasium*, the highest ranking secondary school option in the German public education system. In fact, fewer than 10 percent of all Turkish students (this figure bears in mind that, in Germany, Kurds from Turkey are officially Turkish) make it to the end of Gymnasium and successfully complete the *Abitur*, or general exam. Within Germany's recent immigration policy debate, one of the most harshly criticized practices of many schools was the consistent tracking of non-German children to vocational schools. In fact, one study indicated that majority of children of Turkish descent continue to be sent to Hauptschule, the most remedial of Germany's secondary schools, leaving this majority of Turkish students in Germany with no more than a basic ninth-grade education. The main reason given for this practice of tracking is the low level of German-language achievement among these students, which is attributed to the fact that German is not the primary language in most Turkish households. But let us bear in mind that when Sukriye arrived in Germany, she was nine years old and spoke no German at all. At home, only Kurmanci was spoken. Still, she was able to learn to speak, read, and write fluently in German within a few years of her arrival, in no small part because of her own personal qualities but also because of the society that received her. In a small town, segregation—social, political, economic, or educational—was not possible to the extent that it was in larger cities, which were home to the majority of Germany's immigrants.

The Gymnasium Sukriye attended was over an hour's commute away, in Hannover proper, but Sukriye would not let inconvenience deter her from her education; in fact, she found the possibility of driving by herself to a city extremely alluring. Her Gymnasium days were exhaustingly long; she left the house around 6:00 each morning, and after school she traveled to many of

Hannover's surrounding villages and towns on her social outreach work, sometimes not returning home until 10:00 p.m. As she had with her own family, she now ushered a whole community through the German institutional system—from translating during doctor's office visits and trips to government ministries, to offering counseling and social work at asylum homes and orphanages, to arranging events and attending Kurdish cultural and political festivals. The summer before school started, she worked in the Bahlsen cookie factory to save up money to pay for her driver's license, and the long hours on her feet only cemented in her mind that she had no interest in pursuing a simple factory job, an easy marriage, and a life of contentment among her family and friends in Barsinghausen. She would never stray from her family emotionally, and despite sometimes great distances apart and long stretches without visits, she would always remain connected to them. But she was the only Dogan child to abandon their village, either at home or recreated in Germany, to walk her own path.

When she graduated from Gymnasium, Sukriye was poised for greatness. She had come from a remote, forgotten village to become a successful student, an honored community activist, and, in 1993, a German citizen. When she received her passport and some prize money for her years of community service, she traveled to Kurdistan to freely cross into Syria, where one branch of her family had been cut off from the rest by the international border. It was the first time she had personally seen evidence that the people of divided Kurdistan still retained one shared culture, a culture she wanted to serve and preserve with her own successes. As soon as she returned, she began researching university programs for courses of study in Kurdish languages and history. She discussed her plans with her father, who had no doubt that she would receive a degree and become a great opinion leader who would serve her people and help deliver them from poverty and violence. What neither of them quite understood was that her ambition was centered to a much greater extent on the achievement of personal freedom than it was on any particular career. Her true life's work would be to manage the two dominant themes in her identity—liberation from regressive social restrictions and celebration of what she identified as her culture.

More than any career, Sukriye strove for the freedom to celebrate her culture and serve her people on her own terms. She had no interest in rejecting
her culture as a means of freeing herself from its more conservative dictates,
but rather sought to reject those dictates as the primary signifiers of faithful-
ness to her culture. She chose to focus on concrete aspects of Kurdish life,
such as linguistic fluency, community activism, food, and dance, rather than
intangible social expectations, such as getting married and staying close to
home. She put her faith in formal education as a way to channel her passion
for the Kurdish culture into a profession. When she stumbled upon a course
offering called "Kurdish Language and Kurdish Studies" within the Iranistics
Department at Berlin's Free University, she felt fireworks go off in her head.
She had been waiting all her life to see "Kurdish" printed in a university course
catalogue. "It was the fulfillment of my dream," she says, and she made up her
mind on the spot to travel to Berlin, in the east of newly unified Germany.

Sukriye arrived in Berlin five years after the Wall had come down and five
years before the city once again became Germany's capital city, and there was
a fever of creativity and rebirth in the air. The seat of three totalitarian
regimes and dozens of artistic movements, Germany's most diverse and
complicated city, Berlin holds unique a place in German imagination, as it
does in Germany's immigration history. The city was a wasteland after the
Second World War, reduced to rubble from heavy bombardment and then
depopulated by a mass exodus to the West before East Germany sealed its
borders and erected the Wall in 1961. There were jobs, but no people to fill
them, so both East and West Germany began recruiting foreign guest labor,
albeit on different scales and toward different ends. In fact, some of the first
Kurds to arrive in Berlin came to East Berlin as students through solidarity
exchange programs between socialist countries. But East Germany lacked
the capital and ideology that allowed its Western counterpart to recruit so
heavily and profit so greatly from foreign labor. After the Wall went up in
1961, West Germany was able to offer a monthly pay supplement of DM 400
to guest workers who agreed to work in the city designated as a "Cold War
hotspot," attracting great numbers of immigrants from Turkey, which signed

its guest worker recruitment treaty with Germany that same year. Berlin quickly became Germany's most Turkish city, complete with a "little Istanbul" that would become a stop on city tours decades later. And woven into this Turkish community was a Kurdish immigrant population that was larger than any Sukriye had seen before, estimated at anywhere from 20 to 60 percent of the city's Turkish population. The moment she set foot in Berlin, Sukriye felt her future opening up before her.

She immersed herself in her studies as soon as she had settled in with the Kurdish family her father had arranged for her to live with. But within her first three semesters, she found herself bored and disillusioned with the program. The Iranistics curriculum centered on the study of ancient Persian history and dead Persic languages, only briefly touching on the Kurdish linguistics and contemporary social history that she had dreamed of studying. She realized that although she had always wanted to study and have a career, she had no idea what that career should be. Should she be a professor or a Kurdish historian, a schoolteacher of the Kurdish language, a social worker, or even an archeologist? As she switched from concentration to concentration, she began to look for opportunities to support the Kurdish movement outside of the university, eager to involve herself with organizations that went beyond basic revolutionary agitation.

Even before she moved to Berlin, Sukriye had begun to lose her faith in revolution, after seeing it fail, year after year, to win independence for Kurdistan. "Sooner or later one starts to understand that nothing will be won through revolution and war, but that there are certain structures in the way that politics functions," she said. She still believed in the importance of political action in bringing about reform in Kurdish society and demanding economic and political opportunities for Kurds in Turkey, but she no longer cherished any hope for a free, independent Kurdistan anytime soon. Now, she began to place her hope in diasporic communities of Kurds living in the West, where they had the opportunities for free expression and the resources for scholarly research that could resuscitate dialogue both within and about Kurdish society. These Kurds could preserve a culture that was foundering under hostile politics and a community that was dispersing in flight from war, and might even be able to generate enough awareness and political will abroad to pressure the Turkish government to offer Kurds civil, economic, and human rights as a minority group in their country. Further, Kurds in the diaspora had both the legal and social infrastructure that would enable them to turn the revolutionary mentality of the Kurdish independence movement inward to dismantle sexism, discrimination, and other forms of structural violence within the Kurdish community itself.

Although the sheer size of the Kurdish population in Berlin meant that many Kurds were politically active, Kurdish organizations lived in a kind of existential vacuum. They were highly politicized because only ardently political Kurds chose to be openly associated with Kurdish organizations in a Turkish-majority immigrant population, and they tended to be intolerant of internal criticism for fear of showing a weak face to the surrounding Turkish community. After Sukriye had joined several organizations, she began to see signs of fracture, lack of direction, and knee-jerk conservatism underneath the surface of what seemed to be a motivated and progressive Kurdish community. Instead of being ensconced in an active and proud Kurdish community-based movement, Sukriye found herself alienated from most organized Kurdish activities in what could be called the capital city of Kurdish Germany. She describes a confrontation between herself and an organizer of the gala opening of the Kurdish Institute, which was to be a scholarly institution promoting objective research on Kurdish issues. When she found the organizer hanging a poster of PKK leader Abdullah Ocalan over the director's podium, she recalls saying that if the press corps were to see the poster, the institute would simply be dismissed as another arm of the PKK and not taken seriously, only to have the organizer accuse her of disloyalty to Ocalan, the party, and indeed to the entire movement. Through this memory, we see how she began to construct an identity for herself as a critical voice in a community that had grown, through the collective trauma of war and sociopolitical repression, intolerant of internal dissent.

Shortly afterward, Sukriye joined a political organization affiliated with the Kurdish independence movement, and involved herself with its women's working group. She had repeatedly seen Kurdish women and female party members criticized for adopting Western styles of speech or dress, and accused of losing their identities or becoming morally degenerate. The leadership of this organization was entirely male, and Sukriye felt that it was time to engage her fellows in a dialogue on how women should be included as equals in a movement modeled on socialist revolutionary rhetoric, in which women were described as comrades. Through the women's group, Sukriye and another young Kurdish feminist hoped to address what they saw as a basic hypocrisy in Kurdish politics, and decided to organize an action for International Women's Day, "to criticize the structures in the organization and in Kurdish society, how the regressive social aspects of society were reflected back and advanced through the political groups, how there was institutionalized male violence in the party politics." But the organization's leadership wanted the program to be approved by a committee. "We refused to parade our program for the approval of a bunch of men," she says. Their refusal to seek approval prompted a rumor that they intended to spread rhetoric that would ultimately be divisive to the movement and would serve the enemy's interests. Once again, we see an incident that, in her memory, reinforced her identity as an agent for social criticism, whose efforts were instead perceived as a threat. Unwilling to pander to institutional insecurities or to soften her approach so as to appear less threatening to so-called traditional values, Sukriye chose instead to walk away from organized politics.

She began to move in Berlin's activist circles. A year after she had come to Berlin, she moved out her family friend's basement, and resettled in the city district of Kreuzberg. Under the shadow of the southwest face of the Wall, Kreuzberg was one of the districts in the city center that had suffered most under the Second World War bombing campaigns, and whose empty buildings had been repopulated by guest workers and squatters in the decades after the Wall was erected. Now known as the ghetto for its 34 percent non-German population and 40 percent male unemployment rate, Kreuzberg was home to dozens of Turkish import-export stores, Mediterranean bakeries and kebab shops, Turkish sports clubs and cafes, a Turkish-style *hamam* or women's bathhouse, anarchist settlements, and more social justice projects than any other part of the city. Rather than a troubled, decrepit ghetto,

Kreuzberg actually felt to Sukriye like a vibrant, alternative paradise, a place where all people who didn't "fit in" with mainstream conventions could relax and thrive. She moved into a living community of feminists and progressive activists, fitting in comfortably with the mohawked lesbians and aging punks, the artists and political organizers, who had gravitated, like herself, to Kreuzberg from all over Europe and even from Kurdistan. A few months later, she moved into another living community a few blocks away, a graffiti-decorated, colorful, self-proclaimed "man-free space," thrilled to be surrounded by feminists as passionate as she was.

Sukriye had come to Berlin with a clear idea of what she needed from the city, but now she was beginning to see that no existing organization or program offered her the opportunity she needed. She herself was changing; now she was no longer interested in just being involved with just any organization that spoke out in favor of Kurds and Kurdistan. She wanted real change, and, like her father, was willing to look to German society for the political will and institutional infrastructure the Kurdish people needed.

Sukriye sat in a subway car, bound for home one cold, darkening autumn evening in 2000, thinking about honor, hope, and the future. She had just left a gynecologist's office, where she had been translating for a Kurdish woman who was to be examined for proof of the multiple gang rapes she had survived at the hands of the Turkish soldiers who had occupied, then destroyed her village, and who had guarded her prison cell. The examination was evidence required by the state to corroborate the story she had given in her application for asylum in Germany. Because she was a refugee from Turkey, she had been sent to a Turkish German doctor, who had explained to Sukriye that the refugee's story was impossible, because, as she claimed, Kurds were neither tortured nor raped in Turkey.

The patient to whom Sukriye had to pass on this statement had not been able to sleep a full night in over a year, because she lived in fear not only of her nightmares and her shame, but also of being sent back to Turkey to relive it all over again. Sukriye knew that rape of Kurdish women was widespread in Turkish prisons, and that honor killings committed to cleanse the families of the rape victims' shame continued largely unchecked by the Turkish criminal code, which classified rape as a felony against public decency, not a felony against an individual. But she had never believed she would see the day when a Kurdish rape victim would have to risk having her asylum application in Germany rejected because of the prejudice of Turkish officials in German institutions. Sukriye left the appointment exhausted and disheartened. Despite her scarves, two sweaters, and thick, black denim pants, her muscles felt chilled, so much so that her bones ached. The subway car smelled faintly of dried sweat.

In the last year, Sukriye had begun to feel a creeping sense of anxiety about her future, which correlated directly with her anxiety about the future of Kurdistan. Nearly six years after enrolling at the university, she hadn't even begun research on her thesis topic. She had tried to set up a meeting to organize a research seminar on the Yezidi, a long-persecuted, somewhat insular Kurdish religious minority with a large presence near Hannover, whose stringent caste system was driving many of its German-born youth to suicide or to running away. She had pasted bright yellow posters with "Kurds*Gender*Exile" printed in provocative block letters all over Kreuzberg, intentionally posting them next to Turkish markets and kebab shops. Even though a handful of people, most of whom were her friends, came to the meeting, only three people actually showed up for the first seminar meeting at the university: two formerly East German students and one American exchange student. Within a month of the first meeting, one of the former East Germans, a nervous, high-strung woman struggling to redefine her identity after German reunification and within her marriage to a Muslim Kurd, exploded at Sukriye over a fairly minor organizational issue, and then left the group to start a separate research project on exactly the same topic, only with herself in charge. Her project seemed to be falling apart and her academic program seemed to have no end in sight. Sukriye worried that she was failing her father. Although he was as loving as ever, she noticed that he had begun asking her when she planned on completing her studies, and after every trip home, a tiny part of her shriveled at the thought of disappointing him, her greatest champion and role model.

But her community service work had taken over her life, leaving her with no time and little emotional strength for anything else. What had been just a continuation of her own informal community service efforts had become a professional activity shortly after her arrival in Berlin, when an acquaintance from the university had asked her if she would accompany him as a translator during a mandatory therapy session that he was required to attend as part of his asylum process. The session was the first of hundreds she would interpret for Kurdish asylum seekers at the Treatment Center for Torture Victims, a unique psychotherapeutic consortium founded in 1992 to meet the needs of the vast numbers of refugees flooding into Berlin from the Balkans, and now expanding to provide treatment for other war refugees. In order to verify the accuracy and consistency of asylum claims, the German government had begun requiring asylum seekers to attend therapy sessions with German psychotherapists, and the treatment center was now in dire need of a Kurdish-language interpreter. At this first session, Sukriye not only translated for the patient but also provided the therapist with context and background information to understand what the patient was talking about, and was promptly invited to interpret for Kurdish patients at the institution on a regular basis. It was the first time she had been offered payment for something she would have done for free, and it awakened her fascination with psychotherapy as a practical way to address the problems that Kurds, as a community contending with collective posttraumatic stress, were facing.

The compensation she received at these therapy sessions and at administrative meetings with these torture survivors helped a little, and before long, she was able to move into her own apartment on a quiet side street, a bit dark and cold during the long wintertime, but nonetheless her first place all to herself. Still, she couldn't help but feel that she was stagnating, expending her time and energy on a path with no future. There were limited well-paid career opportunities in social work, and she couldn't afford to study psychotherapy, which would qualify her to do what she really hungered to do. She knew she was a vital part of the overall process helping individuals recover from what they had suffered, but she grew frustrated that her efforts were not making a difference at a systemic level. There just was no political will, either in Turkey or in Germany, to change the basic conditions that had allowed these people to be tortured, and once they had fled, to guarantee their safety. Slowly, her feelings of frustration had grown into a kind of existential doubt. This feeling had only worsened since the PKK leader Abdullah Ocalan had been captured and extradited to a Turkish prison in October of 1999. She would never forget the desperation she had felt all around her at the candlelit vigil in front of the Greek embassy, the three Kurdish protestors who had been shot by guards in front of the Israeli embassy, and worst of all, the sound of her mother weeping as if her heart would break over the telephone late that night. There was no denying it; Kurds everywhere had felt somewhat lost since that day, as if their hope for an independent homeland or for at least some measure of dignity and freedom had been crushed to death.

Despite her growing feeling of impotence and her personal grief since the end of the Kurdish revolution, she had soldiered on with her faith that reform would still be possible, and that her assistance was still necessary. She provided something of a pillar of strength and very intimate courage to the people she worked with every day. Most of the people she translated for were not necessarily fervent believers in therapy. Many had not heard of therapy before, many could not understand what purpose it could serve. In fact, many of the people she worked with vastly preferred to repress their memories of imprisonment, torture, rape, and flight than to talk about them with strangers. One man told her that he only felt worse after therapy sessions, that it did him no good to go out there once a week, drag all his sorrows up from sweet forgetfulness, only to be left out on the sidewalk a mere hour later, alone with his flashbacks and anxiety attacks.

For some time, she translated almost exclusively for male patients. Since more men than women had been directly involved in the Kurdish nationalist movement, it had been easier to identify them as at risk of torture and political persecution. But, over time, she began to work with more and more female Kurdish patients. Nearly every one had experienced some extreme form of sexual violence at the hands of policemen, soldiers, prison guards, or "village guards" in Turkey. At first, there were only intimations, coded allusions as to what was happening. Throughout Germany, Kurdish women sat in front of German lawyers, often with Turkish translators, and implied that something horrendous had happened to them in Turkey, something that they were terrified of facing when they returned. Slowly, she had begun to see a pattern by which rape was used as a weapon of war. One woman she had just translated for had been imprisoned for mouthing off to a village guard, where she had been raped by the prison guards keeping her, and when she was released and fled to Germany to seek asylum, she was so filled with shame that her husband had accepted her back that she had become suicidally depressed. Sukriye knew that for every woman who escaped with her life after a rape, many more would have been killed by her brother or father in defense of the family's honor. Since few in the German state apparatus knew of what many human rights activists have described as systematic rape as a weapon used in the Turkish-Kurdish war, Sukriye shuddered to think how many rape victims had been sent back to Turkey.

For some time, she had been able to combat the exhaustion and occasional depression residual from her work with a sense of purpose. "It was very difficult . . . but I saw it as an opportunity to bear witness, document what was really happening." But most important, she truly believed that the earnest desire of German psychotherapists and social workers to help these refugees might outweigh the cynicism and callousness she had so often encountered in government ministries. In addition to her work at the treatment center, she had soon begun translating regularly at the Paul-Gerhardt Home for families of war refugees and torture survivors, the only home of its kind in all of Berlin. The home was a sharp departure from most of the asylum homes she had seen in the city's outskirts—desolate, hulking boxes dropped in the middle of the vast, underdeveloped landscapes of the former East German countryside, many of which had recently fallen prey to a wave of racially motivated attacks, vandalism, and arson. The Paul-Gerhardt Home was warm and cozy, with each family assigned to individual multiroom apartments, a space where the residents lived as tenants in a regular apartment building, only with social workers at their disposal, group activities, and support in making the transition to life on their own. Sukriye channeled a good deal of her time and energy into working in this home, even helping to organize a type of "theater of the oppressed" for the women residents to celebrate International Women's Day, and felt gratified to see Kurdish children adjusting to the school system,

Kurdish women standing up to stop domestic violence in their own homes, and Kurdish families emerging intact from the brutality of war and the trauma of flight. Some of the home residents eventually became her closest friends and community, almost a surrogate extended family here in Berlin.

By the time the subway pulled into her station, Sukriye had fallen asleep, and the demographics of the car had shifted entirely. Now, she was surrounded by Turkish teenagers in tight jeans, or if in headscarves, with snugly fitting skirts, elaborately lined eyes, and frosted lips. She jerked awake, dully conscious that her mouth had fallen open, and hurriedly gathered her bags together. She knew she should read for her university coursework tonight, but she also thought that she might just get to it tomorrow.

By the time the century ended, Sukriye's ambition and focus was flagging under a weak but persistent dejection. She saw how German bureaucratic procedure repeatedly forced Kurdish refugees from an increasingly brutal war into working with Turkish doctors, lawyers, and social workers, many of whom refused to believe that the Kurds they represented and worked with had suffered torture, rape, and ethnic cleansing at the hands of the Turkish military, or worse still, perceived Kurds as potentially violent terrorists. As much as it saddened and angered her that Kurdish society had turned the violence it had suffered inward, forcing its own women to suffer penance for its collective humiliation, she held the Turkish government responsible for the pain it had caused her people, and the German government responsible for supporting official Turkish positions toward the Kurds. At times, she felt helpless with outrage to see Turkish German activists angrily denounce Germany for its historic marginalization of immigrants but continue to impugn Kurdish minority rights activists as supporters of terrorism. It did not help matters that Germany had listed the PKK as a terrorist organization on its internal ministry file, making it even more difficult for PKK supporters to gain asylum in Germany. She turned thirty with a feeling that she was plodding along, trying to find a career in support of a cause that had been forgotten by the world and was slowly being abandoned by the very people who had fought hardest to bring it to the world's attention.

Sukriye's minority consciousness, her identity, and her sense of purpose in life were all built around being Kurdish. Although she was aware that there was a broader clash-of-civilizations dialogue emerging among Muslim community activists, the entirety of her own activist sentiment was directed at the expansion of secular minority and human rights, both in the homeland and in Germany. She shook her head at ignorant statements by German press and professionals, predicated on generalizations about purported "Muslim" behaviors or pathologies, but she constructed both her personal identity and the barriers to her emotional integration primarily around her Kurdish national identity, both as a Kurd from Turkey and as a Kurd in an increasingly pro-Turkish Germany.

CHAPTER 6

REJECTING THE BURDEN
OF HERITAGE

Rafiqul and Nishat arrived in New York City in the summer of 1996 with tourist visas. But there would be no trips to the Statue of Liberty or Rockefeller Plaza for them. From the moment their airplane touched down at John F. Kennedy Airport, they had only one aim: to earn enough dollars to forestall the family's financial collapse in Bangladesh. Rafiqul had plans to enroll his daughter in an American school, with the hopes that she might build a long and prosperous life in the United States, but he had little ambition for himself to achieve anything from this trip but fast money. He believed that, with simple faith and hard work, he could pay off his debts, leave his daughter comfortably set up, and return home in comfort. He had no qualms about pulling Nishat from university in Bangladesh; certainly she would have better opportunities in life with a degree from an American university.

Almost as soon as they landed, Rafiqul began to look for work in Queens. He and Nishat moved in with some family friends from Bangladesh, sleeping on the living room floor of their one-bedroom apartment in Elmhurst, Queens. When he started working, Rafiqul was careful not to disturb the couple and their small baby daughter on his way out early in the morning, conscious that, in this country, charity had its limits. He had been able to find a full-time job, but he soon realized that undocumented immigrants could scarcely expect to earn the kinds of wages people gossiped and dreamed about back home in Dhaka. Even when he factored in profits from the international exchange rate, he earned nowhere near enough money to

155

support himself and his daughter, and still have enough to send home to his wife. He needed Nishat to help him earn, not take money from him for tuition and books. Within weeks of arriving in the United States, Rafiqul had abandoned his hopes for both himself and for his daughter, and had surrendered to the hard reality of his choices.

Rafiqul had to admit to himself that he had fallen for the promise of America instead of carefully considering the consequences of his choices and the opportunities he could realistically expect. With no legal documentation, he had little to separate himself from the thousands of other undocumented workers, some who had never seen a school building before and some with multiple PhDs, all competing for factory, retail, food service, and domestic service jobs throughout New York City's five boroughs. His personal code of honor made it possible for him to preserve his dignity in underpaid manual labor, but his wife's expectations of the American income scale made him anxious of a failure he had not anticipated.

The so-called American Dream is an almost mythic force in international popular imagination, one of the most powerful arguments to migrate from home. Coined in 1931 by an American historian, the term has since been redefined so often that it has morphed into a kind of metaconcept with psychological, emotional, and nationalist dimensions. That so many people continue to debate the legitimacy of the American Dream as a social contract to new immigrants only emphasizes that many new immigrants understand it as such. The American Dream, as a social contract, is largely something imagined or understood, not the stuff of actual political or economic reality. Even though recent studies have shown that credentials such as fluency in English, legal status, educational attainment, and wealth at arrival can have a significant bearing on an immigrant's prospects, the idea that a person with no resources can make his fortune with hard work and persistence is widely accepted in immigrant communities in the United States.

Immigration policy in the United States has almost exclusively focused on its borders, leaving the job of integration to individual immigrants and to the communities receiving the greatest immigrant inflows. Although early immigration policy sought to regulate the country's ethnic or racial character, the present-day immigration system came into existence through a series of amendments in 1965. Since then, public debates on immigration have related primarily to border regulation and illegal immigration, with public opinion on immigration shifting in direct response to perceived threats to the country's economic health, national character, and national security. As immigrants from all over the world labor to convince consular and immigration officials to let them into the United States as students, skilled and nonskilled workers, refugees, or family members of other immigrants, the hundreds of thousands of immigrants who do not fit into any obvious immigration preference categories have found creative ways to enter and stay in the country. They, like documented immigrants, have tapped into whatever network they already had or could establish for jobs, housing, schooling for their children, and medical treatment. About a quarter of all immigrants coming to the United States have done so illegally, and the overwhelming majority of these immigrants have been absorbed into the economies and societies in which they live, albeit at a lower average pay scale than their documented or citizen neighbors.

Rafiqul and Nishat had no interest in the immigration debate or the political landscape of the country they had moved to. In a surprisingly short time, as they realized that it would take them longer than anticipated to earn a substantial amount of money in New York, their interests in America shifted from the short term to the middle term. And still, they saw no need to weigh in on the immigration debate in order to achieve their goals. In fact, legality didn't seem to offer them much more than they had been able to achieve off the books. It was only after crisis struck in New York that their immigration status became a barrier to their full integration into American society. And it was only then that they began to concern themselves with American immigration policy.

Nishat keeps no signs of the past. Her walls and shelves are devoid of any maps, art, or documents from home, and her albums hold no pictures of her family in Bangladesh. Instead, the pictures and knickknacks cluttering her walls, her doorjambs, her shelves, and her refrigerator are all in homage to the life she has lived in the United States. She arrived in the guise of a child and a tourist, bearing none of the mementos or keepsakes immigrants normally bring to remind them of where they come from. Instead, she surfaced in New York as if she had no past, and in a certain sense, her arrival in New York was the moment her own life began. Nishat had been in New York for less than six months when she met Mohammad Junaid. Mohammad was the first man who had ever noticed her, and from their very first conversation, Nishat was ready to fall in love with him.

By American standards, Nishat, at twenty-two, was well into adulthood by the time she arrived in the United States, but she had never lived on her own or made independent choices about anything, from what she ate to what career path she should pursue. The decision to migrate or stay at home was not hers to make. Yet almost as soon as she had arrived, she found herself thrust into a world with none of the familiar restrictions and obligations that had defined her behavior. Within a matter of weeks, she had completely recalibrated her image of herself, constructing her identity on the basis of her understanding of American life. The act of migrating can lead people who have lived with no personal autonomy to experience a kind of psychological rebirth, and while it may be assumed that Nishat's identity was fully formed by the time she migrated, she essentially began to live as an adult only after she had arrived in the United States.

When Rafiqul had filled out their visa applications, he had listed Nishat as fifteen years old. With her small frame and narrow face, she could easily pass as a teenager, and a terrible illness at the time of her arrival had taken more of her weight and most of her spunk as well. Rafiqul hoped that, while he worked, she could attend high school and eventually feed directly into the American university system. While Nishat languished with a fever her first three weeks in America, he set out into the city to find out what he could. But when she recovered, Nishat learned that the education she'd been promised was out of the question, because her family at home needed whatever meager income she could earn more than they needed her to be educated. Rafiqul could not possibly know how drastic a decision this was; Nishat would never return to college, and would find herself struggling to make a living and to make her peace with the choice that had been made for her. At the time, she did not question her father's decision, in part because she believed that she

REJECTING THE BURDEN OF HERITAGE   159

would eventually go back to school, but also because she had been raised to believe that incredible amounts of money could be made in America. She was mildly disappointed that she had not been allowed to finish her schooling, but also thrilled at the thought of earning her own money and acting as an adult woman responsible for her family's well-being. A certain kind of autonomy of thought came with this responsibility, and it was this autonomy that made it possible for her to fall in love with Mohammad.

She met him at her job. On a lark, she had responded to a "Help Wanted" sign hanging in the window of a small bar in Elmhurst, Queens. When she was hired, she told her father that she'd found a job, but she didn't tell him where. He himself had begun working long hours at a factory job, and was so preoccupied with saving enough to send home and pay down on an apartment of their own, that he didn't bother to police her. He had enough faith in her somewhat conservative upbringing to believe that she would be demure and incapable of what he saw as improper behavior. In the little dive bar, a dark hole in the wall where local Pakistani taxi drivers hung out after their twelve-hour shifts, Nishat wiped down tables, washed dishes, and served liquor for $2 an hour. She noticed immediately that many of the men who ordered drinks from her were Muslim, but she didn't think much of it. Already, and unbeknownst to her father, the realities of her life in America had subtly altered her perception of proper and improper, if not of right and wrong. Back home in Dhaka, under the watchful eye of her mother, Nishat and her sisters had been completely occupied by their studies and chores. There had been no time to daydream about boys, let alone meet with them, and Nishat would never have dared to bring shame on her parents by walking to or from school with a boy, the way some of her classmates would. Even though she was working more hours in the United States than she ever had before, life without family or studies now left her with a lot of extra time to daydream. Still more importantly, in the absence of her traditional family structure, the fear of social retribution that had regulated her behavior no longer had the same weight.

Throughout her life, her father had always been a kind and caring but ultimately marginal presence. Even in the last ten years, when he had lived with the family in Dhaka, he had been a quiet, almost apologetic figure in their loud and busy household. Her mother had been their primary care-giver and disciplinarian, giving them love and guidance, dispensing the rules and shaping their identities. Their father was more affectionate and sup-portive of his children than many fathers she knew of, but he had spent most of their childhood working far away from them. When he had returned, it was only to fail. Nishat had always respected her father, but some very small part of her resented that she'd been pulled from school after one year with-out being consulted, and had then been sent to work in a menial job far from home. Nishat found the lack of family structure and its obligations pro-foundly disorienting. Long after she had gotten over her sickness and adjusted from her jet lag, Nishat woke in the middle of the night with no idea where she was. After twenty years of sleeping in the same house alongside her sisters, then waking to a strict schedule of studies, school, tutoring, chores, and then bed, her life was both lonely and formless. She enjoyed earning money, but her days felt aimless and empty, with no real clear plan for the future.

It was the early spring of 1997 when Mohammad walked into her bar. As was her personal policy with the customers, she did not pay too close atten-tion to him when he sat down to order his beer. But she did notice that he sat there for a very long time. Finally, as she was wiping down the bar, he spoke.

"What's your name?"

"Nishat."

"Are you Muslim?"

"Yes."

"What's a nice Muslim girl like you doing working at this kind of place?"

Nishat paused in her work and, looking him straight in the eye, shot back, "What's a nice Muslim boy like you doing coming to this kind of place?"

He laughed and blushed. "I didn't mean it that way, I just meant that you should be working somewhere with respect and dignity." She noticed that he had warm brown eyes and a sweet smile. "I'll get you a job with respect," he continued. Nishat thought he was charming, and she agreed to let him help her. Within two weeks, she was working at a Dunkin' Donuts shop in a shady, suburban neighborhood in Long Island, making $5 an hour. And within two weeks after that, she had begun falling in love with Mohammad.

From the beginning, theirs was a relationship of practical considerations, based on real interactions and mutual respect. At their very first encounter, they spoke with each other as equals, in English. If they spoke in Urdu, they used the informal, familiar "you" with one another; if she had had a traditional arranged marriage, she would have been expected to address her betrothed in the formal "you." She soon learned that he was three years younger than she was, but he had a steady job as well as a certain savvy that appealed to her. He managed a wholesale perfume store in Manhattan, and he made good money. Like her, he was undocumented, but he knew the system, and he was physical proof that one could make a perfectly solid livelihood without papers. This was New York, he said, and she was all but surrounded by people with no papers, from that grocery store clerk to that cab driver to that manicurist. Could she spot them on the street? Well, he said, neither could the police.

Mohammad had come to the United States on a tourist visa in 1994, and had just this year moved to New York from Texas. That he was already managing a successful midtown store impressed Nishat, who was still a little nervous to take the train and to work in the middle of the city with no papers. He had great, soft eyes and a thick mass of silky black hair, and, at eighteen, his face had still not outgrown its baby fat. Nishat, on the other hand, was a slight, narrow-hipped woman with high sloping cheekbones, keen eyes, and tiny wrists and ankles. Next to him, she felt small and delicate, pretty and protected. He was the middle of three sons. She liked that he would have neither the arrogance of an eldest son nor the childishness of a youngest. After all of her months of loneliness and her disappointment with the drudgery of her life in America, he did not have to persevere too long to win her affection.

For all of its practical, egalitarian beginnings, their relationship soon took on the flavor of a Bollywood melodrama. They spent the summer meeting secretly in the various neighborhoods of Queens. They walked and talked and let their hands brush together for the occasional surreptitious clasp. He began bringing her fancy perfumes as gifts, which she hid as well as she could. Nishat, who had never owned luxury cosmetic items, who had never defied her family, found herself lying to her father every day. She made up shopping trips and work schedule changes. She said all kinds of things, just to sneak a few moments with Mohammad. She fell in love hard, replete with dizzy spells, no appetite, and heart palpitations. She fantasized about their life together, him working, her keeping house, spending evenings together window shopping in Jackson Heights and weekends together in Corona Park. The only thing that could clear her brain fog was a meeting with him. By the end of the summer, he told her that he wanted to marry her. If being in love gave her life meaning, hearing Mohammad propose gave her life structure. Now, she had something to work toward, a goal of her own. She would marry Mohammad, and together, they would build a happy, middle-class life together. It was only after she met Mohammad that Nishat emotionally migrated to America, and it was only after they fell in love that she felt the true allure of that elusive American Dream.

On June 4, 2000, Nishat Islam married Mohammad Junaid in the apartment they would share. She sat against the wall with her face yellowed with turmeric paste, her head draped with a glittering red and gold cloth, clad in a red sari. Mohammad's mother had come from Pakistan, and several Bangladeshi friends and neighbors had come to witness the marriage, which could not be registered with the New York City clerk. During the wedding ceremony, when Nishat and Mohammad entered into the Shari'a contract of marriage, Nishat kept her eyes downcast and thanked Allah in silence. It had taken nearly four years for Rafiqul to agree to the marriage.

The small apartment was just upstairs from the family friends Rafiqul and Nishat had first lived with. Ladies from the neighborhood had hung a riot of streamers and silk flowers from the ceilings and doorjambs. Dozens of people sat shoulder to shoulder on the living room floor, eating sweets and catered Punjabi food late into the night. Nishat looked about her and saw a community of people supporting her and celebrating with her. Although she understood that there had been historic troubles between Bangladeshis and Pakistanis, those divisions didn't exist in America, she thought. Mohammad had crossed that division hundreds of times to prove her love for him. He had approached Rafiqul for Nishat's hand over and over again since 1997, so many times, in fact, that Nishat lost count. Nothing meant more to Nishat than the way Mohammad fought to win not just her heart but her father's. Rafiqul had been outraged that Nishat had gone behind his back, and he was mystified that she wanted to marry someone without papers. But the thing he could not accept was that she had chosen a Pakistani.

New York City, in particular the boroughs of Queens and Brooklyn, had in the last decade become home to a large Bangladeshi community, estimated at anywhere between 50,000 and 150,000. Settled near other South Asian immigrant communities, the Bangladeshi community in New York had nonetheless worked to preserve its identity, establishing storefront and basement mosques in which prayer was conducted in Bangla, and shops selling Bengali food staples. Beyond these external signs of a community, anthropologists have suggested that maintaining a unique cultural identity within the home is of particular importance to Bangladeshi immigrants in diasporic communities, largely because Bangladesh had so recently won its war of independence, and through it, its people's right to an internationally recognized national identity. Like many of his compatriots, Rafiqul felt deeply that his own national identity was something worth valuing and cherishing, and believed that, as long as his family retained its inherently Bengali character, then Bangladesh, the homeland, or *desh*, could not suffer under the pressure of emigration. In his heart, allowing a Pakistani man to become the head of his household would, to some extent, undermine his hard-fought right to be a Bangladeshi.

But Nishat felt that in America there was no difference between Bangladeshis and Pakistanis; as immigrant communities, they faced the same challenges and struggles, and strove for the same vision of prosperity. In her heart, she believed in one of the most powerful myths surrounding immigration, which holds that by migrating to a new home one can overcome restrictions imposed by religious, ethnic, or gender status in the country of origin. This myth does not always come to fruition, but in certain cases it can. In those instances where it does, it results from a complex dynamic between the specific choices of an immigrant and the natural influence of the host country's culture on the second generation of an immigrant family. Immigrants fleeing persecution or oppression may actively renounce the culturally mandated restrictions of their homeland, or they may involuntarily lead their children to distance themselves from these restrictions simply by pursuing socioeconomic opportunity and assimilating certain aspects the host country's culture. In Nishat's case, she both actively renounced certain cultural restrictions and also felt a greater distance from them because she belonged the generation after her father's. She did not directly experience the brutality of the 1971 war for independence the way her father did, nor did she voluntarily choose to leave her homeland. Marriage with the enemy of her countrymen was possible because she had no personal context for forming a bias against Pakistanis, and because as the child of an immigrant, she adopted what she perceived as an American attitude toward marriage: love and personal compatibility trump cultural or financial considerations.

Mohammad belonged to a fairly young and growing Pakistani population in New York, a population that had nearly tripled in the last decade, according to official statistics. But the official number of legal immigrants hardly accounted for the actual number of Pakistanis almost equally divided between the boroughs of Queens and Brooklyn. In the summer of 2002, community affairs officers and community leaders in the Midwood neighborhood of Brooklyn estimated that the Pakistani community there alone exceeded 100,000, while official statistics tallied the city's total Pakistani population at 36,000 Pakistanis; undocumented Pakistani immigrants tended to cluster where their legal countrymen had settled. The spike in Pakistani immigrants in New York after 1990 may be attributed to many causes, but one of the main reasons identified by Pakistani embassy officials was the change in the global migrant labor market. Many Pakistanis who had worked in Persian Gulf countries as guest workers found themselves jobless as opportunities dried up following the 1991 Gulf War. Although some returned to Pakistan, straining urban centers already overburdened with unemployment, some became second-degree migrants in classic immigration destinations such as New York. Many of the Pakistanis in New York hailed from the areas around Lahore, the capital city of the Punjab province in Pakistan. They were primarily economic migrants who had followed friends and family members who had settled in an earlier wave of migration from Pakistan. A frequently observed pattern of migration occurs when immigrants from a certain village or city quarter settle near an established community of immigrants from the same village or city quarter, plugging into a network of experienced compatriots who assist them in navigating and integrating into their new environment.

Mohammad, on the other hand, came from Karachi, the capital of Sindh province and the former capital city of Pakistan. Karachi was home to Pakistan's largest population of *muhajirs*, or Urdu-speaking Muslims from India who had crossed into Pakistan as refugees during the Partition. Mohammad's family was muhajir. Since the mid-1980s, a nationalist movement predominantly among the urban youth in Karachi had led to the formation of a muhajir ethnic and political identity, as well as of a powerful and militant political party, which came into increasingly violent conflict with the native Sindhi population of the city through the decade. Almost coincidentally with the abrupt closing of the Persian Gulf and the return of jobless men to Pakistan's urban centers, the militant urban youth movement ascended to power and unleashed a reign of terror. After the Pakistani army retaliated to assist in crushing the movement, a widespread backlash against the muhajir population followed. The muhajir community in Karachi became the target of a program of systematic state harassment and intimidation, and the conflict between militant muhajirs and Sindhis continued to paralyze the city as a whole.

Mohammad was fifteen years old when he fled to the United States, and he left behind an economically crippled and dangerous town he could hardly think of as home. Since 1965, the avenues for legal permanent migration to the United States had remained fixed: one could be sponsored by a family member, spouse, or employer; one could gain political asylum through a mass refugee resettlement program or on an individual case-by-case basis; or one could win a slot in the diversity lottery, a pool of visas made available to immigrants from countries underrepresented through other immigration channels. Employers were most likely to sponsor highly trained, highly skilled people recruited to fill a certain position, not a high school dropout like Mohammad. He had no family here, and Pakistan's relationship with the United States made it unlikely that any of its groups struggling against systematic violence or poverty would be made the subject of a mass refugee resettlement program. The odds of winning individual asylum or a diversity slot were outlandishly small. So Mohammad calculated his options and decided that his best bet for a life in America was to overstay a tourist visa.

During the rise of the muhajir nationalist movement, a muhajir identity was invented, in which muhajirs came to see themselves as one ethnic group that was diasporic, persecuted, cosmopolitan, middle class, and more liberal than its other ethnic counterparts in Pakistan. Within this context, it may be understood that Mohammad would feel comfortable with an outsider status, less likely to seek to establish ties within the Pakistani community in New York. It was easy for Mohammad, an Urdu-speaking Karachi muhajir among a large, proud, and slightly insular Lahori Punjabi-speaking community, to feel comfortable with non-Pakistanis. Bangladeshi immigrants, by and large poorer and newer than their fellow immigrants from the South Asian subcontinent, legal and undocumented alike, settled within or adjacent to Pakistani and Indian communities. They were Sunni Muslims, as he was, and many Bangladeshis, Rafiqul and Nishat included, spoke Urdu.

Although we have examined how context and proximity might lead a Bangladeshi and a Pakistani to marry each other, we must also consider the practical question of how Mohammad and Nishat, as two undocumented people, calculated the financial and legal security of their life together. Surely, they would not have chosen to marry if they did not believe that it was possible for them to live a stable and reasonably prosperous life without papers. They married during a period of unparalleled prosperity in the United States, which coincided with a liberalization of national attitudes toward immigration. It seemed that the country was finally emerging from a particularly hostile anti-immigrant moment that had begun in the mid-1990s, prompting a loosening in some of the more restrictive legislation that had been passed in the meantime. Cubans and Nicaraguans who had lived illegally in the United States since 1995 were granted blanket amnesty in 2000, and a new act permitted undocumented immigrants who were sponsored by relatives, spouses, or employers to wait for their visas in the United States rather than return home, prompting a marriage boom in immigrant communities nationwide. Nishat and Mohammad were not the only undocumented people who believed that if they waited long enough they might luck out during a blanket amnesty or change in immigration policy. As they settled in to wait for the US government to come around, they tapped into their circle of friends and acquaintances to find paid work, a place to live, health care, and even a car.

Their lives were textbook examples of the social networking phenomenon immigration scholars have identified in immigrant communities around the world, which largely account for the channels through which undocumented immigrants acquire social security or government identification numbers, bank accounts, and leases. Through friends, family members, and acquaintances made within ethnic communities, undocumented immigrants not only gain access to the tools they need to build a livelihood but these networks also provide all immigrants, regardless of status, with the necessary equipment to integrate into a foreign political, economic, and cultural system. Even without language skills or civic orientation, new immigrants can achieve a high level of social integration through informal networks, even in the absence of a comprehensive national integration policy. But the integration and social cohesion provided by informal networks can be impermanent and, in the worst of cases, deceptive.

The history of US immigration policy making can be described as a cycle of alternating liberalization and restriction, in response to discriminatory sentiments and corrective impulses among the electorate. Traditionally and almost like clockwork, hostility toward immigration and immigrants has tended to follow economic recessions, rises in unemployment, or a widely perceived external threat. But the widespread anti-immigrant feeling of the mid-1990s, which led to some of the most restrictive anti-immigrant legislation in decades, took place during a period of great prosperity, high employment, and relative peace. Immigration specialists have attributed the change in public mood to aggressive media reports and to negative pop culture archetypes. California's vote in favor of the unconstitutional, nativist Proposition 187 showed national politicians that they could win elections on strong anti-immigrant platforms, and on the eve of the 1996 general election, three major pieces of immigration legislation were signed into law, all of which called for some restriction on the rights and benefits available to immigrants, whether legal or illegal, and to their US citizen children.

Many of the legal and policy weapons that would be turned against immigrant communities in the coming eras of political crisis and economic difficulty were passed during this era of immigration reform. That these laws were passed largely out of political opportunism rather than in response to real difficulties in the immigration system makes the consequences borne by immigrant communities all the more tragic. Although they had arrived in the thick of this era of anti-immigrant lawmaking, neither Nishat nor Mohammad had been aware of the changes in the political environment. As far as they understood, being illegal in the United States was challenging but nonetheless commonplace enough to be acceptable. In fact, legal scholars have pointed out that neither the 1994 nor 1996 immigration reform laws actually changed the numbers of permissible immigrants or went after existing undocumented immigrant communities. Unable to reach consensus on border control measurements, Congress instead went after legal immigrants who had not yet been naturalized into US citizens.

The immigration debate had followed quite a different cycle in New York, where every aspect of the city's culture and economy depended to some extent on immigrant labor, documented and undocumented alike. New York's immigrant neighborhoods were plentiful and visible, like a cluster of tiny villages, each with its own language, cuisine, goods for sale, and borders. And New York's government had often taken positions that were, if not in direct confrontation with official US immigration policy dictates, based on an informal don't-ask-don't-tell position toward undocumented immigrants. In fact, until the autumn of 2001, no federal government agencies based in New York required proof of legal immigrant status in providing health care, social services, or educational enrollment for city residents.

Unlike cities in Germany or even parts of the United Kingdom, where new residents in a given neighborhood had to register their presence with a wide array of bureaucratic and law-enforcement bodies, and present multiple proofs of identity in order to participate in any social institution, life in New York could be as official or unofficial as an individual chose to make it.

Mohammad and Nishat's daughter Ayesha was born in May 2001, less than four months before the September 11 attacks on the World Trade Center and Pentagon changed the US government's approach to immigration completely, and the full weight of the immigration legislation passed in the mid-1990s was brought to bear on the Muslims of America. Nishat had suffered from major complications during the pregnancy and had spend the majority of it in bed, unable to work. When Ayesha arrived, she was born without a soft-spot and, when she was just a few weeks old, had to undergo corrective brain surgery. While America's political landscape changed to accommodate the new reaches of the war on terror, Ayesha's life hung in the balance. Nishat chose not to return to work, but instead to focus on caring for her daughter while her husband brought home their livelihood. In the meantime, Rafiqul, a long-term heart patient, had to receive a major bypass operation. Mohammad and Nishat were so occupied with caring for their daughter and Nishat's father, paying their bills, and making up for the loss of two main income streams, that they hardly took time to think about the world around them. They did not think about it until they had to.

On May 19, 2003, Mohammad got up earlier than usual. He had a stop to make in downtown Manhattan before heading to work in midtown Manhattan, where he still managed the same wholesale perfume shop near Times Square. So as his wife Nishat slept, he slipped from the bed and walked into the kitchen. He set a small saucepan of water and teabags to boil on the stove and rummaged around in the refrigerator for breakfast. In just a few hours, he was scheduled for a Special Registration hearing, part of a program authorized by the USA PATRIOT Act to register all men from twenty-five different countries, including Pakistan, who were not citizens or permanent residents of the United States. Aside from North Korea, the rest of the countries on the list were predominantly Muslim.

Mohammad had not slept very well the night before. As an undocumented immigrant with no legal right to have lived in the United States for the last ten years, he did not relish the thought of exposing his immigration status before a court. For weeks, he had tried to keep up a brave and jovial face, telling Nishat that if he cooperated, he might be able to win amnesty for both himself and for her. Who knows, he told her, they could both be green card holders by the end of the year! But he was nervous that things would not go as he hoped, and he was nervous that, if the hearing took too long, he would lose his job. He had already spent one entire day waiting for a hearing only to be told to return today, and his boss might not be as sympathetic this time. These days, many people who had employed undocumented workers in the past were wary of drawing unwanted attention from the government. More troubling than this was the possibility that he might be detained. In the months since Special Registration had begun, many of the men who had gone to voluntarily register, in hopes that cooperation would spare them any troubles, had been detained on the spot and never returned.

Just a few feet from the kitchen, in the bedroom, Nishat groaned softly and dragged herself out of bed. She was four months pregnant with their second child, and Mohammad pampered her in the mornings. Although his daughter Ayesha was now his pride and joy, a pudgy little bundle with his round cheeks and eyes and his loose curls, he still secretly hoped for a son. Mohammad carried a mug of thick, milky tea to the bedroom and placed it by the bedside for his wife. He stopped by the crib to kiss Ayesha's forehead and then went back into the kitchen.

In the living room, Nishat's father Rafiqul, whose movements had slowed since his bypass surgery, was folding up the bedclothes on the small twin mattress where he slept. He tired easily, but did not like to stay in bed later than his son-in-law. He knew this would be a difficult day for his daughter, and a decisive one for their family. If Mohammad was able to use this registration as a starting point to seek amnesty for his family on grounds that his daughter required special care only available in the United States, then Rafiqul would know that Nishat's future was secure, and that he had done right to bring her with him. He himself had been required to register under the program, but had little fear that he would be deported. After all, he was sixty-two, a heart patient, and aside from overstaying his visa, he had done nothing wrong in the United States. But the uncertainty of their lives made him uneasy. He hoped that today's hearing might resolve his son-in-law's status and put all of their minds at ease.

Mohammad did not normally pray, except during the major festivals. Nishat was more likely to turn to religion to ease her fears or look for meaning in hardships. But today, as the sky turned from dark to pale blue, Mohammad muttered a few verses of the Qur'an under his breath. He dropped his tea mug in the sink, threw a quick glance at the clock high on the kitchen wall and reviewed the directions to 26 Federal Plaza, the vast building that housed the New York City branch of the Department of Homeland Security's Division of US Citizenship and Immigration Services. Calling to Nishat that he would call her as soon as the hearing was over, Mohammad shrugged on his coat and stepped into the hallway to press the button for the elevator. Nishat walked into the kitchen bleary-eyed and drowsy, and turned her face upward to receive Mohammad's kiss on her forehead. She wrapped her arms around her body and leaned on the doorframe, waiting with him for the elevator. When the elevator door had closed on him, she turned back into the dark apartment to wake Ayesha for breakfast. With so many undocumented Muslims going into hiding or fleeing to Canada, she could not help but think that appearing before immigration authorities was sheer folly. She hoped that Mohammad was right.

The last year and a half had thrown New York City's Muslim communities into a state of tumult. As soon as news of the attacks on the World Trade Center towers on September 11, 2001, hit the airwaves, every Muslim immigrant in New York had been on the watch. Documented or undocumented, legal or illegal, Muslim immigrants throughout the city waited for the inevitable detentions, arrests, sweeps, and reprisals. Moroccans, Afghans, Egyptians, Algerians, Senegalese, Somalis, Turks, Pakistanis, and Bangladeshis gathered in their respective mosques and restaurants to speculate and consult with one another. Undocumented gypsy cab drivers and stockroom workers and waiters and clerks met all over the city in furtive groups, circulating news and rumors about changes in immigration policy. Throughout the history of the United States, wars abroad have led to the targeting of immigrant communities at home. Whether through law enforcement or policy changes, immigrants' prospects to enter and stay in the United States have been compromised each time the country has faced hostilities or national security threats from abroad. And so, as it had always done when threatened, the United States turned on its own neighborhoods as the federal governments authorized blanket sweeps of Muslim immigrant communities.

Within days of the September 11 attacks, night raids had begun. Almost overnight, New York City's traditional stance of looking the other way on immigration status had buckled under the weight of national security pressure. Throughout Muslim neighborhoods in New York and New Jersey, FBI agents and police conducted broad sweeps, arresting several men in a neighborhood on any given night. Across the city, basement and storefront mosques were closed and boarded up. Every week, news broadcasts and neighborhood publications in dozens of languages told of young men living four to a room in run-down apartments who disappeared without a trace, women who had not had time to cover their heads watching as their husbands and sons were driven away in unmarked Lincoln towncars, toddler US citizens left suddenly fatherless, households cut off from their sole income streams. But there were no images of these arrests, of the faces of the many detained and disappeared, of the families left behind to fend for themselves, because most of them were taken in the middle of the night, without warning, without warrants.

Thousands were detained in the initial sweeps. When the immigration detention centers had been filled to capacity, the immigrants, many arrested without being charged and many charged only with administrative violations, were held in federal prisons alongside violent felons. Reports trickled out that many of the detainees were kept in stress positions, deprived of sleep, hassled by guards. Many were charged using so-called secret evidence, which was withheld from the defendants, their lawyers, and the public. Many detainees were held without being charged at all. But none of these truths prompted any mass public displays of outrage. While Muslim, Arab, and

South Asian activist or advocacy groups staged protests, organized outreach and assistance to detainees and their families, compiled media projects and exhibits, and published blogs and email circulars on the disappearances, detentions, abuses, deportations, and ethnic profiling, there was no widespread national backlash against the clampdown on immigrant communities.

Although Amnesty International came out with reports of wholesale abuse in detention centers and prisons, the legal retaliation against these initial detentions took years. Some of the most notorious instances of abuse were reported in the Metropolitan Detention Center in Brooklyn, where eighty-four men were held in the months after September 11. None of these men was charged in the September 11 attacks, and most were deported on civil immigration infractions. Five Department of Justice investigations, most of which were never publicized, described prisoners' heads being smashed against a T-shirt with an American flag on it taped to the concrete wall, beaten without provocation, denied medical attention, and locked up barefoot without pillows, mattresses, blankets, or shoes. Five years after the detentions and abuse, a Bureau of Prisons spokesperson said that the warden had retired and that thirteen guards had been disciplined. And two former detainees would file what some saw as a potential landmark case against the federal government and senior George W. Bush administration officials.

Although Nishat and Mohammad knew of people who had been detained or had disappeared in the months after the attacks, they were happy that they had not been affected. As news of the arrests and terrible rumors of beatings and torture spread, they reacted by lying low. Like so many people in their neighborhood, they kept their heads down and counted their blessings, secretly telling themselves that the disappeared and deported were somehow different from them, so different that they would surely be safe. Detainees and deportees were surely criminals, not like them, who had overstayed visas illegally but had since integrated into society and paid taxes regularly. Their daughter was a US citizen, they told themselves, surely the United States wouldn't deprive its citizen of her parents.

And of course, their lives were full. Although Ayesha had flourished into a plump and chatty little girl who could even coax a grin from the brusque check-out lady at the Korean grocery store where they shopped, she still required constant attention and care. It was agreed that Nishat should stay at home indefinitely and abandon the thought of returning to work. Although not their primary income stream, Nishat's wages from Dunkin' Donuts had brought in much-needed money for household expenses. But with longer hours at the perfume store, Mohammad earned enough to pay the rent on their roomy apartment, to furnish it with matching bedroom and living room sets, and to support a wife, infant, and father-in-law. He had almost forgotten that he was not a legal resident in New York. As the months passed, and the night raids trailed off of the headlines, it was easy for Mohammad and Nishat to believe that they had emerged unscathed from the worst period of profiling that Muslim immigrants had ever faced in the United States.

Then the federal government launched Special Registration. Officially known as the National Security Entry/Exit Registration System (NSEERS), the program was authorized under the USA PATRIOT Act, and called for nationals of twenty-five different countries to register with US immigration authorities. There were three different registration deadlines between December and February of 2003, for men from three different groups of countries. Pakistan was included in the last of the three groups. When the program was announced, published in newspapers, and circulated through local government offices, community and religious leaders encouraged the men to cooperate. They had no way of knowing how destructive the program would actually be.

As the sun rose high over Queens, Nishat prepared herself for her day. She had made no other plans but to take care of the baby and wait for her husband to call and tell her that everything was fine. She propped Ayesha between her thighs, clenched a plastic comb between her teeth, and began to rake her fingers through her daughter's thick mass of curls. As she worked baby oil into Ayesha's scalp, she designed her daughter a new hairstyle to surprise Mohammad. She would dress Ayesha up, put jingly silver anklets and golden bangles on her plump ankles and wrists, and line her eyes with black *kajal* to welcome her daddy back home that night. If she felt up to it, she might apply henna to her own palms before she made dinner.

It wasn't until 6:30 p.m. that Nishat received the collect call from a county jail in New Jersey. When Mohammad's voice came over the line, it sounded distant and robotic. "They held me, honey," he said. He had been detained and slated for deportation. As an undocumented immigrant herself, she would not be allowed to come visit him. He would never come home again. They had been married for three years.

Mohammad was held without trial in Sussex County, New Jersey, for five months before he was deported. Although he had lodged an appeal soon after his detention, his chances for winning were slim from the outset. He had been detained not as a terrorism suspect but as an absconder, a person who ignored a deportation order. In 1997, just before he'd moved to New York, he had been ordered deported in absentia by a Texas immigration judge. Ignoring a deportation order was a criminal offense, the immigration judge in down-town Manhattan had told him, and so he was detained immediately and slated for deportation on the earliest possible charter flight back to Pakistan.

Mohammad insisted that he knew nothing of the earlier deportation order. He later told Nishat this story: he had been working in Houston and living with a few other young men. One day, he had gotten into a fight with one of his roommates, and a third roommate had overreacted and called the police. Mohammad was arrested and held in jail for two days while his parents in Karachi sold their car to raise money for his bail. And of course, he was found to have overstayed his tourist visa by three years. Although he had briefly attended high school in Houston before dropping out to look for work, first in Texas and later in New York, he claimed that he had not spoken English well enough to understand the subpoena for his deportation hearing, or to understand the immigration officer who hand-delivered it. During his Special Registration hearing, he requested that his 1997 deportation hearing be reopened, so that he might defend himself in person. The judge denied his request. He had not been a minor at the time of his previous arrest, the judge said, and the case had been closed fairly.

Nishat struggled to make peace with new information that she had married a man who had already been ordered deported when she first met him.

Initially, she was furious that Mohammad had not told her of this vital obstacle to their future in the United States, but in the end, her loyalty to him won her over. She firmly believed that marriage was once and for a lifetime, and she knew that she had chosen him against her father's opposition, her ethnic loyalty, and sheer rationality. For an undocumented woman with no college education to choose a partner in the same situation, let alone one in an even more tenuous situation than her own, she had clearly made a choice based on intangible benefits. How she assessed these benefits gives us a real insight into both her core psychology and how she was reacting to the challenges and alienation of her first months in New York.

When Nishat first met Mohammad, she had been uprooted from a warm and intimate home life during a period of family crisis. He had made her feel special and noticed at a time when she felt like just another invisible person in a strange city. He was also broad shouldered and fair skinned, with large, dewy eyes and a thick mop of soft, blue-black hair. His attention was flattering to Nishat, who had been raised to admire fair skin and voluptuous figures in women more than her own angular physique and ochre skin tone. Their secret courtship appealed not only to Nishat's inner romanticism, penchant for drama, and hunger for love, but made her aware that she was willing to fight for what she wanted.

And Nishat was willing to fight for her marriage. To defend a marriage founded on love rather than a mutually advantageous socioeconomic arrangement, she would have to become Mohammad's strongest advocate and ally, and support him with fierce loyalty. That was how Nishat loved, like a prize fighter. So, while other wives of men detained during the voluntary registrations stayed hidden at home, relied on the support of friends and family, or returned to their home countries, Nishat worked on her English, reached out to several local activist organizations, and gave interviews with the American media. The steps Nishat took to fight for her marriage and to fight her husband's deportation fundamentally altered her sense of self and relation to her world in both good and bad ways.

The scope of Nishat's world changed drastically after Mohammad was detained. Where her domain had formerly been the kitchen, the housekeeping,

the health of her daughter and care for her unborn child, she was now responsible for keeping her family from total disintegration. She had no legal right to
work, no college degree or vocational training, and no support system. But in
these weeks, she discovered her capacity for survival. She was forced to turn to
community organizations for financial assistance to supplement the state
assistance she received for Ayesha's rehabilitation. As she struggled to educate
herself about the US legal system and run a household on handouts, Nishat felt
herself slowly begin to awaken to her own strength, but also to her crushing
burden. Personal growth is never easy, and so Nishat was by turns optimistic
and nihilistic, proud and generous, needy and bitter. As she struggled under
the weight of her responsibility to free her husband and care for her family, she
underwent a psychological change about her own abilities, her own strengths,
and her contribution to society.

One major channel for this change in her psychology was her affiliation
with one particular community-based activist organization that was assist-
ing her. This group and others like it attempted to organize coalitions and
programs of resistance to harsh immigration and security policies and
enforcement practices that were crippling immigrant communities across
the country. Mostly led by the grown children of immigrants, these groups
often espoused ideas that were unfamiliar to the communities they served,
ideas based in neo-Leninist solidarity movements, post-Civil Rights Era
identity politics, and post-Cold War critical theory. In attempting to
empower into political action people whose lives had previously centered on
home life, low-wage work, and avoiding detection by the law, these groups
often fundamentally altered the political consciousness of the people with
whom it worked. As the group Nishat joined persuaded the wives and children of detainees to contest unfair and abusive detention practices and to
organize campaigns seeking changes in immigration legislation, Nishat, who
had never been involved in political action, soon began participating in
demonstrations and street fairs, acting as a media spokesperson for the
group, and writing letters to local and national elected officials.

Mohammad's life, on the other hand, was now entirely in someone else's
hands. Down to the smallest details of what to wear (an orange jumpsuit) or

when he might eat, he listened to someone else's orders. Even phone calls home had to be made collect. Although the immigration judge had denied his request to reopen his deportation hearing, with the help of the lawyer Nishat had found him, he filed an appeal with the court. He premised his appeal on both political and humanitarian grounds. He filed for political asylum, saying that he had been attacked as a teenager by political militants in Pakistan, and sought parole on humanitarian grounds, stating that his pregnant wife and disabled daughter needed him. But every day was a brutal cut to his masculine pride. He smarted that while he stagnated in jail, his wife relied on the support of community groups run by strangers and women. And he irrationally worried that the blow to his masculinity might repel his wife, perhaps even driving her to seek solace in the company of other men. If he should remain locked up, or eventually be deported, would she follow him? Or would she find another partner to help her wait out the years until she could apply for a green card and join her children as citizens? He kept these doubts to himself, but he kept them nonetheless.

Mohammad was to be deported on a charter flight in July 2003, but Nishat, with the aid of a Pakistani diplomat and an immigration attorney, was able to get Mohammad off the flight. He was returned to the county jail, where he was faced with a complicated choice. The only way he could stay in the United States was behind bars, waiting for his appeal to be heard in court. And he would have to wait indefinitely. If he left the United States, he expected his wife to bring his children to him in Pakistan, where they would not have the same opportunities they would have here. Ultimately, he decided that an indefinite existence in prison was far worse than capitulating and being sent home.

In September 2003, just before his son was born, Mohammad told Nishat that he was abandoning his appeal to remain in the United States. He would be deported within a few weeks, he said, and he expected Nishat to join him in Karachi as soon as she recovered from childbirth. When she heard this, Nishat felt a disappointment that was strangely similar to disdain. She had been fighting for him, why wouldn't he fight for himself? She had found him a lawyer and gone back to work for as long as she'd been physically able, she had gotten his story in the *Chicago Tribune* and the *Washington Post*, and she was in touch with both Pakistani and US government officials on his behalf. She tried to swallow her disappointment and reconcile herself to follow her husband. But she soon learned that disappointment doesn't go down easily.

Nishat had not troubled herself with politics or thought about immigration policy before her husband had confronted the US immigration system. She had trusted in her father's decision to bring her to the United States, and she had trusted in Mohammad to navigate the rocky path of illegal immigrant life for their family. Most of all, she had trusted in her instinct to have confidence in the men in her life. Just when she felt her life most secure, she found herself left without any support from the country that she had chosen as her home, but more importantly, from the men who had guided and validated this choice. Her husband, it seemed, had lied to her about his own knowledge of the legal system, and her father had grossly overestimated her opportunities here. Just as she faced the fact that she had been misguided by the men she trusted most, and misled in her faith that America was a land of unbounded opportunity, it became clear to her that her ethnicity and her religion, the two other cornerstones of her identity besides trust in her family, now further destabilized the security of her existence.

Because of a geopolitical crisis, she had been thrust into a state of personal crisis, and with it she began a complex reassessment of her understanding of her familial, cultural, and religious obligations. She would eventually reconfigure her identity once again, as a woman on her own, and as an immigrant in the United States. The convergence of personal and political disappointment in her own life had the very real effect of awakening Nishat to her own agency in her life, but also to the hopelessness of the situation that she had allowed to develop. By the time the mayhem was over and the dust had settled, she found herself a single mother at twenty-eight, with no education, no way of earning a living wage, and no way back home.

PART III

ALIENATION AND ACCEPTANCE

CHAPTER 7

SHARIF GOES HOME

Sharif slouches in front of his computer in a robe and socks, his eyes red and tired. It is almost 5:00 a.m., and he has barely moved from this spot in the last twenty-four hours. He thinks about little else but war, destruction, and suffering throughout the Arab world. If there is indeed a clash of civilizations, it plays out every day in media reports he monitors and analyzes through the media advocacy organization he chairs, Arab Media Watch. Through his work, he sees how even the most respectable and professional of Britain's media organizations consistently forgo objectivity and balance to feed the public a slanted and dehumanizing picture of Arabs. The more he works, the more work there is. Slowly, what started out as a passion becomes an obsession.

He can't let himself off the hook, can't drag himself from his computer long enough to eat or shower, let alone spend time or money socializing. Since he is living on savings, and there is very little to do in London for free, he chooses to stay at home instead. But he doesn't relax at home, he just keeps on working around the clock, fighting to prove himself right for choosing activism over a career, but also as a worthy suitor to his girlfriend's parents and a competent critic of the media establishment. Slowly and steadily he withdraws from human society and retreats to a world of ideas and ideologies.

More and more frequently, he does not go to bed until 7:00 a.m., often not until noon or even 2:00 p.m. When he does, his head fills with checklists, existential anxiety, and general anger, and he can't sleep. His body constantly aches, his temper is short. But it seems that the worse he feels, the better Arab Media Watch does. As his money and prospects dwindle, Arab Media Watch's membership, coverage, and impact skyrocket. So he asks himself, what right does he have to turn his back on his idealism, his dreams, and his project?

In spite of his crates full of records, his closet full of nice clothes, his fancy car, his attractive and successful girlfriend, his handsome home, his loving and supportive family, and the undeniable success of his project, Sharif descends into a deep depression. He feels isolated and alienated. His enviable personal life collapses under the weight of his political disillusionment and his sense of professional disintegration.

He keeps on going, out of obligation, but he wishes for a way out.

In the summer of 2004, Sharif made the drastic decision to move to Palestine. Initially, the move was just to take on a short-term consultancy with the UN, but he knew that if he were able to regain his sense of purpose and direction, he might stay on in Palestine indefinitely. This decision was a departure for Sharif, both personally and professionally. He had always preferred to stay close to his family in London rather than live overseas. As a journalist, he had worked in well-appointed offices in London, editing dispatches from distant wars, and he had never directly reported on any of the conflicts he monitored for Arab Media Watch. But nonetheless, at this critical juncture in his personal and professional development, he believed that he might be better off living and working in Palestine than in London, his hometown.

In the two years after he had abandoned his career in journalism to build up Britain's only organization dedicated to monitoring British media coverage, first of the Israeli-Palestinian conflict and then, after the Iraq war began, of Arab issues in general, Sharif had constantly been doubting his decision. Although the project had grown in scope, he had not been able to secure a steady source of funding to maintain, staff, and house it. To keep the project running, he tapped into his savings from previous jobs, questioning the direction his life was headed each time he made a withdrawal from the bank. As his savings drained away, taking his self esteem with them, he began to fight more and more with his family. His future with his girlfriend, whom he planned to marry, seemed increasingly tenuous. He was always preoccupied, constantly busy, but felt that he was making no progress toward personal and professional security.

In January 2004, around the tenth anniversary of his father's death, several events came together to bring his self-doubt to a crisis point. His girlfriend, whose mother died after a long battle with cancer, underwent a personal transformation and suddenly ended their three-year relationship, breaking his heart. One week later, his mother checked herself into a hospital and then barely escaped death with an emergency heart operation. He worried that he could not support his family if something should happen to her, he worried that she would die and leave him. He worried about Palestine, he worried about Iraq, he struggled with the value of what he was doing. He came to resent compliments from other British Arabs, who he felt were unwilling to give of their own time and money to help him succeed. By early summer, he was all but crippled with alternating depression and anxiety. He could not sleep, sometimes for many days at a time, and he began to find it easier to think about death than the future. Something had to give.

When a friend told him about a program sponsored by the UN that placed expatriate Palestinian professionals into Palestinian Authority institutions as expert consultants, he jumped at the opportunity. The office of the Palestinian prime minister was launching a media monitoring project, and he had exactly the qualifications to help develop it. In the weeks following his application and acceptance, he had no time to dwell on his fears. He had no plans of permanently abandoning Arab Media Watch or his family. But he had come to associate his life in London with fear of professional failure and personal stagnation, and, if he looked deeper within himself, with fear of loss and abandonment. The thought of living out his life in a place where his work was undervalued and his personal life both isolated and impoverished was naturally distasteful to him. He felt no sense of community and belonging in his hometown. And so, even though he was not by nature an adventurer, thrill seeker, or misery tourist, he viewed his move to Palestine with more hope than wariness. He looked forward to being directly involved in developing the country, and hoped to meet like-minded people who shared his passion and vision for the future of Palestine.

Rather than as an escape from the stresses and pressures of his life, Sharif saw his decision to move as an opportunity to continue working in his chosen field, and for a paycheck. Since he would be working as a media consultant, he would be furthering the goal of Arab Media Watch as well as providing for his family and his future. In many ways, this move to Palestine was a culmination of a lifelong process of identity formation, but he was not the kind of person to make a major life decision for political reasons or to resolve an identity crisis. The fact that he spent all of his time thinking about injustice and suffering may have contributed to his overall anxiety and depression, but his existential crisis was much more practical. He worried that he had chosen a dead-end career, that he would not be able help his mother or support a family, and that he would end up a failure. His personal losses were what pushed him from tension and professional anxiety into depression.

Practical and personal though the causes of his crisis may have been, Sharif could not deny that he was fighting a losing battle on the ideological battlefield. In spite of significant academic efforts to debunk the clash-of-civilizations idea, it seemed to have nonetheless become the dominant paradigm of media representations, policymaking, and public perception. In the years since he had founded Arab Media Watch, the public appetite for moderation and tolerance toward Arabs and Muslims seemed only to be shrinking. Through his work, Sharif saw increasingly skewed and biased reporting on Arabs and Muslims in the aftermath of the September 11 attacks in the United States and the US-led invasion of Iraq, in which Britain was the staunchest supporter of the invading force.

Even as media reports, popular films, and television programs continued to conflate widely diverse Arab and Muslim groups with terrorists and fanatics, more and more Arabs and Muslims were beginning themselves to conflate the occupations of Iraq and Palestine. Even Sharif, who fought against bias, generalizations, and inaccuracies in the British press, saw the occupations of Palestine and Iraq as part of one continuum. As he prepared to travel to Palestine, Sharif said, "When you look on TV, what's the difference between Gaza and Fallujah? It's shocking. Sometimes I kind of wake up and realize there are now two Arab countries occupied by a Western force."

Meanwhile, the Palestinian uprising continued to gain purchase as a "Muslim" cause. On May 1, 2003, the British media reported that two suicide bombers, Asif Mohammed Hanif, twenty-one, and Omar Khan Sharif, twenty-seven, who killed three people at a Tel Aviv bar, were actually British passport holders believed to be of Pakistani descent. These were the first wholly foreign suicide bombers in Israel, reported on at a time when Western policymakers and media analysts had begun discussing the growth of a global Islamist movement. Two years later, in June 2005, the predominantly South Asian body and leading voice for Muslim activists in the United Kingdom, the Muslim Council of Britain, refused to send delegates to attend a Holocaust memorial at Westminster out of ill-conceived solidarity with Palestinian victims of oppression in Israel. The Palestinian resistance to Israeli occupation had traditionally been socialist and secular, but as the power of Yasser Arafat's Fatah party began to wane and the Muslim humanitarian and resistance movement Hamas grew in influence, Palestine as both a real and symbolic cause would come to be associated with Muslim identity. Palestinian support for Islamist groups, many of them openly militant against Israeli settlers and civilians, rose from 17 percent before the Intifada began to 35 percent by the middle of 2004. Many historians have suggested that Christian Palestinians, believed to comprise some 10 percent of the current Palestinian population, were instrumental in the formation of the Palestinian national movement during the late nineteenth century. Some of the most prominent contemporary voices for Palestinian rights and independence are Christian, including Hanan Ashrawi and Edward Said, whose death in September 2003 was considered a tragedy among both Muslim and Christian Palestinian expatriates everywhere. Still, within the new global discourse, Palestinian independence would be increasingly viewed as a Muslim, even Islamist, cause.

Sharif had always thought of himself as both Christian and Muslim, although his mother had described her children, the children of a Muslim father, as Muslim. When he was at his lowest point, after his girlfriend had broken his heart and his mother was ill, Sharif found himself turning to religion as one of many ways out of his depression. He remembered how peaceful and meditative his father had looked performing his daily morning prayers, and so he checked out books to learn how to perform *namaz*. Ultimately, he found it simpler and more peaceful to light a candle and meditate in a church than to memorize the ritualized worship and verses of Muslim prayer, but even though he worshiped as a Christian, he still retained both his Muslim and Christian identities. He eventually devised a more secular coping mechanism, instituting a regular schedule of heavy workouts and rededicating himself to his work with Arab Media Watch. Although the peace and simplicity of religion may have appealed to him in the dark of depression, the cleansing labor of hard work and pure faith in the righteousness of his cause made the most sense to him in the light of day.

The airplane touched down in Ben Gurion Airport in Tel Aviv on August 2, 2004, with a soft jolt. In the pale, early dawn light, the landscape beyond the brown tarmac was barely visible through the airplane window. Sharif leaned back into his seat and closed his eyes while the airplane taxied down the runway. His eyes were dry and his body sore. Although the flight had not been especially long or turbulent, Sharif had not slept at all. Today was the beginning of a new chapter in his life; he was moving to Ramallah, the capital city of occupied Palestine. It was not just apprehension at leaving his family that had kept him awake for the past two nights. In just a few minutes, he would be face-to-face with Israeli security officials, and he worried that if he said the wrong thing, he would find himself detained in a foreign prison.

He exited the airplane and walked across the tarmac toward a shuttle bus bound for the main terminal. Inside the terminal was a large concrete hall echoing with loud chatter. To the right of the entrance, Israeli citizens lined up in front of a row of automats for rapid immigration processing. Sharif joined a long line of foreign nationals leading to a row of booths. In the weeks leading up to his departure, he had made several attempts to contact the United Nations to find out how he should negotiate his way through Israel and into Palestine, but with no luck. The day before he was scheduled to leave, a contact from the United Nations had called him with advice that could be described as cursory at best. He was told that when he arrived, he should come straight from the airport to the UN Development Program (UNDP) office in Jerusalem, but was given no details on how to get there. He was simply advised to not tell Israeli airport officials that he was going to Ramallah, and to not mention what he would be doing when he got there.

When he stepped up to the small booth, a young woman in a pale blue shirt glanced at his name and asked him where he was from. "Britain," he replied curtly, without a moment's hesitation. He was officially one-quarter Palestinian, but he had grown up in London, and he saw himself as both British and Palestinian. Often, in his travels in Arab countries, he told Arabs he was British to cover for his lack of fluency in Arabic. In Britain, he had crafted a profession out of his Palestinian identity. He slid fluidly between these identities, claiming whichever label would best serve each situation. The official questioned him on his travels for twenty minutes before waving him on to two more officials standing on either side of an opening to the cordoned-off baggage claim area. He handed his passport to another young woman in a pale blue shirt. She took his passport, told him to stand to the side of the rope, and wait there for just a moment. He waited for close to an hour, shifting his weight from one leg to the next. Clusters of families in long black coats pushed loaded carts past bare-midriffed students slightly stooped under huge backpacks, and single businessmen scattered herds of tourists. The official returned. Sharif remembers the following exchange:

"What is the purpose of your visit?"

"I'm working with the UN in Jerusalem."

"What will you be doing with the UN?"

"I'm a media consultant."

"What exactly will you be doing as a media consultant with the UN?"

Sharif tried not to break eye-contact with the official as he thought how to answer. "I'm not sure," he slowly answered.

"What do you mean, you're not sure?" she retorted, with no small amount of sarcasm, thought Sharif.

Slow-moving knots of tension began to form in his stomach. "I haven't been briefed yet."

She stared at him with open incredulity and said, "So you come to this country and you don't even know what work you're doing."

He clenched his jaw and repeated that he had not yet been briefed. She repeated her question in different words several times, and each time he stubbornly repeated that he hadn't yet been briefed.

He was then asked to collect his baggage and then bring it back for inspection. While he waited, a group of officials wearing latex gloves dug through his things, taking each item out, scanning bottled items for explosive material, and dumping them back into his bags in disarray. Although such searches have become standard practice in airports, Sharif noticed no one else undergoing such detailed inspection. He felt certain that he had been singled out because of his Arab name and his travel to other Arab countries.

As his shampoo and lotion were being screened, he happened to glance over one official's shoulder and saw the parents of one of his closest childhood friends from London, who were Jewish, approaching the baggage claim area. He felt a sudden rush of embarrassment at what they might think to see him standing there and being interrogated. In London, he would have caught their attention. But here, he could feel that they were on opposite sides of an invisible divide. He saw them hand their passports to an official, who glanced cursorily over their paperwork before waving them through. He knew that he would not feel comfortable discussing his plans to live in Ramallah and work for the Palestinian Authority with them, and that they would most likely have no intention of visiting the Palestinian territories during their visit. In a country he saw as the illegal occupier of his homeland, they were welcome guests. He turned away, avoiding the possibility that they might see him there. As they walked past, chatting with each other, his embarrassment turned to anger. He had been friends with their son for fifteen years, they had gone to the same schools and moved in the same circles. Their son had stood beside him at his father's funeral and in the bitter months that followed. Their son was like a brother to him. And yet here, at this airport, in this country, their son was a welcome guest and he felt like he was being treated as a criminal.

Alienation is not just internally but also externally determined. Emotional and political solidarity with one people rarely occurs without being accompanied by resentment or even animosity toward those perceived as enemies of that people. Sharif had, for most of his life, lived and worked closely with Jews, many of whom had been supporters of the state of Israel's right to exist, even if they had also supported the right of Palestine to coexist with it as a neighbor state. He had had Jewish friends and girlfriends, and Arab Media Watch had Jewish members. But Sharif, who had for most of his adult life worked to ensure that Palestinians would be respected as equals in any real and lasting peace between themselves and the Israeli people, saw the right of return for exiled Palestinians living in decrepit camps in Lebanon as a core problem of the conflict, and the linchpin of Palestinian dignity, respect, and humanity. He knew that many of the refugees cherished the hope of returning to homes within Israel, which would upset Israel's demographic balance and compromise the Jewish character of the state. In fact, within Israel, advocating for the right of return, which has been guaranteed under international law, is seen as a radical position tantamount to advocating for a single state with a Jewish minority, in which Israel would no longer exist as a Jewish state. He worried that that a government that regarded his people as a fundamental threat to its existence would never be able to treat them as equal partners in peace. As such, he expected to be treated with greater suspicion at the airport and checkpoints than he would have as another British traveler, and so, when he encountered certain questions and delays at the airport, he reacted with both specific and general frustration. Thus, a delay that might have just been frustrating to another traveler became a symbolic source of alienation.

Nearly three hours after his arrival, Sharif exited the airport and made his way toward a line of shared vans bound for Jerusalem. Slowly, the van filled with other travelers, all of whom were dressed in the long black coats and brimmed black hats worn by Hasidic Jews. Sharif was certain he was the only Arab on the van, and his feelings of alienation and frustration mounted. The van rattled to a raspy start, and they set off, first to Tel Aviv, and then toward Jerusalem on a broad highway flanked on either side by dry, dusty hills. They entered the West Bank, its border marked only by a small checkpoint made of indifferent tin slats and sandbags on the lane leading toward Tel Aviv.

Atop the dry hills, Sharif saw sprawling new Israeli settlements, with flowering trees and evenly spaced street lights lining broad, paved avenues. On the same hills, but a little farther down, he saw Palestinian villages, with black water tanks on each rooftop and the occasional crumbling, bombed-out shell nestled between other buildings. The thin, ragged roads trailing from the main highway to the Palestinian villages were blocked off by crude piles of rocks. Since the beginning of the latest Intifada, Palestinians living in the West Bank had been prohibited from traveling on or traversing the roadways connecting the settlements, and they contended with increasingly frequent water and electrical shortages. The growing number of Israeli settlements, outposts, and bypass roads cast a wide net over the landscape, leaving Palestinians to live in increasingly smaller and more isolated spaces between highways and settlements. Sharif had read many accounts of the worsening standard of life for Palestinians cut off from resources, farmland, jobs, schools, and services in these "Bantustans," as they were known to human rights activists.

The van descended into a Jerusalem he barely recognized as the same city he had visited almost five years before. Throughout the eastern and predominantly Palestinian half of the city were Israeli soldiers and police carrying loaded semi-automatic weapons, and so-called flying checkpoints could be seen. The van let off its passengers on the western side of town, in an Orthodox Jewish neighborhood. The driver told Sharif that he would not cross into the eastern part of town, that there were troubles there, so on his first day in Palestine, Sharif found himself trudging despondently through narrow passageways under the high late afternoon sun, dragging his luggage in the direction of the golden dome of the al-Aqsa mosque in the Old City, with no idea how to get there. After over an hour of wandering aimlessly, Sharif was approached by an older Palestinian man, who led him to the hotel of his father's cousin, whom he had visited on his last trip to Jerusalem. As he sat in the hotel lobby, listening to the older man's long-winded conversation with his cousin, he was eager to get on with his trip; but he couldn't deny how much more relaxed he felt to hear Arabic all around him, for he was now on the Palestinian side of the city.

Conventional wisdom tells us that divided cities are tantamount to a crime against humanity. Fed with images of Berlin's weeping, laughing masses tearing their own wall down bit by bit with their bare hands, it is difficult for us to conceive that a reunified city could not be better off than a divided one. But many Palestinians Sharif would meet over the coming months yearned for a return to the officially divided Jerusalem that existed before the 1967 war. Over dinner one night some months later, one of Sharif's aunts, who lived in Jerusalem, described the wall that had divided the city from 1948 to 1967. "For Palestinians," she said, "life with the wall was much better, before 1967. . . . [The mayor of Jerusalem from 1967 to the late 1980s] kept saying that a divided Jerusalem was not a happy city, that the city wanted to be united and free. This was not true." Jerusalem had been unified under Israeli rule, essentially placing its Palestinian residents there under occupation. Her husband was arrested seven times in one year during that mayor's term in office. Now, the city officially reunified was unofficially divided by differentials in prosperity and power.

Even in the few brief hours Sharif spent in Jerusalem before heading on to Ramallah, he found the tension of occupation as palpable as the heavy heat of the summer afternoon. As he made his way to and from the UNDP office, he saw Israeli soldiers with loaded weapons on the ramparts of the Old City. After a brief dinner with his uncle's family, he boarded another shared van bound for Ramallah, eager to end his journey. His arrival in Ramallah was bittersweet; before he passed into the capital city of Palestine, he saw for the first time the great grey wall lumbering across the Palestinian landscape, and this was no wall a Palestinian would wish for. The Israeli government called it a security fence, but Sharif thought of it as partly an annexation strategy, partly an excuse for greater punitive violence and control, partly an outdoor prison for his people, and above all an apartheid measure. Condemned by the United Nations and declared illegal by the International Court of Justice, the thirty-foot-high wall was a gesture of ownership, a statement that this land was Israel's to do with as it saw fit.

Past the wall, he crossed through the Kalandia checkpoint, where just a few weeks later a car bomb would be detonated by Palestinian militants amid a

waiting crowd, providing another justification for draconian security measures. Then he was in Palestinian Authority-controlled land. To either side of
the checkpoint, surrounded by lengths of barbed wire, lay the Kalandia
refugee camp, home to some ten thousand refugees of the 1948 war, who had
thrown paint bombs and written graffiti on the wall's massive surface. Sharif
looked past the wall, the poverty, the ravaged roadway, the barbed wire, and
raised his head to look at Ramallah; for the first time since he entered the West
Bank he saw no Israeli soldiers or police, tanks, or barricades.

Within one month of living in Ramallah, Sharif was more at home than he had
been anywhere in years. His first two weeks whirled by in the tumult of moving
from the flat he had been assigned in the suburbs to the city center, and getting
his projects up and running. Since he was not in the habit of living on his own
or cooking for himself, he chose to avoid the chaos of the vegetable market at
the *souk*, but he hardly had time to tire of living on roadside *shawarma* sand-
wiches before he began receiving invitations to join new friends for dinner.

Ramallah was a glittering, charming town on a hilltop, full of boutiques and
intimate restaurants, outdoor cafes and internet parlors, crowded open-air
markets and hip bars, roadside bakeries and spice shops, full of elegant neighborhoods and far removed from the poverty and chaos depicted in Western
media coverage of Palestinian life. The city center buzzed with life and activity,
its air saturated with the aroma of dates, Arabic coffee, and exhaust fumes.
Sharif found Palestinian culture warm and welcoming, and Ramallah society,
with its heavy international media and NGO presence, to be both cosmopolitan and intimate. During his three months there, Sharif saw bombed-out
Palestinian government buildings, often heard distant gunfire, and once, while
dining at an expensive restaurant near his apartment, witnessed a shootout
between a couple of Israeli soldiers and some Palestinian men, but he learned
that life in Ramallah was remarkably free from the military incursions,
poverty, unemployment, and violence that had come to define the Palestinian
experience in many other cities. Palestinians from other cities and refugee
settlements such as Nablus or Jenin often derisively called Ramallah a wom-
anly city, an aberration from the general Palestinian experience.

Sharif, who this time scheduled no trips to refugee camps or other stops of misery tourism, found the comfort and hospitality of Ramallah life both pleasant and also particularly Palestinian. Friends he made at work, in cafes, and even in the gym he joined immediately incorporated him into their own social circles, and he went out almost every night. After the frenetic, expensive, and planned socializing of London, he marveled at the simplicity and ease of social life in Palestine, where cool evenings were spent in effortless conversation over mint lemonade and fragrant Arabic coffee, pleasantly smoking *nargileh*. His problems in London began to seem distant, impossible, and strangely insignificant. His life fell into an easy pattern of work and leisure.

In spite of the warmth of his relatives and new friends in Palestine, and in spite of his optimism for his work, he daily ran up against the hardships and frustrations of Palestinian life. He had always regarded Palestinian leadership as woefully inadequate, corrupt, and ineffective. Before Sharif arrived to work for the office of the prime minister, Ahmed Qureia, independent Palestinian legislators had alleged that leading Palestinians, among them Qureia's family, had reaped huge profits by supplying concrete for the construction of the separation wall, even as Qureia publicly condemned the wall for enforcing apartheid and violating human rights. Sharif brought these allegations up in conversation with his colleagues at the ministry on his first day there, only to be met with silence. He found the work atmosphere stagnant and bureaucratic, dominated by petty rivalries and a general unwillingness to address broader problems. Later that week, he attended a demonstration for reform in the Palestinian Authority in Ramallah's main square, al-Manara and, surrounded by waving flags and beating drums and a festive, cheering crowd, he listened to Mustafa Barghouti, a leading Palestinian prodemocracy activist and medical doctor, and a founding member of the moderate "Third Way" political coalition. The rally was much smaller in scope than the massive rallies protesting the US invasion of Iraq he had recently attended in London, but he reveled in sharing a moment of public criticism, hope, and demand for moderation among his people whose government was dominated by the corruption of Fatah and the fundamentalism of Hamas. By the time his contract with the ministry ended three months later, Sharif said his disillusionment with Palestinian leadership had increased drastically.

If his interactions with the Palestinian authorities frustrated and disillusioned him, his experiences with Israeli soldiers enraged and even frightened him. The day he had arrived in Jerusalem, he had reconnected with the relatives he had met during his first trip to Palestine—his father's cousin, a Nashashibi who owned and operated a successful hotel in East Jerusalem, his wife, and their two daughters. He began visiting them on Fridays, and found in them a close and loving family to take the place of his own. Although he looked forward to the delicious home-cooked lunches and the close companionship he had developed with the family's older daughter, who was about his age, he increasingly came to dread the waits at the checkpoints between Ramallah and Jerusalem.

One of the best days Sharif spent with the family, a day trip to the Dead Sea during his first month in Ramallah, also turned into one of his worst memories of life under Israeli occupation. He left early on the day of the trip, but when he arrived at the Kalandia checkpoint, he found a long line—more like a motionless, bored crowd than a line—stretching several hundred yards from the checkpoint. The late-summer heat scalded the metal cages and concrete pavements, and rose in waves from the mass of bodies pressed against one another. Expressionless and hushed, students and professionals, stooped old ladies and small children, people of all kinds stood waiting for the checkpoint guards to begin letting them through. Here and there, Sharif heard the muffled cries of babies. Along the sides of the line, groups of soldiers sat and stood on cement blocks piled up to form makeshift viewing platforms. Sharif scanned a group of soldiers, who were laughing at some joke or comment one of them made, until his gaze came to rest on one single soldier standing by himself, whose loaded semi-automatic rifle was pointed directly at the crowd of people waiting to pass through the checkpoint. Many residents of the Palestinian territories do not have official Israeli paperwork to pass legally through the checkpoints, but sneak in and out of Israeli territory to work jobs as day laborers or to visit family and friends. But all people with official business, studies, or medical care in Israeli-controlled land must pass through the checkpoints each day. There is no logic to back-ups or jams; what Sharif perceived as a massive line and an oppressive situation was in fact quite run-of-the-mill for Kalandia.

He finally arrived at the counter hot and cranky, and an official asked for his identification. When he had registered with the UNDP in Jerusalem, he had submitted his passport to have his tourist visa changed into a work visa, but the Israeli Foreign Affairs Ministry still had not returned his passport to the UNDP. Until now, he had not had any difficulty passing through check-points when he had simply handed over his UN identification card, but today the official eyed his name and refused to let him pass. He told the official that the Foreign Affairs Ministry was causing the delay and that he was powerless to do anything until the Israeli government got back to him. The official questioned him on his background, whether he had family in Palestine, what he did for a living, what he had been doing in Ramallah and why he wanted to go to Jerusalem. A lengthy argument ensued before the official finally let him pass, and he boarded a hot, crowded van bound for Jerusalem.

The van stopped at the second checkpoint between Ramallah and Jerusalem, where an individual soldier came to the van and watched as all of its passengers held up their identification and passports. The soldier, who was Israeli, then called Sharif out of the van and began questioning him in Arabic. When Sharif replied in English that he didn't understand, choosing as always at checkpoints to present himself as a foreigner, the soldier continued to ques-tion him in Arabic. He felt that the soldier believed he was an undocumented Palestinian sneaking through on a fake ID, and was trying to trick him into responding in Arabic. Suddenly switching gears, the soldier finally asked in English where he was from. When Sharif replied that he was British, the soldier paused, read his name out loud, and then asked him again where he was from, and then over and over again. Sharif replied each time, with grow-ing irritation, that he was British. Then, the soldier switched tack, asking Sharif who had issued his identification, and a perplexed Sharif said that, as the identification card read, it had been issued by the United Nations. Then this question was repeated in different configurations, each time eliciting the same answer from Sharif. The questioning continued for about forty-five minutes, and then the soldier flung Sharif's UN identification card back at him before turning away. He turned over one shoulder and said "Go," before joining the other soldiers at the checkpoint. Sharif felt hassled and humiliated, and asked himself if, as a UN employee, he could be questioned like this, what must the Palestinians without proper identification face each day? When he arrived in Jerusalem and told his story, his relatives were sympathetic but also amused at his irritation. He had gotten away easy, they told him. The family's house was just a few blocks from their hotel near the Old City, and they had been waiting for eight years to receive permission to build an extra room onto their own home. They were well acquainted with the powerlessness of life as a Palestinian. Even with wealth and education, one still had no power.

Since Sharif had been delayed in arriving, they reached the Dead Sea at dusk. Sharif joined his cousins and two of their cousins for a swim, and soon darkness swallowed up the horizon line. He floated in a warm, black sea, listening to the soft slap of water and the muted cadences of Arabic chatter. Slowly, stars glowed to life across the whole canopy of the sky, and reflected on the water's surface. The five swimmers' conversation ebbed into a low murmur. Sharif floated on his back, surrounded by a velvety black night, alone with a silent riot of stars, and for the first time in almost two years, he felt completely at peace. When the swimmers returned to the shore, theirs was the only group left at the beach. They gingerly stepped over the rocky beach to a grassy area which, by day, held a bar and restaurant for beach guests, and joined their family for a picnic dinner on the empty tables and chairs.

After eating, they all started packing up. Sharif and his cousin picked up some things to carry back to the car and headed off toward the parking lot together, deep in conversation. When they reached the parking lot, they noticed that theirs was the only civilian car there, but an Israeli military jeep was also parked at one end of the lot. Five soldiers sat inside. Sharif and his cousin continued toward the car, averting their eyes from the jeep, and continued with their conversation in Arabic. Sharif says he heard the jeep's ignition start, and as he and his cousin stood by the car, the jeep full of soldiers began driving around them in slow, tight circles. As he recalls it, one soldier in the passenger side stared at them, a strange smile playing at his mouth, as he let his empty machine-gun magazine report in a steady, staccato chatter. They stood frozen, and Sharif remembers thinking that if those soldiers had decided to hurt them, there was no one to help them. Then, without warning, the jeep veered off and disappeared into the night, and the rest of the family joined them, laughing and chatting. Sharif was silent the whole ride home.

That day Sharif spent at the Dead Sea summed up for him so much of what life in Palestine had come to mean—a feeling of perfect peace and belonging always just a simple incident away from a feeling of complete powerlessness. After all that he had read, he had expected to be delayed at checkpoints and to see signs of military occupation throughout the West Bank. But he was not prepared for the rage he would feel looking at the faces of Israeli soldiers. Each time he saw a soldier laughing, he felt a surge of humiliation, certain that he and his people were the subject of laughter, and each time he was questioned, he felt angry that he was being treated as an inferior. Although he was well paid and fairly free from persecution, the realities of occupation did redefine how he chose to live and move in Palestine, and he visited Jerusalem less and less often as his stay in Palestine progressed. The experiences of his youth and early adulthood had given him a great deal of autonomy, and on the basis of the identity he had developed for himself, Sharif was used to striking out on a fairly individualistic life path. Even his experiences as an outsider—in school and in the workplace—had never impinged on his academic or career success. His opinions may have been unpopular, but he had never experienced any physical or legal restrictions to his personal development. Confronted with a situation that negated his individuality and also placed him among the ranks of the occupied brought a new dimension to the outsider identity he had previously developed—being an outsider is quite different from being marginalized. Even though his wealth, status, and life circumstances separated him from the experiences of the majority of Palestinians—who lived without identification, work, education, running water, and under the constant threat of violence—he soon learned that wealth and status do not rid one of the humiliation of occupation.

Whatever his personal experiences may have taught him, Sharif learned the greatest lessons on the complications of being Palestinian from the friends he made. Just a few days after his Dead Sea trip, a muscular young man approached Sharif in the gym with some unwelcome pointers on his form. Sharif had felt diffident in this gym, whose members all looked like professional bodybuilders, and had largely kept to himself while he worked out. But before long, the young man, who introduced himself as Mosab Hassan, had cracked Sharif's shy reserve, so often mistaken for arrogance, with his easy intimacy and quirky sense of humor. At first glance, Sharif had taken in Mosab's muscular shoulders and square glasses and thought he was some sort of a stern, bossy know-it-all. But within a few minutes, he noticed that a childlike grin played around Mosab's mouth and that his round eyes were filled with welcome, and soon the two were laughing and teasing each other like old friends. The next time they ran into each other at the gym, Mosab invited Sharif to join him and some of his friends for lunch the following Friday, which as the holiest day of the week in Islam, was weekend for most Palestinian offices.

As Mosab had directed, Sharif took a taxi to a small village at the edge of Ramallah, where Mosab and was helping one of his friends add a floor to his mother's house. Sharif joined a group of about a dozen men, hungry after a morning spent lugging and laying bricks, around a table with one large dish of *maqloobeh*, a Palestinian national dish of spiced chicken and rice with cauliflower and chickpeas. In the Palestinian style, they all ate out of the same dish, and then after lunch, they wandered outside, plucking and eating fruit from the trees blanketing the land. As they sprawled on the ground under the trees, Mosab pointed out to Sharif a low, nondescript building surrounded by a barbed-wire fence. It was an Israeli detention facility, he said, where he had been held for six months.

Then Mosab told Sharif that he was the eldest son of the West Bank spokesman for Hamas, Sheikh Hassan Yusuf, considered to be the organization's most senior political official in the West Bank. Sheikh Yusuf, known widely in the Palestinian villages as a man of great compassion, wisdom, and charity, but described repeatedly in Israeli and Western media reports only as an "ultra-Orthodox" Hamas official, had been arrested fourteen times without charge during Mosab's lifetime, had spent nearly seven years of his life in Israeli prisons and detention facilities, and had once been officially deported to Lebanon. When Sharif met Mosab, Mosab's father was in administrative internment in Israel, and his mother, who was struggling to support her family, had decided to apply for a social worker certification program. Mosab was struggling to establish his own career to be able to help support his family. He loved jazz music and English-language literature, and was more interested in marrying a nice girl and starting a lucrative business, maybe real estate, than in Palestinian politics, but he had spent many months of his life paying for his father's political position. Just ten days before his high school exams, Mosab had been arrested and held for nearly a year. By the time he was released, his father was back in jail and Mosab was in charge of the household. He had little time to prepare for his exams, and although he passed, his score was one percentage point lower than the minimum score required for admission at the highly regarded Birzeit University. He was disappointed, but was satisfied to enroll at al-Quds University. Then, after just one year at school, he was arrested again and held without charge for six months in the detention center he now showed Sharif, before he was transferred to a prison in the middle of the Negev desert. As he now struggled to find investors for his real estate business and dreamt of starting a family, Mosab was encountering few people who wanted to invest in a company whose CEO was under Israeli scrutiny, and few Palestinian families who wanted their daughters to marry someone who might spend the rest of his life in and out of jail.

For Sharif, it was jarring to see his new friend so matter-of-factly discussing such a drastic and surely traumatic experience that had happened so close by to where he was voluntarily spending his free time. But Palestine was a small place, and just as Israeli settlers and Palestinian refugees lived practically on top of one another, the joys and tragedies of individual lives there often occurred in the same places. For the rest of the afternoon, as they followed their picnic with an hour-long horseback ride through the fragrant orchards and then lounged under fruit trees to sip tea and smoke nargileh as they watched the sun set, Sharif thought about what Mosab had told him.

Sheikh Yusuf would be released from prison the following December, and just days after his release he gave interviews to the local and international press, declaring Hamas's support for the creation of a Palestinian state that could peacefully coexist with its neighbor, Israel. But on the eve of Palestinian Authority elections, in September 2005, his diplomatic work and humanitarian efforts in villages impacted by the separation wall would be cut short, as Israeli officials arrested him and 206 other Palestinians in an attempt to deter the election to power of Hamas. International media continued to state that Hamas officials called for Israel's destruction. Mosab himself was arrested again in 2005.

Mosab was by no means the only friend Sharif made who had been arrested or detained in an Israeli prison. Indeed, everyone he met had experienced some problem, harassment, or intimidation resulting directly from the occupation. And very few people he met actually knew any Israelis, let alone had close Israeli friends. Security measures and mutual suspicion resulting from Israel's military occupation and Palestine's increasingly desperate fight for independence had only driven the two communities farther into their opposing corners. It was amazing how completely realized the segregation had become between two such economically and socially intertwined communities. Even as a large and diverse cross-section of Israeli society continued to protest the settlement and occupation of the West Bank and Gaza, even as the majority of Israelis favored a withdrawal from occupied Palestinian land, the majority of Palestinians only saw the face of Israeli occupation and colonization. The prevailing Palestinian view of Israel was as its rampant and brutal oppressor, home to a universally prosettlement, prooccupation population, and the majority of reports Palestinians read in Western media outlets did little to undermine their perspective. As the Israeli-Palestinian conflict continued to increase in international symbolic significance, actual understanding of the complexity and diversity of all interested parties decreased, and the opportunities for compassionate conflict resolution diminished. Sharif met intelligent, thoughtful, and compassionate Palestinians who firmly believed that nonviolent resistance was an impossible dream, and that the Palestinians' only hope for economic and psychological liberation was through armed resistance and violent uprising.

In spite of the struggles and frustrations he saw all around him, Sharif made up his mind to stay on in Palestine after had been in Ramallah for two months. He knew he would miss his family, but he had never felt so personally or professionally fulfilled in his life. He did not miss London and, as he prepared to return home for a vacation, it dawned on him that he did not at all look forward to seeing his hometown. He decided to pursue opportunities for extended work in Palestine, seeking out various people, many of whom he had respected from afar for years. He would sometimes scan through his cell phone directory and smile at the names and numbers he had personally accumulated, such as the journalist Amira Haas, nuclear nonproliferation activist Mordechai Vanunu, as well as Hanan Ashrawi and Mustafa Barghouti, whom he'd seen speak at the first rally he had attended in August. He set about extending his contract with the UNDP TOKTAN program by another three months, and he also met with Barghouti to discuss the possibility of working with his organization, Palestine Monitor, instead of the ministry. When he returned to London, he only planned to spend enough time there to take care of some administrative tasks, hand over official leadership of Arab Media Watch to the man who had been managing the organization on a temporary basis, and spend some time with his family before returning home to Palestine.

Why did Sharif want to return to Palestine? One might expect that the ambivalence of his experience would sour him to the prospect of living and working there, where each trip might be interrupted by an interrogation, where the possibility of violence was never far away, where any of his friends might be arrested, and where, if he chose to leave the protective umbrella of the United Nations, he might even expose himself to the risk of arrest. But Sharif was able to separate his feelings for Palestine from his feelings for the occupation. He had found Palestinian society to be more welcoming and intriguing than any he'd known before, and he savored the perspective he gained by monitoring Western media coverage of Palestine from Palestine itself. Although one could easily lose perspective on the rest of the world and even on life in Israel from Palestine, where the largest issue on everyone's mind, the proverbial elephant in the room, was the occupation, the immediacy of events and access to Palestinian reactions on the ground was invaluable to Sharif's work. The full immersion in the Palestinian perspective was, in sum, the full realization of the journey Sharif had been on since he had learned he was Palestinian. His experiences in Palestine had validated and reignited his passionate outrage, which gave meaning to the activism that had driven his life and had been so stifled by contrary political realities and sheer apathy in London. He thought that he might not decide to settle in Ramallah permanently, but for the time being he was prepared to call it home.

Sharif arrived in London in November 2004, just before Yasser Arafat's death, and as he ran from meeting to meeting, filling what he thought would just be a brief visit to London with as much Arab Media Watch business as he could, he wore his discontent with the cold and the bustle like an ill-fitting shirt. But then, in December, Arab Media Watch finalized a source of funding that would pay for a full-time salary for Sharif, as well as for a handful of full-time staffers, for a full year. Sharif sadly acknowledged that, although he had looked forward to returning to Ramallah, he could not turn his back on an opportunity to run Arab Media Watch for a salary. He was deeply disappointed that he would not return to Ramallah, but he had to acknowledge that his life work, his home, and his calling were, indeed, in London. And in the coming months, he would have his work cut out for him.

Early in 2005, after Arab Media Watch published a comprehensive analysis of bias against the Palestinian perspective in BBC's coverage for October 2004, hackers Sharif believed to be pro-Israel activists would cause the group's Web site to be shut down. As they struggled to get the Web site back and running, Sharif and his team continued to monitor the British media, now in partnership with the Council for Arab-British Understanding. Their reach expanded and their impact grew. With each crisis in the Middle East in the coming year, from the reorganization and rejection of the Palestinian government following the death of Arafat, to the Israeli bombardment of Lebanon, to the steady descent of Iraq into a bloody civil war, Arab Media Watch had its hands full in its efforts to steer the British media away from selective reporting and to provide the British public with resources and background information from the Arab perspective.

Even as Arab Media Watch kept its eyes trained on the Middle East, calamity struck at home. During the morning rush on July 7, 2005, four bombs exploded in London's public transportation system, killing fifty-two commuters and the four suicide bombers who detonated them. The attacks brought to the forefront of public debate and media coverage two simultaneous phenomena that had been emerging in British governmental policy since the September 11, 2001, attacks in the United States, phenomena that can be understood within the global clash-of-civilizations discourse. Experts have pointed out that throughout the 1990s, while the British government focused its energies on combating Irish nationalist militants, intelligence and law enforcement bodies were well aware that Islamic militant groups were using Britain as a base for coordinating global activities, but as these groups were not considered a domestic security threat, they were allowed to exist. Only after the US attacks did the British government begin directly developing a national and international strategy for combating Islamist militant groups. As the foremost and most prominent ally of the United States in its so-called war on terror, Britain enthusiastically implemented existing anti-terrorism laws to combat the so-called Islamic terror threat, officially sanctioning a drastic increase in ethnic and racial profiling throughout the country. Even though Britain's 2000 Terrorism Act prohibits law enforcement officers from discriminating against ethnic minorities, it also permits officers to consider ethnic background as grounds for stopping a person as a terrorism suspect.

Much to the chagrin of Britain's many ethnically diverse Muslim communities, a Home Office dictum published in 2004 suggested that Muslims were a single community, and in March of 2005, a Home Office minister publicly stated that Muslims would just have to accept the reality that they would be stopped and searched more often than others, prompting an outcry by South Asian, black, and Arab community leaders, themselves representing various configurations of ethnically, nationally, racially, and religiously diverse populations. Studies have indicated that the number of British South Asians, regardless of religious affiliation, stopped and searched by law enforcement officers tripled in the eighteen months after the September 11 attacks.

The shooting to death of an undocumented Brazilian immigrant as a potential terror suspect within weeks of the tube bombings sent shock waves through Britain's minority communities. Arguing that religious affiliation is not readily visible in ethnic or racial makeup, community activists suggested that Britain's antiterrorism strategy relied on an inappropriate and racist conflation of ethnic background with religious fundamentalism, and religiosity in turn with terrorist affiliation. But the institutional legitimization of prejudice in the combat of the terrorist threat would continue. The four suicide bombers who attacked the London transport system were revealed to be middle-class, well-educated, British South Asians who, from all appearances, were well integrated into the British way of life and British values system. Just days after the background of the bombers made its way into the press, a secret British government document surfaced, describing a trend of increasingly "disaffected" but economically integrated Muslim youth susceptible to an increasingly aggressive al-Qaeda recruitment program on university campuses. The government proposed a multipronged operation, code named Contest, to engage the "Muslim" community, identify its most sensitive social and political issues, domestic and international alike, and to inculcate among its youth a sense of loyalty for British cultural and political values.

In the frenzy of public debate and minority interest-group formation that ensued in Britain, a public policy dilemma emerged that was unique to the clash-of-civilizations era. Who exactly were these disaffected Muslims, how could they be identified, and what were they so disaffected about? Ultimately, any political strategy devised to identify and target a disaffected Muslim community was flawed; there was less likely to be a community of disaffected people than disaffected individuals scattered throughout different communities. Although the Operation Contest dossier suggested that "Muslims" felt alienated by oppressive foreign policy decisions affecting "Muslim" countries, it was also true that a large segment of the native English population expressed deep anger and frustration at British policies toward Iraq and Palestine, and in relation to the United States. One Arab media analyst criticized the government for associating terror with the religion Islam, whereas it had avoided calling Irish militants "Catholic terrorists" during the peak era of IRA attacks on London targets. Now, in a sort of ontological twist, just as Britain's largest Muslim community began to claim Palestine as a Muslim issue, so now public perception began to accept Britain's largest Muslim community as its only Muslim community.

When Sharif returned from Palestine, the beginnings of a British Arab lobby had begun to emerge. Most notably, the National Association of British Arabs (NABA), headed by Dr. Ismail Jalili, in which both Sharif and Muna were active, attempted to develop a lobbying agenda that centered on domestic political issues such as the creation of a census category for Arabs and the passage of race relations legislation. In doing so, NABA hoped to cultivate local and domestic electoral influence for an Arab interest group. For the majority of 2005, British Arab attention would, however, continue to be captured by crises overseas rather than by the issues of profiling, detentions, and hate crimes against Arabs in Britain. Still, as a second generation of Arabs, born or raised in Britain, began to coalesce into one identity group despite the diversity of their national, racial, and religious affiliations, the possibility still remained that they would take a greater interest and role in domestic politics. But in the clash-of-civilizations era, as the national government pursued strategies aimed at pacifying and indoctrinating disaffected Muslims, and as the dominant Muslim community was South Asian, it would be South Asian community activists who would set the so-called British Muslim agenda. Sharif, as a secular Arab interested in the doctrines of universal justice, tolerance, and human rights, would strike a separate course, a sort of "Third Way" of his own.

Sharif had spent much of his life constructing his identity from a framework of ideas, ideologies, and political theory, then filling it out with his real experiences to form a clear, concise narrative of both alienation and belonging. As disappointed and frustrated as he may have occasionally felt with his life in London, his adult persona was clearly informed by London culture. From his personal style, to the way he moved, even to the kinds of music and television programs he enjoyed, he was very much a son of London. But he had consciously worked to develop emotional and psychological roots in

Palestinian culture, largely because the shock of learning of his Palestinian heritage during the violent exuberance of the Intifada meant that, at the cusp of adolescence and coming into his identity as an adult, he had learned of a major loss in his family's collective past. As he passed from adolescence into adulthood, he channeled his passion for and knowledge of his homeland into a career that gave his life direction and meaning, but also kept him intimately connected with the very issue that had been the centrally defining feature of his identity. By 2006, Sharif was securely settled into his profession as well as his political beliefs, and had struck a clear balance between his involvement with Palestinian and Arab issues and his life in London.

A well-read, articulate man who had spent the majority of his adulthood thinking, reading, and talking about issues of homeland, politics, and identity, Sharif was able to craft his immigrant narrative into a clear story line, a narrative arc with a major revelation, an ideological struggle, personal loss, formative experiences, professional experiences, and personal resolution. As a voice for minority rights and against stereotypical representations of Arabs, he did find himself embroiled in the clash-of-civilizations debate on a professional and intellectual level, but the debate itself had little bearing on his sense of personal belonging in British society. If anything, it was his absolute grounding and ease within British political and media institutions that allowed him to vocalize his outrage against damaging generalizations about the so-called Muslim and Arab worlds. In no way did Britain's political approach toward its Muslim communities or toward Muslim-majority countries abroad pose an existential threat to himself or his family. And because of this, he was able to see himself as an advocate for those who did face an existential threat from these policies. It was precisely his ease with his British identity that allowed him to advocate on behalf of his Arab identity.

CHAPTER 8

SUKRIYE FINDS LOVE

Sukriye trudges through her days like a robot. She is sleep-deprived and losing money fast. And she has fallen in love for the first time in her life. He is perfect in every way—intelligent, gentle, literary, and a fellow Kurd whom her parents are bound to adore. He just happens to be living in Syria. In a few months, the home for traumatized refugees where she has worked for four years will close, leaving her jobless. She has no backup plan. In fact, she has only one plan. Get the man she loves out of Syria and into Germany.

The entire topography of her life has changed. Before she fell in love, her house was constantly full of guests, feasts, music, and dancing. Now her stovetop is often cold and her refrigerator often empty. She divides her time between work and the endless bureaucratic runaround, trying to secure her beloved's legal migration to Germany.

Sukriye has always seen the personal as political, and has struggled to embody in her own person the liberation of her people. By educating herself and freeing herself from the binds of conservative thinking, but without distancing herself from her pride in Kurdish culture and history, she walks a fine line between criticism and uplift. She is profoundly aware of political discourse in everyday life, but has always focused her political attention on the liberation of Kurdistan. To her, the clash of civilizations is a false modality, one that has little to do with the political struggle that has defined her personal and her professional life. After all, Kurds are not just Sunni Muslims, as she is, but also Shi'a, Alevi, Yezidi, and Jewish, to name a few of the religions observed by her compatriots. She believes in the so-called Western values of religious tolerance and human rights, but she believes that these are values that should be broadly applied throughout the world. It is more important to her that Kurds as one people have a chance at freedom and cultural unity than that Muslim identity becomes a political category applied toward serving the interests of the majority Muslim community where she lives.

As Germany's Turkish community has used its influence to lobby for accession into the European Union, claiming that anti-Muslim sentiment is what is keeping the EU member states from accepting it as an equal member in their exclusive club, Sukriye has held that Turkey's continuing failure to grant its Kurds full political, cultural, and economic freedom poses the stronger argument against its accession. When the so-called Muslim world protested the US-led invasion of Iraq, Sukriye supported it as a means to win security and long-term autonomy for Iraq's Kurds.

But now her thoughts are no longer filled with abstract political ideas. The political has in fact become personal. She has nowhere near the same patience she did with the people she helps through their asylum processes. She often finds herself on the verge of exhausted tears in the middle of the day, unable to stand the bureaucratic rigmarole she has to endure, unable to find the energy for political debate. She has never, at any time during the Kurds' long and often bleak struggle for freedom, felt this thoroughly hopeless. She wishes she could just go to sleep and wake up with her beloved beside her, on the far side of politics and bureaucracy. But she doesn't give in and let go. She gets up every morning to get through the day, willing herself forward until she will have him at her side.

Sukriye met Nezir Suleiman during a visit home to Kurdistan. When she met him, she was thirty-two years old and almost compulsively single. It was July 2003, and she was leading two German psychotherapists on a research trip through Kurdistan. The day she saw Nezir, she had no interest in anything but her work, no responsibility but to the German researchers she was leading, and no long-term commitment but to her freedom. Within six months of their meeting, she would have no greater passion than Nezir.

Sukriye had dedicated the last ten years of her life to the therapeutic care of refugees, and had just been hired as a full-time social worker at the Paul-Gerhardt Home, where she had started out as an interpreter for Kurdish refugees. But one job was never enough for Sukriye; in addition to her full-time work and the constant unofficial translation and counseling she provided to her wide circle of friends and acquaintances, she had continued to work with the Berlin Society for the Advancement of Kurdology, participate in programs organized by several women's rights groups, and maintain close ties with the Treatment Center for Torture Victim. For some years, the center had wanted her to lead a trip to research whether Western psychotherapy had been able to help Kurds cope with the traumas they and their society had lived through, and now funding had been secured for the project. The researchers would travel to Kurdish villages and interview the men and women who had struggled under occupation, arrest, and even torture, and who had undergone psychotherapeutic treatment in Germany before returning home.

Now, as many refugee rights organizations were urging Turkey to set up a formal return program for Kurds displaced during the hostilities, Sukriye and other Kurdish rights advocates hoped that rehabilitation of the Kurdish region might now begin, and wanted to understand what role psychotherapy could play in that rehabilitation. Since PKK militants had declared a cease-fire in 1998, the German research team hoped that travel within Kurdistan might now be safe, as long as the team avoided the villages bordering Iraq, where the US-led occupation was well into its fourth month. They would take as their home base the village where Sukriye's oldest sister, the last of the Dogans' children remaining in Kurdistan, lived with her family. Her sister's application for asylum to Germany had been rejected on grounds that the war in Kurdistan was officially over. But when they arrived, the researchers found that although the ceasefire had been declared and martial law officially lifted, life in Kurdistan was still very much dominated by the military, and its people still lived as if they were in a state of war. There were checkpoints everywhere, curfews and rules limiting their movement, and regular clashes between militants and soldiers throughout the countryside. When the researchers tried to enter the village, gendarmes blocked them and told them to report to the nearest military base for interrogation. There, they were kept waiting, intimidated, questioned, told to come back, and ultimately told that they were not welcome. The message was clear: if they pushed forward with their research, they would find only trouble. They had no choice but to call off the research project and head back to Sukriye's father's house in Nusaybin.

Sukriye's frustration had several layers; she was frustrated that her project had been shut down, she was frustrated that Turkish military bureaucracy still stood in the way of economic and social development in Kurdistan, and she was frustrated that the rest of the world believed that the war was over. This frustration had ruled the better part of her adult life, and she could see no imminent end to it. She enjoyed showing her colleagues the beauty of her homeland and thought it was important that they see the constant stress its residents lived with, but she knew that without true research, no rehabilitation would be possible. She believed that no research would be possible until people working for social and economic development in Kurdish communities in Turkey were no longer perceived as suspicious by the Turkish government.

Like many human rights activists, Sukriye believed that international scrutiny and pressure might ultimately hold the Turkish government accountable for rehabilitating the war-torn region. But now, with Turkey in EU accession discussions, Sukriye had begun to realize how small a role the Kurdish experience in Turkey played in determining Turkey's eligibility. As the debate progressed in the coming years, Turkey would release high-profile Kurdish political prisoners, allow some Kurdish-language television broadcasts, and permit small private courses in Kurdish languages to be offered. But Sukriye found these to be cursory nods to minority rights at best, and was saddened to see European officials appeased by them. Germany, home to a great number of Turkish Kurds, would serve as Turkey's staunchest supporter in its accession bid, proving to Sukriye how little political influence the Kurdish community had managed to accumulate in all its years there.

After they had arrived in the city, Sukriye decided to salvage the trip with a little diversion, a visit over the border to Syria, where a branch of her mother's family lived in a small town less than twenty kilometers away from Nusaybin. Long before there was a border between Turkey and Syria this area had been home to Sukriye's family, and long after the border had been drawn, it had failed to destroy the intimate connection between the family it divided. Although the houses on the Syrian side were made of clay while in the north houses were now mostly of stone, even though in the south they lived among Arabs while in the north they lived among Turks, they were still one family and one people, who had continued to visit and marry one another in the years since their separation. They were still northern Kurds, compared to the southern Kurds in Iraq, who spoke Sorani, and other Kurdish subgroups, who spoke Kermanshahi, Gorani, Laki, or Zazaki. On both sides of the Turkish-Syrian border, Kurds spoke Kurmanci. And on both sides of the border, Kurds lived in fear of the state.

But the day Sukriye and Nezir met, fear took a back seat to the pleasure of good company and an unexpected reunion. It had been many years since Sukriye had had the chance to visit the Syrian side, and her arrival was eagerly anticipated. She arrived, full of stories and with two strangers in tow, and caused a stir. Her aunt's house was full of people, sitting in groups on rugs spread out across the floor. Older men sat along one wall, rolling strands of prayer beads through their fingers, and women shuttled in and out with fresh plates of fruit, bowls of snacks, and canisters of hot water to freshen the tea. Not very many outsiders came to this town, and without interrupting the natural flow of conversation and activity, the visitors became the focal point of all attention. The long struggle for Kurdish nationhood has passed unnoticed through much of the world, and as in gatherings of Kurds throughout the world, these outsiders who had taken an interest in the rehabilitation and development of Kurdish society piqued the curiosity of the group.

Nezir sat quietly with his friends and relatives, listening to Sukriye talk. His house was next door to her relatives' house and they were distant cousins, but they had never before met. As she carried on her conversation with those around her, Sukriye's attention was divided between her frustration with the progress of their research and her delight, as always, to be back home in Kurdistan. But Nezir's attention was focused entirely on her. He felt a fascination with her that he had never before experienced around any woman. For the first time in his life, Nezir found himself in the company of a Kurdish woman who seemed both spiritually and physically free, who was independent and also deeply attached to Kurdish culture, who spoke with equal comfort to the Kurds and the Germans present. He was impressed that someone who had grown up in Germany should speak such fluent and beautiful Kurmanci. He watched the way she moved fluidly between her family and her professional colleages, the way her identity seemed both wholly Kurdish and comfortably Western, and he was intrigued. Unlike many Kurdish women who had lived in the West, Sukriye did not posture at acting liberated, wearing freedom as an accoutrement of clothing and slang, but respected the customs and traditions of her people while still moving freely about and developing her own political opinions. Her freedom turned his head. Nezir was forty years old, and had spent his life hungering for and cultivating freedom. There was nothing he valued more.

Nezir was one of some 225,000 Kurds living in Syria whose claim to Syrian citizenship had been revoked as part of an aggressive campaign to "Arabize" the resource-rich land in the country's northeast, home to the country's Kurdish population. What had begun as a program of forced assimilation and land redistribution soon became a multipronged ethnic cleansing effort to curtail the visibility, power, and growth of non-Arab minorities, primarily the two million Kurds who comprised some 10 percent of the country's total population. The effort took official and unofficial forms. Syrian Kurds say the ethnic cleansing began in 1960, when a movie theater in the predominantly Kurdish city of Qamishli burned to the ground, killing hundreds of children including Nezir's older brother. Later investigations suggested that the incident was carried out by anti-Kurd militants, but could not confirm whether they had been affiliated with the central government. There would have been no time for Nezir's family to mourn; each day was chock full with work and chores. But Nezir recalls that occasionally, when she broke a dish or pricked her finger sewing the dresses she made for extra income, his mother would close her eyes and call out his dead brother's name.

Then, in 1962, an exceptional census stripped 120,000 Kurds of their citizenship, claiming that they were foreign infiltrators and militants who had fled from Turkey into Syria. Some scholars have stated that the Kurds of Syria were believed to have escaped over the border from the brutal reprisal campaign the Turkish government had unleashed throughout southeast Turkey in retaliation for the 1924 Kurdish uprisings, but Nezir says that his family had always lived in this area that is a part of modern Syria. Of course, they had always seen that same area as Kurdistan, themselves as Kurds, and the internationally recognized border as dividing their own unrecognized country. Now, as stateless people, they were officially known as *ajanib*, or foreigners, prohibited from marrying, owning property, and from official employment. They required special permits to stay in hotels or hospitals in cities and towns where they didn't live. Further, without passports, they could neither travel nor cross borders to legally relocate in a country that might have them. In essence, every aspect of life for a stateless person was made illegal, and as such, they were forced to live in a permanent state of fear and intimidation.

Nezir had lately begun to feel stifled by the circumstances of his stateless life. He had always made an effort to transcend the legal and physical limitations of his life through his outlook and through education, but he, like Sukriye, felt the deep frustration of realizing that change may not come soon, if ever, to the people of Kurdistan. He saw Sukriye as someone with greater personal freedom than himself. He thought she might know of some opportunities for someone like him—a highly educated, intelligent, and hard-working man interested in helping his people, who could not legally work anywhere. And he wanted to hear what she, as a person who had studied and traveled, had to say about the future of the Kurds.

As the sun waned and people came and went, Sukriye and Nezir struck up a conversation. Almost immediately, the two felt an easy, comfortable rapport with one another. Just as he was taken with her freedom, Sukriye was instantly struck by how easy it was to talk to him, person to person. He treated her like an individual, not just as a woman; his conversation was driven by intellectual curiosity and a shared interest in Kurdistan's culture and politics, not inhibited by gender roles and shame. They talked about politics, comparing life to the north and south of the border, and sharing anecdotes about their travels in Kurdistan. As the gathering broke up to prepare for bed, Sukriye found herself hoping she might see Nezir again before they left. Nezir found himself thinking of how he might stay in touch with her after she had gone.

Where did this easy rapport come from, one might ask? Both Sukriye and Nezir were Kurds, even distantly related, but their daily circumstances could not have been more different from one another. Out of very different personal histories, Sukriye and Nezir had managed to construct similar personal narratives, to locate themselves similarly within the Kurdish political and social spectrum, and to have even developed similar personal identities.

Born stateless, the year after his family lost their citizenship, Nezir grew up in a region he describes as forgotten by all but poverty. His hometown, Amouda, was just three kilometers south of the border with Turkey. As a child, he remembers fantasizing about escaping over the border into the mountains, which were the Kurds' symbolic home and historic refuge. He was fascinated by the border, and his childhood heroes were smugglers—as Sukriye's father had been—men who braved gunfire and arrest to provide for their families and, in some small way, keep Kurdistan united.

Amouda had a long literary and philosophical tradition; for centuries, the town had been home to some leading Islamic scholarly orders, and was renowned throughout Kurdistan for its many writers and poets, and for its famous literary evenings. Sukriye, who had visited Amouda three times before, remembers the lively discussions on the town's characteristic wooden balconies with great fondness. Because of its literary tradition, education was a big part of Kurdish life in the town, even as conservatism and gossip held sway over many aspects of its society. All the boys of the town went to school and many, including Nezir, went on to pursue degrees at major universities across Syria; Kurds were allowed to attend school, although they were barred from legal employment after graduation. Statelessness imposed a good number of restrictions on Nezir's childhood and youth, but education helped to set him free. Even as a teenager, he and a group of friends read about the lives and strategies of revolutionaries like Che Guevara, and used their knowledge to form an informal action group with a revolutionary ideology hoping to establish contact with Kurdish activists across the border. Later, he realized that he was achieving little with direct political action and would only expose himself to great personal risks if he continued with it.

He completed his degree in agricultural engineering at the university in Aleppo, but was forced to earn a subsistence living as a seasonal laborer, for which he was grossly overqualified. But he began cultivating a personal philosophy and lifestyle that, unlike political organization and other pro-independence work, could not land him in jail, and allowed him to feel free in spite of the restrictions of his circumstances. He chose to pursue intellectual and spiritual freedom instead of succumbing to limitation and living in fear. He made it a point to meet people from different walks of life, to read and write and, whenever possible, to travel outside of Amouda. He read Dostoyevsky and was inspired to write a collection of short stories, which he did in a camp for seasonal laborers under the starry sky when his long days of physical labor had ended. He edited a Kurdish-language magazine published in Lebanon. He conducted qualitative research studies on the cultural practices and challenges faced by Kurdish minority communities. He distanced himself from the conservative practices of his community, but remained intimately involved with his culture. Just as Sukriye had done, he had chosen personal liberation as his contribution toward the liberation of his people. And just like Sukriye, Nezir dedicated his life to personal development, political and social work on behalf of his people, and cultural celebration through literature and language. Although she had been born under Turkish rule and raised in Germany, and he had been born under Syrian rule and raised stateless, they had somehow wound up on similar life paths.

In envisioning the quest for personal liberation and individual freedom as a way to serve their people, Sukriye and Nezir both managed to strike a balance, meeting the emotional demands of their nation as well as themselves as individuals. In some ways, it is the pursuit of individual satisfaction that is so characteristic of modern life that has made the Kurdish nation vulnerable in the modern era. After all, pursuit of individual satisfaction detracts from the binds of collective obligation, which itself forms the very foundation for pre-serving the culture of a nation with no homeland. A Kurdish identity can never be taken for granted, because there is no Kurdistan to which Kurds can return if they feel they have become unhinged, uprooted, or distanced from their culture. Immigrants from many countries struggle to strike a balance between family and self, community and individual, tradition and innova-tion, and often contend with fears of losing their sense of cultural identity. But the existence of a home country can serve as a kind of subconscious sol-ace, an anchor to which an immigrant is tethered, no matter how thin the tether may have stretched. To people with no homeland, however, the tie to home must be consciously constructed.

The Kurdish nation itself is spread across several countries and has, in each of them, faced some existential threat. As a result, all Kurds must con-sciously choose how they will relate to their nation, a choice motivated by sentiments as diverse as fear, outrage, love, pride, hatred, ambition, right-eousness, and morality. Even in their countries of origin, Kurds have had lit-tle opportunity for formal political cohesion and cultural expression as a single people. Because of this, the assertion of Kurdish identity often trans-lates into a lifestyle choice. Both in their countries of origin and in immi-grant communities, Kurds have often had to choose between three possible paths: assimilation, political activism, and cultural traditionalism. Many Kurds have chosen to disappear into a broader society that either denies or is ignorant of their existence, but many others have fought to preserve their culture in their homes or to advocate Kurdish political autonomy. Sukriye and Nezir, both disillusioned with political organization and unwilling to limit their opportunities for personal growth with traditional social obliga-tions, seem to have found a fourth path.

Both Sukriye and Nezir constructed their identities as Kurds by relentlessly questioning their definition of Kurdishness, by learning about the Kurds through study and travel, by embracing the religious and linguistic diversity of the Kurdish people, and by criticizing and working to reform the more repressive Kurdish social practices. Both have worked to forge a separate Kurdish path, one by which the Kurdish nation may flourish even if it never

achieves independence. They both wish for the freedom of Kurds from political repression and economic hardship, but they are willing to accept a free
Kurdish nation that does not have a state with internationally recognized borders. The quest for freedom, says Nezir, "is the search for wisdom, not a piece
of nation." Both he and Sukriye believe that if all Kurds work to liberate themselves from regressive and repressive traditions, and educate themselves
enough to raise their families out of poverty and fear, then the Kurds as a
nation will never run the risk of extinction. Because of this belief, the Kurdish
nation has no boundaries to either of them. And because they share this
belief, it was easy for them to transcend boundaries to find their way to each
other. "At the time that I met Sukriye, I was in a very different state of mind,"
says Nezir. "I had never before had a place where I belonged. I was always on
the move, always in search of something new. And through my constant travel
and searching, I overcame many of my boundaries. I found freedom. My only
thought was to free myself, to liberate myself. I thought, when I free myself, I
will find someone who is also free. This is what I found in Sukriye."

Sukriye and Nezir met several times over the course of her visit, always in
the company of a large group. But their affinity for one another was undeniable. Although their conversation never strayed from politics, culture, and
literature, they were both happy to have found someone they could relate to,
and they quickly began to behave with the easy companionability of old
friends. Sukriye liked him, and was glad to have found a friend within her
distant family circle. She thought it might be nice to stay in touch, and to get
together when she came to visit. But Nezir had other hopes. Within days of
their first meeting, he could not ignore what he was feeling. He had fallen in
love with her. After forty years of confirmed bachelorhood, the restlessness
of new love felt at times uncomfortable. She was constantly in his thoughts,
as if superimposed on every other thought he had and everything he saw. He
felt an inexplicable desire to write poetry. He had always been open to new
experiences, so he embraced what he was feeling. But he instinctively felt that
nothing would drive Sukriye off sooner than telling her what he felt.

To Sukriye, marriage was no simple matter of love and companionship.
Both her personal and professional experiences had invested her definition

of marriage with deeper significance. She had seen many women within her community and family circle trade in their intellect and personal aspirations for the unending labor of housework, limited by conservative views of marriage roles and women's traditional obligations. Even in the political and academic world of Berlin, far removed from her parents' family circle, she had found it difficult to engage in honest dialogue with Kurdish men about empowered gender relations. But it was her work with Kurdish women who were victims of rape and torture that led her to realize how deeply the trauma of war had infected gender relations in Kurdistan. Instead of sympathy and collective healing, many rape victims she met had encountered revulsion and even violence from their families. In the interest of protecting women from violence and community from dishonor, many Kurdish families had taken to restricting women's rights and freedom of movement even further. Her work opened her eyes to the cycle of violence and repression that dominated many women's lives, and awoke in her a distaste of any hint of male control over her own personal freedom. From a very young age, she had equated marriage with an end to her self-determination. Now, she believed that it was patriarchal institutions and male violence that kept Kurdish women, and thus Kurdish societies, unfree. She grew fierce in the defense of her freedom. She began to believe that avoiding an unhappy marriage was both a personal and philosophical necessity; it was a very personal way that she could promote both her own freedom and the freedom of Kurdish women everywhere.

This set up a challenge in her personal life: she would only marry if she shared true love and respect with someone. She also knew in her heart that she would only want to marry another Kurd, who would share her intimate passion for Kurdistan, and who would fit in with her family. Yet even though she could not bear the thought of bringing shame on her parents by openly dating an assortment of strangers, she also could not allow them to arrange a formal introduction with someone from their community. She would not have the luxury of taking her time to get to know someone she met through a formal introduction, and the risk of agreeing to spend the rest of her life with someone she eventually found she couldn't love or respect was too great. She had been disappointed to find how difficult it was to find single Kurdish men who shared her beliefs and values at the university or the political scene in Berlin. And she had never imagined herself marrying a man imported from home just to be her husband. She had seen too many such marriages fall apart because of cultural conflict, mismatched expectations, and wounded pride. As she grew older, she occasionally longed for companionship and love, but not at the cost of compromise. As time passed, the cost of compromise grew only greater; after all, she had held out so long, why should she relent now? And so, as she grew older, she grew more and more sensitive to marriage inquiries and proposals, which she perceived as attempts to curtail her own freedom.

Nezir sensed this and knew that she would only agree to marry him if she truly loved him herself. He felt that she would perceive any of his advances as a kind of aggression, and above all, he didn't want to hurt or upset her. And so he resolved to establish a friendship with her, nothing more, and to keep his feelings to himself until he sensed that she might feel something for him. He looked forward to corresponding with her, to talking about politics and literature with someone who was accomplished, well read, well traveled, and passionate. On some level, he knew that they were kindred spirits. She would have to recognize this in time. "I never made a conscious decision to love her or not love her. I just noticed that I spent all my time in my thoughts with her," he says. "I just wanted to give my love to her, and I knew that I would have to somehow slowly show her my love."

Meanwhile, word had spread that two foreign doctors were in the area, so early each morning, people from the town began arriving in search of medical advice. Although the German doctors were psychiatrists, most of the problems that were brought to them were matters of general health care, and so from daybreak until the evening, Sukriye stayed busy translating for people who rarely had access to medical professionals. Sukriye hadn't seen Nezir for a couple of days when she had a late-afternoon visitor who almost ruined his chances at her hand. When the visitor, an older woman who was an acquaintance of Sukriye's parents, came to the house where Sukriye and her colleagues had set up a makeshift consultation room, Sukriye assumed she had come for medical counseling. Since she was a family acquaintance, Sukriye sat with her in conversation before asking the reason for her visit. Suddenly and without any preamble, the woman announced, "You know, you've studied, Nezir has studied. You're both unmarried. You should marry each other." She patted Sukriye on the knee, telling her to think it over.

Sukriye felt ambushed. She felt certain that Nezir must have sent the woman to inquire on his behalf, and since this did not fit with what she had come to understand of his character, she was disappointed. The fact that she had actually liked him annoyed her more. She reacted to her disappointment with anger and, as was her normal reaction to anger and disappointment, she grew expressionless and still. Sukriye was not one for hot flashes of temper or angry outbursts; she was firm in her opinions and passionate in her feelings, but she kept them to herself unless she felt safe showing them. She usually made it a point to avoid situations that exposed her to people who disrespected her boundaries, and so had managed to live life on her own terms without offending anyone in the community. She was incensed that Nezir should have misread her so, but also that he should have put her in a position to have to spar with one of her parents' friends. Keeping her face blank, she told the visitor that she had not come back to Kurdistan in search of marriage, and had no interest in having one brokered for her. The subject was closed, she said, hurrying to take her leave of the visitor. She found the situation distasteful, they tinged her memories of conversation with Nezir a putrid color, and she put him out of her mind.

The next day, when Sukriye returned from a picnic in the fields with a group of her cousins, she found Nezir waiting to speak to her. The picnic had put her in high spirits, but when she saw him, she grew distant. She received him politely, and coldly. He spoke quietly and directly, hiding the terror in his heart that his chances with her were ruined. She should know that he had not sent the woman to her, he said, and if he had any such intentions, he certainly would have approached her himself. He made it clear that he did not believe in such old-fashioned formalities and indirectness in matters of marriage and love, but rather felt that love should be approached with openness and honesty. Sukriye was impressed, and the directness of his speech warmed her heart. She replied simply, "It's a good thing you told me. I thought it was strange." They smiled at each other, and their friendship was restored. They exchanged email and postal addresses, and agreed to stay in touch with each other. A few days later, it was time for Sukriye to return to Berlin.

Theirs was a twenty-first-century love story, unfolding through email and cell phone conversations. Without the immediacy of modern communication technology, they never would have come to dominate each other's daily lives within a matter of weeks the way that they did. There were still challenges: Internet connections came late and inconsistently to Syria, and were operated by a state-run company. There was only one Internet café in Amouda, where the connection was slow and regularly down, where the lines were long, and where many of the Kurds were wary that their messages or search history could be monitored. But after Sukriye left, Nezir became a regular fixture there, and almost immediately after her arrival in Berlin, Sukriye received her first email from him. He'd written a piece about Kurdistan, he said, and he wondered if he might send it to her for her impressions. Sukriye was always interested in literature about Kurdistan, so she replied that she would like to read he'd written. The next day, she found a poem in her inbox. When she read it, she was surprised to see that some of the verses were about her. Nezir was not by profession a poet, and so the poem was not the greatest she had read. But it was the first poem that had been written specifically about her and for her. She was not blind; she could see what Nezir was indirectly telling her. But the next day, when Nezir wrote asking her impressions, she carefully avoided taking the bait. She told him that she had found his point of view interesting, and that she had enjoyed reading his work.

They began to email regularly, and although most of their letters focused on politics and personal philosophy, they became more and more intimate with each other. Sukriye found herself telling him about her own vision of homeland, and of her personal interpretations of Kurdish values. Slowly, his messages became more affectionate and loving. He told her that he had found her sweet from the first time he had met her, and how amazed he was at her character, her fluency with the language, her familiarity with current Kurdish politics, and the nearly perfect balance she seemed to have struck between German and Kurdish culture. He never thought that it would be possible for a Kurdish woman who had grown up in the West to have such close ties with home, and at the same time to be so knowledgeable and critical of the problems with Kurdish society. He was touched that she made the effort to bring Germans with her to show them her homeland, even in the face of great political obstacles, and managed to show them what was loveable and beautiful about Kurdistan. She, in turn, was amazed that such a man as Nezir was possible. This can't be an Oriental man, she thought. She wondered that he was born and raised in a closed-off part of the world, lived there still, and nevertheless had such a cultivated and progressive outlook. "I thought to myself, such a gentle, sweet person! A person could fall in love with him after all."

Within a few weeks, they decided to continue their conversations over the phone. Nezir got hold of a Turkish cell phone that, so close to the border, could pick up a decent signal. Sukriye mailed him prepaid cards for Turkish cell phones, available at Turkish- and Kurdish-owned news stands and international call centers all over Berlin. Before long, they had completely abandoned political and cultural discussions and openly began speaking of their feelings. Sukriye bought herself a little pocket notebook, and she began to collect all the Kurdish words she had never had any reason to learn. "I never knew so many names of flowers before," she says with a wry smile. They spoke from late at night, after his parents had gone to sleep, until dawn paled the sky. Sukriye dragged herself wearily from bed one morning in early September, running late for work after a long night running up her cell phone bill, and as she turned on the radio to Radio MultiKulti, set tea on the stove, and pulled on her dark blue corduroy pants, she realized with a shock that she was in love. That night, she and Nezir confessed their love for each other into their phone receivers. A fluorescent light in the vestibule of Sukriye's building cast a whitish glow on the wet cobblestones in the sidewalk, and at the same time, a nighttime breeze stirred some of the yellow dust on Amouda's streets.

The first glow of romance carried them through the next few days. Neither of them slept or worked much. Their phone charges grew and grew. One day, it occurred to Sukriye, for all the money she had spent on phone bills, she could have flown to Kurdistan three times and back. And just like that, her patience with the long-distance relationship ran out. His voice wasn't enough. She wanted more. They began discussing how they might meet. And so they passed out of the safe haze of new romance into the hard, cold reality of figuring out how they might actually have a relationship. They had already discussed marriage. They both believed in marriage, and knew that if they wanted to build a long-term relationship and a long-term alliance between their families, they would have to marry. But they both felt that they wanted to see each other one more time in person, just to see if what they were feeling was real.

There was no place they could physically meet without transgressing some law, whether societal, religious, or government-imposed. As a stateless person, Nezir could not legally travel outside of Syria. But Sukriye could not visit him there without her family finding out that something was going on, and she did not want any gossip to reach her parents. Nezir was willing to entertain the possibility of sneaking over the various borders crisscrossing Kurdistan in order to meet with her, but Sukriye did not want to risk exposing him to legal troubles. For someone with his status, travel outside of Amouda was risk enough, but if he was unlucky enough to be caught crossing international borders, he could be detained and disappear. Meanwhile, an unacknowledged state of war continued to reign in Turkey, and the military and political situation in Iraq seemed to be growing more fraught with each passing day. The conflict between various militant groups and the US-led occupation forces had increased security concerns, and transborder movement drew the attention not only of Turkish military forces but also of Iraqi Kurdish authorities keen to prevent diplomatic and military troubles with Turkey at any cost. Kurdish cross-border traffic and trade into Kurdistan-Iraq would continue freely even after a bloody suicide bombing in February of 2004, the costliest of the occupation era to date, but long before this, Nezir and Sukriye had decided that, if Iraq could be avoided, it should. Iran was also out. Even if Nezir's status and the political instability of the region had not exposed them to a certain threat, then their love did. In Iran, the one remaining part of Kurdistan not in a state of war, it was punishable by law for unmarried couples to travel or board together.

They began to entertain reckless plans. In a particularly emotional moment, they even discussed the possibility paying a human trafficker to smuggle Nezir into Germany via transport container, at risk of apprehension or even death, where he would then apply for political asylum. Although neither of them really believed that they would ever pursue such a drastic plan, they both felt that they had to exhaust all possibilities before they broached their last possible plan: marriage. But six months after they had met, four months after they had fallen in love, they realized that they were only losing valuable time. If there were immense emotional and bureaucratic challenges to marriage, they paled in comparison to the social and legal barriers to dating. They stood to risk more and gain less by dating than by marriage. And so, without fanfare, without ceremony, without setting a bride price or sharing dates and nuts, without the knowledge of any elders, they decided to arrange their own marriage. They were the first in either of their families to have embarked on adulthood with the intention of avoiding marriage, pursuing freedom, and if marrying at all, doing so only for love. It was as unlikely a story as anyone could imagine. Without trying, without looking, without compromising, they had made a perfect match. Little did they know that overcoming their own personal hesitations would be the easiest part of their journey toward married life together.

Sukriye's plan was for them to marry, and then apply for Nezir to join her in Berlin with a family reunification visa. Nezir never believed that it would actually happen. For a stateless Kurd to marry legally was radical enough, but for him to secure a legal entry visa to Europe as the husband of a German citizen was practically revolutionary. If Syria had stateless populations and strict ideological limits built into its conception of nationality, so had Germany. Citizenship has been a notoriously complex issue in Germany where, until 2000, nationality was predominantly conferred on the grounds of blood ties rather than by birth. Naturalization options did exist, but requirements were stringent enough to exclude a large percentage of nonethnic German immigrants living in Germany, in some cases even immigrants who had lived in Germany for several generations. Immigrants' rights and prospects were still determined by the so-called "foreigner law," and refugees and asylum seekers ran the risk of giving birth to not only foreign but even stateless children while they waited for their asylum applications to be processed. Still, Germany's non-German population continued to grow, through high birth rates and immigration inflows, and just as the European Union began to discuss a pan-European immigration concept, so did Germany begin to reform its own national immigration concept. But the process was slow and met with much resistance from the conservative bloc of political parties, and when Sukriye and Nezir began to discuss their options for a future together, the national sentiment on expanded citizenship and civil rights for immigrants, especially of Muslim immigrants from countries believed to support anti-Western Islamist movements now in the post-September 11 era, was far from positive. It seemed that the resolution of a comprehensive immigration policy still lay in the distant future.

But the first level of bureaucracy Sukriye and Nezir had to overcome was the bureaucracy of family protocol. Before they could officially begin collecting information and paperwork about marriage, Nezir first had to send an official emissary to ask Sukriye's father for her hand in marriage, and the emissary could not mention that Sukriye knew about the proposal. The proposal must be posed as if it was an independent inquiry, made honorably between families. One might ask, if these two were so progressive and independent-minded, why didn't they just approach Sukriye's father themselves and announce their intention to marry? Simply put, Sukriye wanted to do her father at least this honor before his community, so that he might not feel that he had been deceived into accepting something he might consider inappropriate. She knew that her father would never stand in the way of her happiness, but she was wise enough to know that if she was careful to protect his pride and dignity, and to give him the respect of a traditional, familiar marriage proposal, then he would feel more positively disposed to the marriage. She was conscious that he had given her more freedom than many Kurdish men of his background were accustomed to giving their daughters, and she wanted to show him that she had not abused his trust. She wanted him to know that she still honored the traditional customs.

Nezir made his first move in January 2004. He was in Syria, Sukriye was in Berlin, and her father, Mehmet, was in Diyarbakir, in Turkey. Since no one from Nezir's immediate family could cross the border into Turkey, he had to send his uncle, who approached Mehmet one evening with a formal proposal. And then, Sukriye's plan to comply with family protocol backfired. Mehmet smiled noncommittally at the proposal, saying vaguely that he had to get Sukriye's opinion before he could agree to any arrangement. But he thought that he had learned his lesson well enough not to actually approach Sukriye with a proposal; for nearly fifteen years, Sukriye had cut off all conversations about proposals and marriages, refusing to entertain any inquiries. In fact, she had told her parents never to approach her with any proposal at all. So now, even as she tried to play by the traditional rules, her father was playing by her own modern, feminist rules, and nixed the very proposal that she herself had arranged!

Nearly two months passed before Nezir finally contacted Mehmet himself, saying that someone had spoken to Sukriye and she had agreed. In March of 2004, Sukriye finally got to accept the proposal she had waited so long for her father to make, and Mehmet celebrated the engagement with a big party in Nusaybin. The thirty guests he had invited shared sweets and fruits to wish the absent bride and groom a sweet life together, dancing shoulder-to-shoulder late into the night.

On June 3, 2004, Sukriye became Nezir's wife before a Shari'a court in Damascus. Inside a great, square building reminiscent of eastern-bloc government buildings, down a long corridor edging a wide, sun-bleached courtyard, Nezir waited for his wedding to begin. Beside him, stood a short, square-faced, mustachioed man, a lawyer, who was standing in for Sukriye as his bride.

Because Nezir could not leave Syria, he and Sukriye had to be married before a Syrian court in order to be eligible for a family reunification visa to Germany. But since Nezir was classified as a "foreigner" in the eyes of the

Syrian government, his marriage would not be registered in Syria. The strange legal sleight of hand that allowed a native population to be classified as foreign continued, allowing so-called foreigners to be legally married in a Shari'a court, under Islamic religious code, but not formally registered as married in Syrian government records. What this meant was that, unless Germany recognized the marriage as legal and provided the couple with a marriage license, there would be no proof that they were married at all. Since in Germany citizenship was not a birthright, if Germany refused to acknowledge their marriage, it could happen that their children could end up stateless as well. With so much at stake, Sukriye made sure to schedule appointments with representatives at every bureaucratic institution or office that might be remotely relevant to the case. After exhaustive discussions with the Berlin city clerk, the Foreigner Office, the State Department, and the German embassy, she made sure that her marriage would be recognized. It took her another three months to prepare the appropriate materials needed for a legal marriage in Syria. She spent hundreds of euros and countless hours away from her job in line at various government offices to collect proof of her German citizenship, her birth certificate, and proof that she was a Muslim, as well as documentation of an authorized HIV test.

But she spent the most time by far figuring out what type of marriage might be acceptable before German law. She knew that, in the eyes of her family, she would not be married until she was married by their mullah and had celebrated her wedding with a circle dance lasting several hours in a massive hall full of friends and family. A wedding before the court was mere paperwork, nothing to be taken seriously. She had spent so much money on applications, registrations, legalizations, translations, and notarizations, not to mention on phone bills and work hours lost, that she was eager to find the cheapest possible legal marriage. So when one of the many officials she met happened to mention that Syria permitted marriages to be conducted with one of the partners in absentia, and that such a marriage would be recognized in Germany as long as all of the appropriate paperwork was in order, Sukriye decided to save herself the money of a trip to Syria and be married in absentia. All she had to do was send a power of attorney along with all the other documents to be translated, which would authorize a lawyer in Syria to represent her at the marriage proceeding in Damascus. The lawyer could also serve as the witness to the marriage.

Meanwhile, Nezir had spent over three months trying to correct errors on his state-issued "foreigner" identity card. Immediately after the withdrawal of citizenship from 120,000 Kurds and their descendents, the Syrian government was left with the awkward task of creating an institutional system for registering a group of people whose civil existence it had officially denied. Since statelessness carried no civil rights or privileges, there was no need to be particularly diligent in registering these new foreigners. Their documentation was all stored in semi-chaos in the Qamishli municipal courthouse. Foreigner identity cards were often littered with errors, such as misspellings, inaccurate family relationships, incorrect dates of birth, and the like. On Nezir's identity card, his birth year was listed as 1959, and he was actually born in 1963, one year after the exceptional census. He thought that since he might now actually have an official existence, he would like to have correct information listed on his new identification.

But suddenly all hell broke loose in Syrian Kurdistan. On March 12, 2004, just after an interim constitution giving the Kurdish provinces a broad autonomy and veto power in the Iraqi parliament had passed, a riot broke between Syrian Arabs and Kurds at a soccer match in Qamishli. The riots spread across northern Syria in what some Kurds have since dubbed their own Intifada. Government buildings in several towns, including Qamishli, were torched, along with boxes and boxes of disorganized documentation on stateless Kurds. Nezir's identity was among the documentation destroyed in a fire in Qamishli's city hall. Nezir was frustrated by the loss of his documentation, but a friend of his who had studied law advised him that the wedding could proceed as long as Sukriye's paperwork was in order.

Although the so-called Kurdish Intifada had led to the destruction of many identities, to a brutal crackdown against Kurdish communities, and to the withdrawal of the government's promise to reinstate citizenship for up to 30,000 Kurds, many of Syria's Kurds would celebrate it as a historic moment of collective pride. In fact, many scholars have speculated that the Intifada broke out because of a sense of empowerment swelling across Kurdistan, a kind of collective exuberance and national pride in the fact that Iraqi Kurdistan might finally achieve its own freedom. It is often assumed that all Muslims in the world were opposed to the Iraq war. But the overwhelming majority of Kurds, which has been estimated at as many as 40 million people worldwide, the greatest percentage of whom are Muslim, supported the US-led invasion of Iraq. In Berlin, most of Sukriye's non-Kurdish friends crowded on the left end of the political spectrum. In the months leading up to the war, she often found herself sitting through antiwar, and increasingly strident anti-American, discussions. More than one of her close German friends declared that they would never visit the United States, solely for political reasons. But in proceeding with the move against the Saddam Hussein regime in the face of opposition from Turkey, its long-term ally and long-term antagonist of Kurdish pro-independence aspirations, the United States had come closer than any powerful nation to openly allying with a Kurdish governmental body.

Sukriye, for her part, had felt put off by the excessive sentimentalizing of the September 11 events in the Western press, but had no personal argument with the United States that prevented her, as a Kurd, from supporting its actions in Iraq. Sukriye's feelings toward the Iraq war reflected the feelings of many Kurds who were growing frustrated waiting for economic rehabilitation, political recognition, or equal rights in the countries where they lived. Before the war had broken out, Sukriye and some of her colleagues from the Berlin Society for the Advancement of Kurdology had traveled to Iraqi Kurdistan, and although she had been saddened at the plight of Kurds living in miserable refugee camps in Kirkuk, and by the rise of Islamist influence throughout the region, she had still felt a thrill at seeing Kurdish politicians openly debating governance in a Kurdish language. She had collected a rock to take home with her, which she had placed in the small bowl beside her bed, the final part of the Kurdistan she had united on her bedside table. Although few believed that Kurdish autonomy or even independence in Iraq would lead to the creation of a greater Kurdistan, the United States's validation of the Kurdish ethnic and political identity gave many Kurds, particularly Turkish

Kurds, a feeling of hope during a period when their own nationalist movement had lost its leadership and direction.

That summer was also a time of great personal hope for Sukriye and
Nezir. After months of effort and expense, on a sunny June day in Damascus,
a man with no identity married a woman who wasn't there. The Shari'a
court judge, a man with a well-developed sense of humor, told the two men,
Nezir and the attorney who was representing Sukriye, to join hands and
recite from the Qur'an. The men, after a moment of awkward silence, realized that the judge would not proceed with the ceremony until they held
hands. Blushing furiously, they clasped each other's hands, resting their eyes
everywhere but on one another. But the judge still hadn't finished amusing
himself. He called out into the corridor and waved two passers-by into the
courtroom to serve as witnesses to the wedding, noting that, under Islamic
law, two Muslim witnesses were required in a wedding.

Then, he asked Nezir to set a bride price. Nezir was mildly stumped.
Saying no amount of money would equal Sukriye in value, he tried to decline
a bride price. But he was required under law to name some amount, so he
simply said, off the top of his head, that he would offer 500 Syrian lira. Nezir
and Sukriye were declared married, and the two men dropped their hands to
their sides in relief. As Nezir turned to leave, the judge pulled him aside and
asked Nezir if he didn't have something sweet to offer him, to celebrate the
wedding, and so Nezir, grinning broadly, dug into his pocket for 500 lira to
show his gratitude to the judge. The judge grimaced at the bills in his hand
and remained standing in front of Nezir, who was so dizzy with joy that he
slapped another 500 lira in the judge's palm. He chuckled to himself that he
had set a 500 lira price for the bride, and paid twice that much for the bribe.

By September 24, 2004, Berlin is already cold and dreary. The sky is blotchy
and overcast beyond the windows of the Paul-Gerhardt Home, the city's
only residential home for traumatized war refugees and torture survivors,
and their families. When Sukriye started working here as a translator nearly
ten years ago, the residents were all Kurds, like herself. Now, they are mostly
Chechens, and Sukriye has become a social worker. In a place like this, that

means that she is part immigration law expert, human rights advocate, family health counselor, psychotherapist, sister, parent, and friend to every one of the home's residents. Her job does not end when the office closes, and her work is never done. In the basement office of the home, Sukriye's head bends over a sheaf of papers. A milky light leaks into the room, outlining her head with a white glow. In a few minutes, she will have her last appointment of the day, and then she can finally go home. It is barely 4:00 in the afternoon, and Sukriye is mentally and physically exhausted.

These days, Sukriye's seemingly boundless patience with the needier, more self-destructive residents of the home seems to have its limits. She has been married for three months, but securing Nezir's legal immigration has turned into another full-time job. She had been willing to move all the landmass between them to make it possible for them to have a life together. But she had never thought it would actually come to that, and these days, she feels as if she has physically been moving mountains. In the last eight months, Sukriye has spent at least ten hours each week in first the Foreigner Office, then the State Department, and countless municipal and regional government offices in between. Her Shari'a marriage certificate has been questioned and examined and discredited then reexamined. At every office and department she has visited, she has been asked to provide a different set of documentation, and sent on wild goose chases through the land of embassies and consulates. She has called in favors and pulled whatever influence she can muster, and she still does not know when she can celebrate her wedding. In these last eight months, she has lost almost twenty pounds and taken up chain smoking, a habit she had never before indulged. Her home is often empty and unheated, her refrigerator is rarely stocked, and music and dancing rarely fill her living room as it had in the past. Her wedding ring knocks loosely against her knuckle, like a horseshoe in a toss.

After they had finally pulled off the courthouse marriage in Damascus, they had believed the process was nearing its end. In Berlin, a legal proceeding was opened for Nezir to join Sukriye in Germany with a family reunification visa, and Sukriye traveled to Syria in July, where the couple celebrated their engagement with the hundreds of relatives and friends who could not travel to Germany. At the end of the trip, Nezir was to return home with

Sukriye, in time to celebrate their wedding in Barsinghausen and to settle into Sukriye's apartment well before Ramadan began in November. Between planning for the celebration and confronting her own discomfort at playing the traditional bride, Sukriye found much of the trip to be trying and hectic. She had spent an entire afternoon fighting a local beautician to not whiten her skin with cheap makeup, only to find that the photographer had lightened her face in the engagement photos anyway. She had found it difficult to dance in the frilly pink ballgown that was rented for her to wear, and was later chastised for dancing so energetically when she should have been sitting on a platform, demurely averting her eyes. She had so looked forward to putting the double madness of immigration and wedding planning behind her and finally having a simple, quotidian existence with her new husband. But when she had returned to Germany, Nezir was not at her side.

Instead, the immigration proceeding was dragging on from day to day with no end in sight. What should have been a simple approval had turned into a several month-long inquiry into all aspects of their personal life and history. Each time she spent time and money collecting, legalizing, notarizing, and translating a new set of documents, she found herself sent on yet another quest for yet more documentation that was absolutely required. Initially, Sukriye had chalked up the delays to standard bureaucratic inefficiency and to the unusual circumstances of Nezir's case. But then, one dreary early September evening, after she had waited in line at the Foreigner Office for nearly two hours, she met with the office head. Without any preamble, the woman accused Sukriye of a bogus marriage. "When they hear Shari'a court, their ears just perk up. Bride price and such, they just find it shocking." Sukriye believed that the Foreigner Office was indirectly accusing her of attempting to smuggle a terrorist into the country. She felt suddenly deflated.

It was clear to Sukriye that the rules of migration had subtly shifted. Until recently, if immigrants experienced roadblocks or difficulties in securing visas for family members or obtaining citizenship, it was only because Germany had not yet set up the bureaucratic structures appropriate to the major immigration destination it had unwillingly become. Now, she was experiencing difficulties in her immigration proceeding because she was attempting to secure a visa for a Muslim man from Syria. With each passing meeting, more and more aspects of her marriage were questioned. Now, officials from the Foreigner Office told her that her decision to marry in absentia was suspicious, and supported the allegation that the marriage itself was fictitious. One official spent an entire afternoon trying to get Sukriye to admit that Nezir spoke Turkish, even though he lived in Syria and communicated with Sukriye in Kurmanci, implying that as a northern Kurd he must be a PKK supporter, that he must have illegally moved with militants in Turkey. Since the PKK had been named on the German Interior Ministry's list of terrorist organizations, if Nezir had been established as a PKK supporter, his immigration application could be summarily dismissed. Then she was informed that the fact that his identity was unprovable was grounds for further suspicion, even though he himself did not choose to be born stateless. She spent entire days waiting around, only for case workers to speak to her in aggressive, dismissive tones, as if she were somehow trying to put something over on them. "The Foreigner Office has a political strategy to disempower people, to wear them out to the point that they just give up. See, what it's about is that the people who work there can't possibly have an in-depth understanding of conditions in every country," she explains. "So the burden of proof is mine, which means that I must explain everything. But when everything I bring them is questioned, then the whole process is moot. They could very easily contact the ministries themselves and find out what happened."

Amid all these accusations and obligations, the Foreigner Office has now told her that her case must be investigated by the Federal Criminal Ministry. And, on top of it, she must pay for the investigation, even though the Foreigner Office has ordered it. Although Sukriye is frustrated with her own experiences, her true sympathy rests with asylum seekers and refugees, people who have no protection, power, or recourse against a biased Foreigner Office caseworker. And in many cases, all that stands between an asylum seeker and deportation is the good will of a caseworker. Sukriye has seen more than one person be escorted out of the Foreigner Office in handcuffs, slated for immediate deportation, on the basis of a recommendation made in haste by a caseworker who happened to be in a sour mood on that day. "It is a genuinely hard place, this Foreigner Office," says Sukriye. "Look, for me it's one thing, I'm a German citizen. But the poor refugees, for whom it's really about life and death, deportation or visa extension, and they have to just wait there, trembling. Now in my case, legally, they can't make any serious objections because this type of marriage is recognized in Germany, and I registered for it ahead of time. It's only because of internal rules and heightened security measures that they're making this much of a hassle."

Now, this late September afternoon at the Paul-Gerhardt Home, Sukriye struggles to get through her last appointment of the day without yawning. Her entire body aches. In two months, by the end of November 2004, this home is slated to close, and converted into yet another of Berlin's hundreds of senior living communities. Sukriye will be out of a job. She has had no time to do anything more than her job and take on the German immigration authorities, let alone find another job. She can only think so far as actually getting Nezir here. Then, they will just have to figure out what to do next. It will not be easy. If Germany actually allows Nezir in, he will not be eligible to apply for a work permit for at least two years. And if he actually is eligible to apply for a work permit, he will have to demonstrate fluency in a language he had never heard until his fortieth year of life.

As darkness slides over the cobblestone courtyard to the home, Sukriye winds up her appointment and prepares to head home. She turns off the lights in her office and peeks into the activities room next door to make sure that the children have returned to their rooms. On the back wall is a gallery of crayon drawings by the Chechen children who live here. In the pictures are stick figures blindfolded, lined up for execution, clunky tanks rolling over rectangular houses, fires coming out of four-square windows, helicopters shooting red. None of the children who drew these pictures is older than ten. Sukriye turns out the light in the activity room and heads out into the courtyard, then to the street. It has begun to rain. It will take her over an hour to get home. When she does, she will turn on the heat, rummage in her freezer for a frozen dinner, and fall into bed with her phone, and Nezir.

On November 24, 2004, Nezir received a German travel pass, and in January of 2005, he and Sukriye danced at their wedding in Barsinghausen. When he held a travel pass, it was the first time in his life that Nezir had existed legally, and he described the pass as his birth certificate for a new existence. Citizenship is a state of being with both psychological and bureaucratic dimensions. For some, taking on citizenship is a simple functional decision to improve living conditions. In this view, citizenship brings with it freedom, security, and agency: the freedom to move across international borders with impunity, the security to lay down roots in a host country, and agency to influence the host country's political culture. But to some, the decision to take citizenship becomes philosophical, the basis of agonizing internal dialogue on identity and the right of the state to include or exclude. In Germany, citizenship has traditionally been synonymous with national or even ethnic belonging, and so debates on citizenship have included an existential element; redefining citizenship and revising the grounds for eligibility to some degree requires Germany to expand its concept of national inclusion. In many countries, citizen's rights trump universal human rights, and citizens have access to education, work, ownership rights, and social services to which they would otherwise be denied legal access. It is this institutionalization of private choices, the legal structuring of access, that compound with matters of national character to make citizenship such a complex and hotly debated subject in the leading immigrant destinations of the world.

In Nezir's case, taking on German citizenship meant no longer having to live in fear. Never again would any state body be able to question his right to travel within the country in which he lived. Of course, he would still have to wait two years before he could apply for permission to work in Germany, and in the meantime, he would have to learn German and adjust to a completely alien culture. Sukriye would have to apply for welfare to tide them over until she could find another job, and they would not be able to travel to Kurdistan together for many years. But they were together, and, in spite of all the distance and stress, they were still as much in love as they had hoped they would be.

Sukriye had spent her entire life balancing between tradition and liberation, between her loyalty to her culture and her desire for personal freedom. She had ejected herself from the comfort and warmth of her family sphere, with the ambition of having a great career in the service of the Kurdish people, and her parents had supported her decision with the implicit understanding that she would achieve great things and perhaps even play a role in freeing Kurdistan in her journeys. But the tragedy of the Kurdish struggle was that it was largely ignored in mainstream academic and political institutions, and Sukriye soon realized that if she wanted to serve her people it would have to be on a smaller, personal scale. She ultimately made her peace with a smaller sphere of personal satisfaction, content in the realization that she was helping individuals to achieve a measure of security, and that she was a member of a community with enough cultural wealth and strength to survive political invisibility into the indefinite future. As conscious as she was of the truly existential struggles of many of the Kurdish refugees she worked with on a daily basis, she never gave her personal narrative much thought, forming her own identity on a humble and intimate scale. Her national pride, her feminist values, and her professional aspirations were simply themes that emerged in her life story without her own effort to emphasize or analyze them.

To Sukriye, the defining struggle of her life was the Kurdish struggle for recognition and rights. Since the country in which she had settled had given her personal opportunities while systematically ignoring the existence of her people, and because it had never seen immigrants as a part of its collective national imagination, she could never feel German. Still, she had gone to great lengths to succeed as best she could within the German academic and social service systems, and had met many Germans along the way who had made tremendous personal and professional sacrifices to serve people in need. She had already managed to bind her emotional loyalty to Kurdistan and her professional ambition to Germany by the time the clash-of-civilizations discourse emerged. She simply saw it as another element of Germany's resistance to incorporating non-Germans into its national character, just another bureaucratic hurdle for asylum seekers to whom it proved a true existential threat. She already belonged to an identity group unseen and misunderstood by the majority of the world.

CHAPTER 9

NISHAT LETS GO

Nishat barely takes note of news from Iraq, Palestine, or even Bangladesh. For her, the war on terror is neither abstract nor broad, but rather very personal and very intimate. She doesn't think in terms of a clash of civilizations or Islam versus the West. She doesn't see unfair mainstream media portrayal of Muslim men and women, invasions and wars waged in predominantly Muslim countries, and the legitimization of oppressive action against Muslim immigrant communities throughout the West as evidence of one global ideological conflict. The only struggle that is real to Nishat is her own family's struggle. If she has learned any rhetoric from the activist organizations she relies on for financial assistance, child care, networking, legal advice, and emotional support, it is only so that she can better frame her statements to the press. And the only reason she gives interviews and issues statements to the press is that she believes they will convince some politician, any politician, to give her amnesty to become a legal immigrant in the United States. Action based on faith in the possibility of improbable outcomes is one of Nishat's coping strategies.

Nishat develops the following strategies for giving herself a sense of control over her future:

She networks, learns social and racial justice rhetoric, and speaks to the press. She becomes a community organizer with one activist organization. She plays three such organizations against one another to see which will be of greatest assistance to her. She develops high expectations based on the social justice education she has received.

She makes dramatic statements and symbolic gestures. One day, she declares that she will refuse to wear any of the perfumes remaining from the collection Mohammad brought home each week until she sees her husband again. She lists recipes she will only make when she sees him again, buys clothes she will wear only when she sees him again. For a while, she becomes a devout Muslim, and then later abandons this to dress like an American woman as long as she can. On a day trip to Washington, D.C., she photographs her son crying in front of the White House, which she later shows to her American friends.

She abuses her body. Always an erratic eater, she becomes a full-blown anorexic. Her body weight drops to ninety pounds, and her hair grows coarse and thin. She suffers from chronic infections and short breath. She stays awake all night watching TV, falling asleep only as dawn breaks.

She feels completely alone. She loses patience with her children, threatening to hit Ayesha with a hanger just to get her to stop whining one minute, then smothering her with kisses the next. She asks everyone she meets for help with babysitting, researching immigration law, buying gifts for her kids. She periodically rejects old friends for new ones.

She avoids the subway for fear of random searches. She stays indoors most of the time.

On September 24, 2003, Nishat Islam checked herself into the Elmhurst Hospital alone. She was underweight and exhausted, lonely and joyless, and she was giving birth to her second child. Her son Rasha Junaid was born on at 2:30 in the morning of September 25, 2003, a US citizen weighing 7 pounds, 10 ounces. He was introduced to his father when he was eleven days old, through the bullet-proof glass divider in the visiting room of the jail where Mohammed was being held for immigration violations. Less than a week later, on October 11, 2003, Mohammad Junaid was deported. He left the United States on a charter flight late at night a week later with nothing but what he was wearing.

After Nishat had cried for the better part of several days, she took a photo of Mohammad with baby Ayesha from a photo album and put it on the refrigerator door. And then she made a decision. Nishat refused to follow

Mohammad to Karachi. In a compromise wrangled from one of their last conversations, Nishat had promised to send Rasha to live with his father in Karachi as soon as he was weaned. But Rasha turned out to have a developmental delay, and Nishat insisted that he remain under the care of his US doctors. And so, while Mohammad returned home to Pakistan with no work, to listen to his brothers mock him for letting his wife stay behind without him, Nishat, her father, and her two children remained in Queens, locked in limbo. Once a week, Nishat and Mohammad spoke on the phone, hiding accusations of betrayal and abandonment in their standard dialogue of missing each other. He couldn't enter the United States and she refused to leave. Their marriage was at an impasse.

Under the NSEERS program, 83,519 men voluntarily registered, and some 13,000 of these men were tagged for deportation. None of the men who registered was ever found to have links with militant or so-called terrorist activities. Flushing, Queens and Midwood, Brooklyn, two neighborhoods with large Pakistani and Bangladeshi communities, were all but decimated in the three years after the September 11 attacks on the World Trade Center. A study conducted by an Asian American legal defense organization notes that one in three of all men who were deported or detained left families behind in the United States. Many of these families, left without their primary breadwinners or the chance to be legalized, simply followed their men out of the country. For those who wished to give their US citizen children an American life, few options were available.

Strong antiterrorism and restrictive immigration legislation existed before September 11, and mass sweeps of immigrant communities had been a frequent response to national security concerns in the United States. In fact, in the 1940s and 1950s, nearly 2 million suspected communists and sympathizers were detained. But with September 11, New York City changed one of its unacknowledged rules about undocumented immigrants. Before that day, one undocumented immigrant was no different from another. In fact, New York City's economy was so bound up with the fruits of undocumented labor that such immigrants were safer from scrutiny there than anywhere else in the country. As long as they were not implicated in any criminal charges, authorities gave them a wide berth. Suddenly, Muslim undocumented immigrants were perceived as a massive national security threat. Where previously debate surrounding such immigrants largely revolved around economic and national identity issues, now the main question at hand was, were undocumented Muslim immigrants more likely to be Islamist militants? Unable to devise an effective formula for identifying potential terrorism risks in the United States, the federal government simply decided to clean its house of the largest group of Muslim men it could without being held accountable for any legal or social obligations.

According to Nishat, Rafiqul, and Mohammad, who had, respectively, made the conscious decision to falsify a visa application, overstay a visa, and ignore a deportation order, the United States offered them a certain contract even if it refrained from offering them formal documentation. If they laid low, focused on work and family life, and paid their taxes like everyone else, the US government would look the other way. The sense of betrayal Nishat felt was that she had, in fact, achieved the American Dream openly, without any artifice, under the watch of whatever authorities there were. She had worked, been married, and paid rent. Her husband had owned a car and managed a store in the middle of America's iconic commercial strip, Times Square. They had used public resources, like the subway and hospital, and no one had given them any reason to feel guilty for doing so. In Bangladesh, even highly educated people can struggle for a lifetime to achieve things like a home, a car, a permanent job, but here, Nishat and Mohammad had been able to have a solidly middle-class life without legal documentation or college degrees. The world was unjust; until equal opportunities were available throughout the world, undocumented workers like Mohammad and Nishat sought opportunities by any means necessary. America had always been content to incorporate resourceful, driven, often overqualified undocumented immigrants into its service, agricultural, and manufacturing sectors.

Long after Mohammad had been deported, Nishat continued to argue that his detention and deportation had been unjust. Teenaged boys will fight, she said, so what justification was there to order him deported? She was quoted in media reports saying "We figure we work hard, we follow

American rules, everything turn out well," and "In our country, we think America is the dream country. But our dreams are broken. There are no dreams come true here." And she was ridiculed in conservative blogs and online discussion forums for claiming to have followed US rules when she had knowingly been living in the country illegally, and for appealing for sympathy for a man who had defied a deportation order. Her belief that her husband had been robbed of his freedom, and that her family had been robbed of him because of some minor incident in his teenaged years only fed her sense of victimization by and isolation from the rest of US society. In her representation of the incident, Mohammad was a hapless victim of a system designed to criminalize all undocumented immigrants.

This belief illustrates an important point of departure between Nishat's view of undocumented immigrants' rights and the view of those who support border control and deportation in the interests of national security. Nishat did not believe that living in a country illegally was grounds for a person to be viewed as a threat to national security. In fact, she would argue that the fact that she and her husband had lived undetected and unhindered for as long as they had was proof that they had been absorbed into the country's social and economic systems. If a society tolerates and even relies on undocumented immigrants, why should these immigrants become targets of national suspicion and fear? Nishat wondered to what end her husband's deportation had taken place. After all, what sort of message was society sending all immigrants if long-term, economically integrated undocumented immigrants of certain ethnic, linguistic, or religious backgrounds can be singled out as criminal when society as a whole faces indeterminate and often faceless threats from abroad?

The decision to overstay a visa in pursuit of a better life is a violation of US law. Any action that draws the attention of US law enforcement authorities to an illegal resident is then seen as a second violation of the law, making the detected undocumented immigrant a repeat offender. Thus, the decision to remain in the United States illegally is to accept life on permanent probation. An undocumented person must decide to limit his activities to avoid any possibility of detection. The circumstances of detection may be unfair, irregular, or subjective, but an undocumented person has little or no opportunity to contest in favor of a fair trial. The undocumented person is, in effect, vulnerable to the prejudices of individual law enforcement officials, as well as to the prejudices and fears of society as a whole. In March 2005, a Bangladeshi teenaged girl was arrested as a potential suicide bomber when federal agents interpreted her journal entries as suspicious, and was detained for illegally overstaying a tourist visa when she was a toddler. That she would not have been legally recognized as an individual with decision-making autonomy at that age, even as a US citizen, did not figure into the legal calculations leading to her detention. As the United States grapples with its own society-wide fear of Muslims as outsiders, as possible adherents to an enemy ideology, as potential national security threats, its legal system allows little room for interpretation of the law on a case-by-case basis.

In December 2003, the Department of Homeland Security suspended the Special Registration call-in program it had inherited from the Justice Department. Officials said that federal government resources could be better applied to other counterterrorism efforts, but declined to comment on the findings of the September 11 Commission, which found little evidence to support earlier Justice Department claims of the program's success. So ended one of the farthest-reaching instances of legally institutionalized ethnic profiling and mass deportation in over fifty years of US history.

Still, thousands of registrants would continue to fight arduous legal battles to remain in the United States. For years to come, men who had voluntarily registered under a program that had been abandoned as ineffective in its original purpose would continue to be ordered deported from their homes and families to countries they had left behind long before.

Rafiqul had also complied with the Special Registration call-in program. Early in 2003, before his son-in-law had been detained, he too had been photographed, fingerprinted, and interviewed under oath. Since he was found to be out of status, he had been told that he would have to appear for a deportation hearing. The courts were extremely backlogged at the time of Rafiqul's interview, and immediate court dates were all assigned to criminal cases. His own deportation hearing would have to be scheduled at some time in the distant future; he would receive notification in the mail.

While he waited for his court date, he and his daughter had managed to recover from the loss of Mohammad's income stream and cobble together a living for themselves. She turned to activism, and he turned to art. Following his most recent heart operation to receive a pacemaker, he had spent almost all of his waking hours babysitting and making art. Their living room wall was now completely full of delicate carvings and wooden sculptures, giving their living room the feel of a gallery displaying a retrospective of an outsider artist's work. He had placed each piece on an individual wooden platform he had mounted on the wall, and he now began to remove them, one by one, to sell. He made trips to Chinatown in downtown Manhattan to watch the street artists draw decorative nameplates for tourists, shaping letters out of exotic birds and flowers, and practiced drawing nameplates at home. He staked out a spot in the competitive pathway in front of the Central Park Zoo, coveted by undocumented artisans from all over the world, and began selling nameplates and figurines for badly needed supplemental income, pushing the household income to over $1,000 a month. He had to rush to beat the other artists, getting there before 7:00 a.m. He participated in street fairs organized by the activist organizations his daughter worked with. And somehow, he managed to forget that he was pending possible deportation.

One windy day in December 2004, he was called for his court date. As he made his way toward 26 Federal Plaza, he hunched his shoulders against the wind, much stronger and icier down here at the southernmost tip of Manhattan island than at home in Queens. Inside, the building was crowded and chaotic. People streamed around him speaking a multitude of languages, clutching file folders and plastic bags stuffed with papers; some were accompanied by lawyers. Here and there, one could see an expression of hesitant defiance or submissive fear on the faces of the undocumented people who, in general, studiously avoided government buildings such as this. Rafiqul was not too worried as he waited for his case to be heard. But as be stood to receive the judge's decision, he could barely keep his knees from folding. The judge hearing his case was kind and respectful, but firm. He could not find any justification for allowing Rafiqul to stay in the United

States, he said. Rafiqul would have to leave the country by February 25, 2005. The judge then wished him good luck.

Rafiqul had hoped that his hearing might be delayed indefinitely, or at least long enough for a change in federal administration to one that might change existing policies regarding the so-called war on terror. He had hoped that the hearing might be canceled as action against the fallout from the call-in program continued. After all, the call-in program itself had been suspended, and further deportation hearings could only continue to overburden a stretched legal system. He had even hoped that, should his hearing take place, the judge might take pity on an old man, who was a heart patient and whose daughter needed his support. Ultimately, even though he had made a conscious decision to live illegally in the United States, Rafiqul believed that if he willingly responded to the US government's call for help in hunting for terrorists, he wouldn't be forced to leave. But Rafiqul would not openly defy a legal ruling to leave. He would leave the country for good in January 2005.

Meanwhile, Nishat was facing another decision about whether to stay in the United States or go to Pakistan. Now that her father was leaving, taking with him both free child care and additional income, the obvious solution to keeping her marriage alive was for Nishat and the children to join Mohammad in Karachi. But Nishat still had many doubts about this option. Her most pressing concern was the future of her children. Both required special medical care and stood to benefit from the small classrooms and special education programs unavailable in Karachi. Ayesha had just started school in October, and she had blossomed under the positive reinforcement and encouragement of the American school system. The three-and-a-half-year-old regularly sang songs from school and practiced writing numbers and letters for fun at home. Nishat also knew that if she went to Karachi, she was closing the door on her own chances for personal growth. As a Bangladeshi woman in Pakistan, she feared that she would be looked down upon in Karachi society. Her grasp of Urdu was proficient but not flawless, and as a woman with two children and no advanced degrees, she knew she would have to spend her life inside Mohammad's house, under the thumb of the senior women of the household. Instead of having an apartment to themselves, where Nishat ruled as queen of the household, her family of four would live in one room in a house they shared with Mohammad's widowed father, his brothers, and their wives and children.

But the deepest, most intimate source of her concern was how Mohammad might have changed. He had been begging her to come join him for over a year, and was beginning to grow angry with her. He had still not found work in Karachi, and she feared what bitterness and disappointment would have done to his personality, what doubt and frustration would have done to his love and faith in her. When she told him that her father would be returning home soon, and that she was still considering staying on in the United States alone, Mohammad did not react well. He could not understand how she could stay on without any male family members to serve as safeguards of her honor. For the first time since he'd been detained, he accused her of infidelity. Then he delivered his ultimatum. If she didn't wind up shop in the United States and join him within one year, he would, he said, be forced to take steps.

Take steps? How dare he threaten to divorce her? Wasn't she the one who was sacrificing her personal happiness to raise the children with all the amenities and opportunities of a life in America? As she worked herself up, she had to acknowledge that he had touched a nerve. Underneath her outrage, she felt a good deal of guilt. The last year and a half of struggle had left her stronger and more empowered, but also conflicted. Her new circumstances forced her to reconcile what she now perceived as competing duties to her husband and her children. In many ways, she had completely redefined her image of a "good wife," often setting her actions at odds with what she was raised to value. Before Mohammad's detention, she saw her wifely duties as running the household. Now, although she would still be ashamed to let any man cook or clean in her house, her fundamental duties had changed. Her duty to her husband's cause took her out of the home and into the public sphere. She appeared in newspaper articles with her face and head uncovered, denouncing the US government's practices. Doing this caused her to feel a certain amount of guilt, which she expressed by saying that her husband had probably been tortured for what she said to the media. Her activist work also brought her to work closely with men and unmarried couples. She even later said that she expected her children to date in high school and probably outside of the religion; after all, this was America. These changes in her psychology and worldview made it possible for her to imagine a life as a single mother while her husband lived in another country.

Certainly, her mother had lived apart from her father, but not by her own choice. Nishat, on the other hand, had chosen not to follow her husband. But material well-being was far more important to her than the fear of scandal and shame, and yes, more important than love. In her heart, Nishat knew that she was better off here, even as a social outcast and without a husband. She cursed her fate and denounced the United States in the press, but she still had a spacious apartment with matching furniture and cable TV in both the bedroom and living room. The day her husband threatened divorce, Nishat rededicated herself to Islam. She locked up all of her short skirts and short-sleeved tops. She wouldn't get rid of them quite yet, but she did put them all away. She stopped wearing makeup and began wearing a headscarf each time she left the house. She began praying five times each day, and reading from the Qur'an each morning and evening. And she abandoned the possibility of joining her husband in Karachi. She took down the photo of Mohammad with Ayesha from the refrigerator and trained Ayesha to tell guests that she was from Bangladesh instead of Pakistan.

Then, she steeled herself to begin looking for help again. The organization she'd been working with had not been able to help her keep her father in the United States, so she would reach out to other organizations for help. And she would return to the media.

It is December 20, 2004, and Nishat has a full day ahead of her. She has an appointment with the director of a charitable Muslim organization and her interview will be published in the *New York Times*. This is a different organization from the one she has relied most heavily upon, but Nishat has frantically been reaching out for help from all directions. It has been three weeks since her father accepted a voluntary departure judgment, and three weeks since she last spoke with her husband after he threatened to divorce her.

Rafiqul has stopped working in Central Park and has been spending as much time as possible with the children. He hasn't told Nishat, but he has been paying secret visits to Bangladeshi friends he's made over the years, handing out generous cash gifts. Nishat would be furious if she knew, but Rafiqul has never been able to break his habit of giving.

For the moment, Nishat is peaceful, enjoying the still of the early morning. She is wearing one of her standard house uniforms: a T-shirt over a long skirt, gold necklace and bangles, anklets on both feet, rings on several fingers, hair loose. Her T-shirt reads "November 2," a reminder of the latest national general election, in which George W. Bush was elected to his second term. A secondary issue in the campaign had been illegal immigration, and now many immigrant rights groups, including the one Nishat works with, fear that the goal of mass legalizations and amnesty will be unreachable. Nishat literally wears her new political consciousness on her sleeve.

The radiators gasp and hiss. The children are both in bed, feverish from the radiators' heat and from their inevitable winter colds. The television is dark, and the early-morning light plays across Rafiqul's gallery of plywood and balsa sculptures, large parts of which have been sold off in the last few months. Rafiqul sits on the couch in a lungi and drooping undershirt, sipping his tea. Nishat steps over the low plywood baby barrier Rafiqul built in the kitchen doorway, carrying her father's breakfast into the living room, her anklet bells jingling as she walks. A few minutes later, she disappears into her room and reemerges in a navy blue suit she bought on sale, down to $35 from $199, a blue scarf wrapped around her head and neck. She has removed her jewelry and makeup. She puts the breakfast dishes in the kitchen sink and goes back into the bedroom to tuck her children in and kiss them each lingeringly. She grabs a folder and a bag and heads out the door. With her petite frame and slightly awkward movements in a suit, she looks like a schoolgirl going for college interviews. She likes the feel of a suit, and she has high aspirations. She knows that she doesn't have the immigration status or qualifications for anything but under-the-counter menial or service jobs, but she wants more for herself. She will go on telling these activists and journalists that she can't work poorly paying restaurant or bodega jobs because of the high cost of child care, but her little secret with herself is this: "I wasted six month of my life two dollar an hour job. People say there is so much work in Jackson Heights, in restaurant there, but I don't want to do it! Even if I don't have kids, I wouldn't want to do it!" She believes she deserves a chance at a real job, a high-paying job in an office or hospital, where she can make $15 an hour. But those jobs don't hire undocumented people.

She is animated as she walks down the street, waving to neighbors as she waits for crosswalk signals to change. In the subway, she runs into a Bangladeshi woman she knows, and the two joke and chat in bright chirpy tones until she reaches her stop. Just outside of the charitable organization's office, which is attached to a local mosque, she stops. She takes a deep breath, stoops her shoulders, and lets her eyes fill with tears. Showtime.

She walks into the building with short, hesitant steps, looking around with widened eyes. In a tremulous voice, she asks to speak with the director of the organization. She later says "The thing about America, in here they're not gonna let you fall, not like Bangladesh, where if you don't have father or husband you starve . . . but you have to do like that to get any help." If she acts strong and defiant, as strong-willed and assertive as she really is, she believes that the people she is entreating for help would not recognize her as being in need. She also knows that she would not have managed to survive without any income if she had not been savvy enough to figure out where and how to find assistance. When she is seated in his office, the director of the organization leans close, his eyes full of compassion and solutions.

"Has he provided you with any child support payment?" he asks about Mohammad.

"No," Nishat replies, glancing quickly at her hands and then at the corner of the table to express first shame then helplessness.

"That's disappointing," says the director. Failure to provide child support is grounds for separation, he says, adding that any imam would be sure to agree. Nishat nods eagerly, hungry for answers. "But I don't want to advise you to pursue that course if. . . ." His voice trails off.

He resettles himself from a listening to an action posture, and begins to detail different options. She can write letters to elected officials, he says.

Unfortunately, officials in Queens are not as responsive as those in Brooklyn, but she should write the letters anyway. His organization would be willing to write a letter to Mohammad, reminding him of his duties, he offers. Perhaps he could be convinced to join her in a third country?

"He doesn't call me three weeks, he say he don't even want to think about coming until we are there." Tears which have gathered in her eyes rush down her cheeks, making big dark spots on her headscarf.

"Sometimes husbands change after detention. There is a lot of confusion and shame," he tilts his head and pauses, looking warmly at Nishat for a few long seconds. He concedes that child-support levels might be too high for someone from Pakistan to pay. Nishat nods slowly.

He discusses a wide array of possible solutions to her many problems. Her primary concern is money, so he names several possible income streams. She can babysit at any number of local mosques or she can work from home. If the organization can find a way to provide her with a computer, she might be able to look into data entry, medical billing, or translations. It would be difficult to find work in these areas which did not require proof of legal residence, but inquiries could be made. Next, he discusses ways that she can maintain medical care for her children. He advises her on how to seek out emergency Medicaid, which free clinic still won't ask after her status, and which hospitals she should go to for emergencies. He gives her the name of a doctor, who is a Muslim woman herself, who helps his organization provide pediatric and gynecological services to women in need. He asks her to list the different types of assistance she is receiving and gives her several names to contact: a woman outreach worker with his organization, doctors, social workers, contact people in partner organizations in Canada.

Just as Nishat is preparing to leave, the director remembers that he has a copy of today's *New York Times*, which carries a critique of the Special Registration program. The director referred the journalist who wrote it to Nishat. The article opens with a description of Nishat's father, and Nishat's story figures prominently in the piece. She has been quoted, and in the top left corner of the page, there is a large picture of her sobbing, with her mouth wide open, her eyes squeezed shut, and her face glistening with tears. Nishat walks around to the side of the desk and leans over the picture. The two of them gaze at the picture approvingly. It is a powerful picture, they agree, and will be sure to win some attention from influential people. The director hopes that he will be able to help other families through public outcry generated from this piece, but Nishat hopes this article will win her father a reprieve and set her on the path to amnesty. After she takes her leave and is back outside, she stops at the nearest bodega to pick up her own copy of the article. She stands just outside the front door and pores over the article, looking for her own name. After a few moments, she snaps the paper shut. As she makes her way back to the subway, she fumes to herself that the article didn't say more about her suffering, didn't openly state that she should be given amnesty, and won't get her anywhere. She is frustrated that this article won't keep her father with her. "It didn't say nothing!" she mutters.

Before going home, she goes to visit a family friend, a lady she calls "auntie" who used to live in the apartment below her, who housed Nishat and her father during their first hard weeks in New York. Last year, while Nishat was slowly losing her material stability and married life, auntie moved into a nice single family house in Jamaica, Queens. And, although no one openly acknowledges it, auntie has been keeping her distance since Nishat's troubles began. She blames this on the move and on the demands on her time, caring for both her husband and teenaged daughter, but Nishat has gotten the message. She won't be able to ask auntie for money, sponsorship, a place to stay, a job, or babysitting help. Still, Nishat rarely has the chance to visit someone who knows and loves her, and she is making the most of her day out of the house. She walks down the tree-lined avenues and admires the yards and cars in front of the houses she passes. Inside, she sips tea and munches on snacks while auntie looks at the photograph in the newspaper. Auntie's husband finishes his meal and joins the ladies in the living room. The three gather around the newspaper, gesturing and discussing with great intensity what such a photograph could do for Nishat. The husband retreats into the bedroom to get ready for work, and the two ladies quickly run out of things to talk about. On her way out of the house, Nishat stops to touch the thick, dark green leaves of a chest-high lime tree growing in the hall. She turns to auntie in amazement; this tree grew from the seed of a lime Nishat brought from Bangladesh, and gave as a gift to auntie when it was shin high. Nishat reflects on how well the tree has flourished since its arrival from Bangladesh, and briefly thinks of the girl that planted that seed. Then she tightens her head-scarf and steps out onto the street.

Ultimately, Nishat will not pursue any of the director's suggestions. She will collect advice and ideas like trinkets, but she will not take any job, learn computer skills, convince her husband to seek third-country asylum, or even divorce him. In the coming year, her father will leave, she will sublet part of her apartment to a woman from Bangladesh, she will continue with her activism, Ayesha will go to school and Rasha will learn to walk. And Nishat will hold out for amnesty.

Rafiqul left a month later, on January 18, 2005. It was a bright, frosty day. A stinging wind whipped around the corner of their building, knocking pedestrians breathless and tossing dirty snow in their faces. On the side-walks, people clutched their coats at their throats and butted the air with their head. Not a hospitable day, Rafiqul's last day in the United States.

Much had changed in the apartment. Rafiqul's artwork had been removed from the wall, leaving only pocks and scars in the paint. On the weekend before his departure, he built a thin wooden dividing wall to make an extra bedroom in the living room. In the thin balsa wall he built a door-way, framed with a frosted floral wallpaper border, and thumbtacked pen caricature drawings of Rasha and Ayesha on either side. His twin bed and paint-spattered workbench now were in the new bedroom, which Nishat would show to potential subletters. Until hours before Rafiqul's departure, controversy reigned over whether Nishat should rent to a man or a woman. Rafiqul entreated Nishat to avoid scandal and rent to a woman, but Nishat complained that a woman would take up too much room in the refrigerator and too much time in the shower, and would be moody and territorial. A man would help around the house, eat the food she made anyway, and maybe even pay a little extra for it. Three years ago, she never would have considered living without her husband and renting part of her apartment to another man. Rafiqul knew his daughter well enough to worry that she might be considering remarrying for a green card, and his protective, traditional ways couldn't be reconciled with such a possibility.

But this conflict was just part of the mounting tension building up in the apartment in Rafiqul's final weeks in the United States. Just four days before he was to leave, two plainclothes FBI agents showed up unannounced, looking for Mohammad. Nishat was so rattled when she opened the door that when one of the agents asked her if she was Mohammad Junaid's wife, she answered no. When he repeated the question, she managed to squeak out a yes, and that he had been deported in 2003. Someone with her husband's name and date of birth had been using a computer at the University of Alabama, and the agents were investigating. She told them that she had broken contact with him and rushed to close the door. Nishat had not spoken to Mohammad in nearly two months, and the mention of his name, the sudden intrusion of the agents on the eve of her father's departure, all came together to heighten Nishat's sense of fear and anxiety.

The afternoon before Rafiqul's departure, he and Nishat withdrew from each other to mourn. They both knew that they would never see each other again unless Nishat failed to make it in New York. A slender shard of light sliced across the living room floor and splintered over an uneven stack of rope-bound boxes and suitcases. Rafiqul had told Nishat that he was resting for the journey ahead, but he lay for the last time on his sunken twin mattress, weeping in silence. On the other side of the makeshift living room wall Nishat sat on the love seat, twisting and untwisting her feet, chanting from the thick, leather-bound Qur'an open on her lap. A teardrop hung from the tip of her nose. She wiped it away with the lacy edge of her blue headscarf, and rocked back and forth to the rhythm of the verse. In the bedroom, Rasha slept soundly. Ayesha played in the living room, jumping on and off the other sofa.

Within a few hours, people began to arrive in waves. Nishat had summoned people to help carry Rafiqul's baggage and to arrange for transportation to and from the airport. But the main purpose for their presence was that Nishat had reached far and wide for people to come and give her a feeling of family and community at a moment when she was losing the person who had brought her to the United States, and who had been her entire family for the last seven years. She had recruited nearly thirty people to accompany her to the airport, with five cars among them, and eight people to stay with her through the night.

First, Nishat's cousin arrived with his young, fashionable wife and four-year-old son. Then, a friend from her days behind the Dunkin' Donuts counter arrived, a young Muslim man from India. While her cousin and his family settled into the living room to watch Bollywood videos, her friend positioned himself by the side of the stove to help stir a huge pot of chicken *biryani*, a spiced rice dish, which Nishat had made in preparation for the masses of people she had mobilized to help her through this evening and night.

Then, the members of the activist organization that had been supporting her for the previous year and a half began arriving. They were immigrants and children of immigrants from India and Bangladesh, all in their twenties. They fell into two categories; one cluster of youth organizers, who were themselves in their very early twenties, dressed in the standard urban youth uniform of puffy jackets, attractive sneakers, detailed makeup, and tight jeans for the girls, and loose, crisply ironed jeans for the boys; another group of women in their late twenties who had been involved in social justice initiatives for some time, wearing simple clothes, low-maintenance haircuts, and no makeup. The youth organizers chattered away about favorite Bollywood actors, Bikram Yoga, cars, and TV shows, and the social justice activists were quiet and industrious, attending to the babies, serving up dishes of food, discussing carpooling arrangements and answering the telephone. Rasha woke and was carried out into the living room, where Ayesha and her cousin were playing and fighting raucously. Nishat disappeared into her bedroom and emerged a few moments later in her navy blue suit, clutching her elbows.

Meanwhile, another cousin and his family arrived and stood uncomfortably in the entranceway, dressed in festive clothes. Following close behind, a group of Bangladeshi women, some covered and some in brightly colored Bangladeshi *shalwar kameez*, with a collection of teenaged daughters in postures of combined sulkiness and respect, gathered in the entranceway. For a few minutes, Nishat smiled and made pleasant conversation with the women, many of whom she'd seen rarely since her wedding day.

Then, suddenly, it was time to go. Nishat promptly burst into tears. The women looked uncomfortably down at their hands, the teenaged girls turned away, and Nishat's auntie took Nishat's face in her hands. "You shouldn't cry, come on." The social justice activists and youth organizers gathered at the edge of the circle of women and looked on, silently. The rough bark of Nishat's sobs mingled dissonantly with the shrill noise of the TV and playing children coming from the living room. Rafiqul stood in the hallway outside of the apartment, his hands thrust deep into his jean pockets, blinking hard and fast at the elevator doors.

Nishat pulled away from auntie's grasp and crouched down to call Ayesha and Rasha to her. "Tell nana goodbye," she gasped, her voice heavy and gruff.

Ayesha grew confused and upset. She wrapped her arms around Nishat's neck and looked around at the tight circle of legs, and began to cry. "I miss you, mommy," she gulped, and began kissing her mother's wet cheek.

Slowly, the crowd dispersed and different people piled into different cars. Rafiqul sat in the front seat of a car and looked out of the window, chewing his lip.

The caravan of cars, vans, and SUVs pulled up at John F. Kennedy Airport just before 8:00 p.m. People thronged in front of the terminal entrance with piles of luggage and boxes tied with rope and milled beneath a gigantic Calder mobile swaying next to a vast, illuminated American flag. Rows of airline counters filled the hall. A long line coiled back, forth, and back again in front of the Biman Bangladesh counter, and a guard stood checking tickets and passport at its end. Rafiqul eyed the guard nervously and quickly rebuked a younger cousin who started to take pictures of him inside the terminal. While her cousin held a place in the line, Rafiqul and Nishat huddled with her entourage. She began to cry again, and her older cousin chided her in a soft, stern voice. "Come on Happy," he said, calling the weeping woman by her childhood nickname, "Chchch, chch, stop it."

Rafiqul broke away to go register with the immigration officials in the terminal, so that records would show that he had voluntarily departed well before his final deadline. The small crowd, with Nishat at its center, moved to the other side of the airline counter to wait for him. He returned a few minutes later, pale and trembling slightly. The official registering him told him that he was under arrest, and showed him that he had been entered on the computer system as slated for forced deportation. Rafiqul said that he tried to argue that he had only been ordered to accept voluntary departure, and that he would not have to be escorted out of the country in handcuffs. Rafiqul told Nishat that the official finally threw his passport across the counter and said "Now get out of here and never come back." Regardless of what exactly the security guard told Rafiqul, he later remembered this final encounter as how he was summarily dismissed from the United States, a refined engineer and artist treated like dirt by a roughneck.

The group made its way slowly toward the security checkpoint, beyond which only ticketed passengers could pass, and waited until the flight was scheduled to begin boarding. Rafiqul slowly nodded and wrapped his arm around his daughter. She pursed her lips and said good-bye, walking forward with him a few steps toward the security gate. Her supporters remained behind, to give her space to bid her father farewell. As Rafiqul disappeared behind the row of security guards and metal detectors, a deep, throaty roar emerged from Nishat's mouth and she collapsed on the terminal floor in a dead faint.

Her friend from Dunkin' Donuts carried her to a bank of chairs while one of the social justice activists splashed bottled water on her face. When Nishat revived, she began sobbing. Her cousins both shushed her, childing her to stop crying, but several of the activists and organizers told them to let her cry in slightly moralistic tones. Nishat suddenly burst out, "I am all alone! They have taken everything from me!"

A group of people supported her to the escalator, where she passed out again. Her cousin's wife suggested taking her to a paramedic, saying "She has an eating disability, she hasn't eaten all day," but one of the youth organizers jumped in with the suggestion that "She doesn't trust authorities." Nishat, as if on cue, began waving her hand, saying "I hate them, I hate them, no police!" The activists and organizers murmured sympathetically, "No one's going to make you go," "Don't worry, let's just take her home." She passed out and was revived twice more before arriving home.

When the group reached the apartment, Ayesha rushed to the door, having forgotten to be sad, once again bubbling with smiles and stories of games she had played. Nishat collapsed against the wall and dragged Ayesha toward her. Clutching her close against her body, Nishat sobbed into her mouth, "We're alone now. Do you miss nana? Do you miss him? We'll never see nana no more!" She held Ayesha until the little girl was also sobbing in great hiccups, her face bright red.

Later that night, after Nishat had called her mother and Ayesha had forgotten to be sad again, Nishat returned to being queen of her domain. She had lost first one, then another king, and now the apartment was her home, all hers. She reheated the biryani and made beds all over the apartment,then heated milk for her guests. She was a warm and gracious hostess. As her guests slept, she stayed awake to mourn her losses, but also to savor her freedom.

Nishat lasted for another year before she folded, gave up, and left the United States behind. She blamed her decision on the random searches in the subways, the reelection of George W. Bush, the complete loss of her autonomy. But in the end she chose her husband. She said it was America closing in on her, her world growing smaller and smaller. But at her most honest, she said she was afraid of Allah's wrath if she turned her back on her children's father. She knew that if she lost him and America closed in on her any more, she would lose her only means of survival. It was time to cut her losses in America and accept that he was the only hope she and her children had.

Before May 2003, Mohammad and Nishat had both been employed, independent, and contributing to New York City's economy and tax base. After many years of work, Rafiqul had been entering retirement, providing his daughter with child care and a link to her homeland. After Mohammad's detention, Nishat worked until her child was born, and Rafiqul began selling his artwork to help maintain the economic independence of their household. After Rafiqul left, Nishat began living entirely on public and community assistance. Her monthly income broke down this way:

$300 housing subsidy

$450 stipend from a local immigrants' rights group

$200 Supplemental Security Income (SSI) benefits for Ayesha's disability

$270 food stamps

Why would an undocumented woman whose husband had been deported, whose father had been asked to leave voluntarily, whose children were still toddlers, who had no college education and no support system left want to stay on in the United States? Nishat had gone before the press, openly denouncing the United States and publicizing her illegal status, so even though no steps had been taken to deport the families of deported participants in the Special Registration call-in program, Nishat now had effectively blown her cover.

She stayed because she believed that she could make it. It was that simple. Her emergent political consciousness had brought with it certain expectations. She had learned a great deal of social justice rhetoric and taken certain risks to expose her family to public scrutiny, and she believed that she might be able to win amnesty for her family with her rhetoric and actions. Nishat was no more tenacious than many people who brave war, disaster, bureaucracy, and doubt to fight to correct the iniquities of the world. While this education in social justice empowered her to stand up and fight for her principles, it was too rapid to provide her with a broader context for movements dedicated to social change. She only engaged in activism to achieve very specific goals for her family, not to create a dialectic between those with power and those without. But although her limited education in activism allowed her to develop unrealistic expectations and therefore left her disappointed, it also gave her an opportunity to develop into a strong, self-possessed, at times eloquent spokesperson for social change. She was unique among many who shared her experience as women left behind by deported Muslim men after September 11. She fought her own shortcomings and choices, exposed herself to new experiences and to criticism, and endangered her marriage and her belief system to fight, as clichéd as it may seem, for her American dream.

Until the day she left, just after Eid-ul-Fitr in November 2005, she continued to hope for amnesty and give interviews in the media. She had gone back to wearing Western clothes, taken off her headscarf, stopped praying five times a day, and this year, for the first time, she had not fasted during Ramadan. The week before she left, she entertained her new cavalry of friends and colleagues with an almost giddy charm, handing out Ramadan sweets and American cookies. On one visit, an immigration attorney who had consulted with her on her father's case told her about a landmark decision just taken in a circuit court, in which a Mexican woman with a special-needs child had won individual amnesty to stay. Nishat fell into silence.

After a beat, the lawyer said, "Well, you had to make a decision."

Nishat misunderstood and broke into a loud, hearty laugh. "Decision? What decision! I already make decision! Now, I go!" She smiled serenely and sipped her lemon zinger tea, now optimistic at the thought of going home.

By the time she decided to leave, she had put her health, her marriage, and her hope for the future in great jeopardy. But worst of all, she had destroyed her relationship with the social justice organization that first supported her then later gave her a job as a community organizer. When the organization's director had asked her to stay longer hours without pay, Nishat had accused her of hypocritically exploiting her, shaming the director, a respected community organizer and social justice advocate, into tears. Without that support, her self-esteem, feeling of belonging and, of course, savings dwindled rapidly away. She was well aware that she was almost thirty, with no education and two children, bound for a new country where her husband had been doubting her fidelity for two years. Her father had gambled on her future by pulling her out of her university program in Dhaka, and she herself had gambled on love as enough of a basis for marriage between two undocumented people in a country that had, on occasion, turned against its illegal population. They had lost.

But hope springs eternal with Nishat. She put her faith in her husband and swallowed her apprehension. She left for Karachi in a brand new, knee-length black dress with matching shoes and jewelry. She would not wear a shalwar kameez and headscarf and arrive cowed and ashamed to beg her husband for mercy. She would hold her head high, with her children dressed to the nines and loyal to her, and she would expect her husband to treat her like the queen of the house, still.

Nishat had been thrust into personal agency by crisis, when the person who had decided for her and defined her role in life had been removed from the country and from her life. Until that point, she had given little thought to her own life choices, acting on the recommendation of people who had authority over her or on the instinctive desire to be loved. She found herself defining herself and constructing her identity as she struggled with her descent from a secure middle-class life with a loving husband and a supporting father into the life of a single mother with no qualifications or legal rights fighting for welfare funding and the well-being of her children. Hers was a purely existential struggle, not a struggle of ideas or ideologies or competing interests. She drew on a variety of political and cultural modalities to define her own personal losses in a broader scale, in the hope that she might generate enough political will from powerful people to win security and documentation in the United States.

She only began to develop her personal narrative after the clash-of-civilizations paradigm had emerged, and it became a prominent feature of her life story. Although she did not often refer to the West as the enemy of Muslims, she often complained that her circumstances had so suddenly changed as a result of broader geopolitical troubles. In her mind, she was simply collateral damage in a larger battle. She developed her narrative solely as a means to combat an existential threat to her livelihood, and when it was clear that she had lost, that it was time to capitulate and go home, she ran out of stories to tell. As she prepared to go back to her husband, to a country that was not her home, she toyed with the idea of writing a novel about her struggles, but she knew that she never would. Instead, she said that the whole point of telling her story had been to win amnesty, and since she had failed at that, there was no point in talking about the past any more.

EPILOGUE

In 2006, Sharif's professional and personal ambitions finally came together, and for the first time in a long time, he was completely happy with his life in London. He was in the center of an active and increasingly visible British Arab lobby, was writing and speaking out on the issues that moved him more than ever before, and was able to support himself by pursuing his passions. Arab Media Watch, recovering from having its Web site hacked, was enjoying growing fame and success in its efforts, and had joined in fruitful partnerships with both British- and Arab-led lobbying bodies that were making political inroads on behalf of London's 300,000 Arabs. He had also become an editor for Britain's first glossy culture magazine for, by, and about British Arabs. Although in 2006 the Israeli military invaded Lebanon and launched a bombing campaign in Beirut, devastating the city one week after his sister had celebrated her wedding there, and although living conditions in Iraq continued to spiral downward, these tragedies only bolstered his dedication to his work and the need for his organization's voice. By year's end, Sharif was rapidly approaching the prime of his career. He had risked professional stability to pursue his passion, and had ended up with it all: a fulfilling career, a happy home life, and a perfectly realized British Arab identity. After a long and frustrating search, it seemed that he had found his way home to British Arabia.

Sukriye spent much of 2006 recovering from the financial, professional, and emotional strain of the previous year. After a year of outsized expenses on bureaucratic procedure, travel, phone bills, and wedding festivities, she was out of a job and, for the first time in her life, on welfare. But she had finally found love, and peace had settled in her heart. Although her liveli- hood was more precarious than it had ever been before, she faced the future with hopeful optimism. But the couple still had many hurdles to pass before they could consider themselves safe. Nezir's status in Germany remained precarious. Although he had gained admission into Germany, his applica- tion for long-term residency and a work permit was still pending. He had begun to take German language courses, at forty-three trying to navigate through a new language and a new culture, but was still far from fluent at year end. Meanwhile, Sukriye and Nezir found themselves retreating into a small circle of Kurdish friends, activists, and intellectuals who shared their interests and language. Sukriye never consciously chose to withdraw from many of her German friends, but her newly married life was full, and she and Nezir also subconsciously accepted that they simply felt more at home among their own people. Sukriye eventually found herself a fulfilling job working on immigration issues in the office of an elected representative to the Berlin Senate, initiated in response to the new German immigration law that had come into effect in January 2005, and she launched several side projects, presentations, and publications relating to her earlier research on the Yezidis and violence against women, but Nezir faced the future with a certain amount of trepidation. In 2007, to their great relief, Nezir's applica- tion for long-term residency was approved, and he began to look for oppor- tunities to publish in the Kurdish language, both within Europe and throughout the world. As they looked to the future and shared the past, it was clear that their lives had settled into a happy and safe Kurdish world within Berlin.

Nishat had arrived in Karachi in November 2005, and by February of the following year she had fled her husband's home to her parents in Bangladesh. Upon her arrival, the husband she had loved from afar and unintentionally spurned for two years forced her to cover herself completely and refused her permission to leave the house. Within a week, he had begun beating her and Ayesha, out of his frustration with Nishat's inability to adjust to her new circumstances as a second-class figure in a compound household run by his elder brother, and with Ayesha's constant clamoring for the school and life and even snacks she had left behind in America. When she arrived at her parents' home in Bangladesh, Nishat found her father housebound by complications from his heart condition and lingering depression, and a mother whose declarations of love were tempered with expressions of disappointment. Her parents told her that, although they wished they could support her, they were so strapped for money in their old age that they would have to sell their house, and that she would simply have to return to her husband. With a heavy heart and dry eyes, she returned to her husband to accept her fate. So it was that the smartest, most capable Islam child ended up at thirty as a prisoner in her home in a strange, hostile land, an uneducated mother of two, without prospects or a way out. Until her last day in the United States, she had still hoped to salvage her life, but she had feared what would come.

From Nishat's Journal

October 13, 2005

Jaan I am coming to you. But please don't give me any hard time. Definately I also deserve some nice happiest life. Can you give it to me? I don't think so. Because in here you was only mine But over there you with every body. You or not gonna listen to me. Now I have to listen to you all the time.

I already had too much hard time in my time. I don't want to see or take any more hard time.

Over there you gonna conerl on me screem with me front every body and May be you gonna hit me too. That's gonna be happen. And I have cry my whole rest of life.

CHARACTERS

PALESTINE

Sharif Aref and Inaam Nashashibi, parents of Hikmat and one other
  son, two daughters

Jamil and Nura Abdelahad, parents of Muna (Hikmat's wife) and one
  other daughter

Hikmat and Muna Nishashibi, parents of Sharif, Nura, and Omar

KURDISTAN

Mehmet and Adla Dogan, parents of Abdul Rehman, Ramziye, Fauziye,
  Abdul Kader, Abdul Wehab, Celile, Abdul Karim (d. at age 12),
  Hasbiye, Sukriye, and Abdul Selam

Sukriye Dogan marries Nezir Suleiman

BANGLADESH

Rafiqul and Jorna Islam, parents of Farhat Jahan, Nighat Jahan, Nishat
  Jahan, and Kamrul

Nishat marries Mohammad Junaid

Nishat and Mohammad Junaid, parents of Ayesha and Rasha

PRONUNCIATION OF CHARACTERS' NAMES

Jamil Abdelahad: juh-MEEL ab-duh-LEH-had

Nura Abdelahad: NOO-ruh ab-duh-LEH-had

Muna Nashashibi: MU-nuh nah-shuh-SHEE-bee

Maha Abdelahad: MA-huh ab-duh-LEH-had

Sharif Nashashibi: shuh-REEF nah-shuh-SHEE-bee

Inaam Nashashibi: i-NAHM nah-shuh-SHEE-bee

Hikmat Nashashibi: HIK-muht nah-shuh-SHEE-bee

Mehmet Dogan: MEH-met DOH-an

Adla Dogan: AHD-lah DOH-an

Sukriye Dogan: shu-KREE-yuh DOH-an

Hasbiye Dogan: has-BEE-yuh DOH-an

Celile Dogan: juh-LEE-luh DOH-an

Nezir Suleiman: NEH-zeer su-LAY-man

Rafiqul Islam: RAF-i-kul is-LAHM

Jorna Islam: JOR-na is-LAHM

Nishat Islam: nih-SHAHT is-LAHM

Mohammad Junaid: mo-HAH-mehd ju-NAYD

Ayesha Junaid: ah-YEE-shuh ju-NAYD

Rasha Junaid: RUH-shah ju-NAYD

SOURCES

BOOKS AND ARTICLES

Ahmad, Feroz. *The Making of Modern Turkey.* New York: Routledge, 1993.

Aktas, Mehmet, Birgit Ammann, Carsten Borck, Sukriye Dogan, Siamend Hajo, Eva Savelsberg, and Helim Yusiv. *Das Kurdische Berlin.* Berlin: Auslaenderbeauftragte des Senats, 2003.

Aleinikoff, Thomas Alexander, David A. Martin, and Hiroshi Motomura. *Immigration and Citizenship: Process and Policy.* Fourth edition. St. Paul, Minn.: West Group, 2001.

Ali, Monica. *Brick Lane.* New York: Scribner, 2003.

Alt, Jörg, and Ralph Fodor. *Rechtlos?: Menschen ohne Papiere.* Karlsruhe: von Loeper Literaturverlag im Adriane Buchdienst, 2001.

Ameli, Saied Reza. *Globalization, Americanization and British Muslim Identity.* London: Islamic College for Advanced Studies Press, 2002.

Ameli, Saied R., Manzur Elahi, and Arzu Merali. *Dual Citizenship: British, Islamic or Both?—Obligation, Recognition, Respect and Belonging.* London: Islamic Human Rights Commission, 2004, available at www.ihrc.org.

———. *Social Discrimination: Across the Muslim Divide.* London: Islamic Human Rights Commission, 2004, available at www.ihrc.org.

Ammann, Birgit. *Kurden in Europa: Ethnizitaet und Diaspora.* Vol. 4 of *Kurdologie,* edited by Carsten Borck, Eva Savelsberg, and Siamend Hajo. Muenster: Lit Verlag, 2000.

Ammann, Renate, and Barbara von Neumann-Cosel, eds. *Berlin: Eine Stadt im Zeichen der Migration.* Berlin: VWP Verlag fuer Wissenschaftliche Publikationen, 1997.

Anderson, Benedict. *Imagined Communities: Reflections on the Origin and Spread of Nationalism.* Revised and extended edition. London: Verso, 1991.

Ansari, Humayun. *Muslims in Britain.* London: Minority Rights Group International, 2002, available at www.minorityrights.org.

Aufzeichnung sur Auslaenderpolitik und zum Auslaenderrecht in der Bundesrepublik Deutschland. Bonn: Bundesministerium des Innern, 1997.

Battis, Ulrich, Dmitris Tsatsos, and Dmitris Stefanou, eds. *Europaeische Integration und nationals Verfassungsrecht: Ertraege eines Forschungsprojektes an der Fernuniversitaet in Hagen* (Sondereinband). Baden-Baden: Nomos Verlaggesellschaft, 1995.

Bericht zur Integrations- und Auslaenderpolitik. Berlin: Auslaenderbeauftragte des Senats, various years.

"Berlin—Zuwanderung, gesellschaftliche Probleme, politische Ansaetze." In *Migration.* Berlin: Senatverwaltung fuer Stadtentwicklung, Umweltschutz und Technologie und Fakultaetinstitut Sozialwissenschaften, Humboldt Universitaet, 1995.

Bill, James A., and Robert Springborg. *Politics in the Middle East.* Fifth edition. New York: Longman, 2000.

Bird, Christiane. *A Thousand Sighs, a Thousand Revolts: Journeys in Kurdistan.* New York: Ballantine, 2004.

Brech, Joachim, and Laura Vanhue, eds. *Migration: Stadt im Wandel.* Berlin: VWP Wohnbund Publikationen, 1997.

Bruinessen, Martin van. *Agha, Shaikh and State: On the Social and Political Organization of Kurdistan.* Utrecht: Proefschrift, Rijksuniversiteit, 1978.

———. *Kurdish Ethno-nationalism versus Nation-building States.* Istanbul: Isis Press, 2000.

Butterfield, Jeanne. *Practice Advisory: What Does the Patriot Act Mean for Immigrants?* Washington, D.C.: American Immigration Law Foundation, 2001.

Cole, David. *Enemy Alien: Double Standards and Constitutional Freedoms in the War on Terrorism.* New York: New Press, 2003.

Cole, David, and James X. Dempsey. *Terrorism and the Constitution.* New York: New Press, 2002.

Dahbour, Omar, and Micheline R. Ishay, eds. *The Nationalism Reader.* Atlantic Highlands, N.J.: Humanities Press, 1995.

Daniels, Roger. *Guarding the Golden Door: American Immigration Policy and Immigrants since 1882.* New York: Hill and Wang, 2004.

Demir, Mustafa, and Ergun Sonmez. *Die anderen Deutschen: 40 Jahre Arbeitsmiration— Von Gastarbeitern zur nationalen Minderheit.* Berlin: Verlag fuer Wissenschaft und Bildung, 2001.

Esposito, John L., and Francois Burgot. *Modernizing Islam: Religion in the Public Sphere in Europe and the Middle East.* New Brunswick: Rutgers University Press, 2003.

Feinblatt, John. "Concerning New York City Executive Order 124." *Statement of John Feinblatt, Criminal Justice Coordinator, City of New York City, Before the Subcommittee on Immigration, Border Security and Claims.* Washington, D.C.: House Committee on the Judiciary, U.S. House of Representatives, February 27, 2003.

Gardner, Katy. *Global Migrants, Local Lives: Travel and Transformation in Rural Bangladesh.* Oxford: Clarendon, 1995.

Glass, D.V. *Population: Policies and Movements in Europe.* [1940] London: Frank Cass 1967.

Gregory, Frank, and Paul Wilkinson. "Riding Pillion for Tackling Terrorism Is a High-Risk Policy." In *Security, Terrorism, and the UK*, edited by Christopher Browning. London: Royal Institute of International Affairs, 2005.

Gunter, Michael M. *The Kurds and the Future of Turkey*. New York: Saint Martin's Press, 1997.

Gupta, Anjan. "How to Gain Influence and Achieve Political Power in Britain." Paper presented at Group 3, Participation in British Political Life. Third Arab Communities Conference, Arab Club of Britain, London, 1999.

Hafez, Kai, ed. *Der Islam und der Westen: Anstiftung zum Dialog*. Frankfurt am Main: Fischer, 1997.

———. "The West and Islam in the Mass Media: Cornerstones for a New International Culture of Communication in the 21st Century." ZEI Discussion Papers, Center for European Integration Studies, University of Bonn, 2000.

Harrington, Paul, and Andrew Sum, with Sheila Palma. "The Impacts of the Recession of 2001 and the Jobless Recovery of 2002 on the Native Born and Immigrant Workforce of the United States." Unpublished paper, Center for Labor Market Studies, Northeastern University, Boston, 2003.

Hunter, S. T., ed. *Islam, Europe's Second Religion: The New Social, Cultural, and Political Landscape*. Westport, Conn.: Praeger, 2002.

Huntington, Samuel P. *The Clash of Civilizations: Remaking of the World Order*. New York: Simon and Schuster, 1996.

Hutter, Franz-Josef, Anje Mihr, and Carsten Tessmer, eds. *Menschen auf der Flucht*. Opladen: Leske und Budrich, 1999.

Jacoby, Tamar, ed. *Reinventing the Melting Pot: The New Immigrants and What It Means to Be American*. New York: Basic Books, 2004.

al-Jalili, Ismail. *Arab Population in the U.K.: An Ethnic Profile*. Stamford, U.K.: National Association of British Arabs, 2004.

Jassat, Iqbal. "Bombings Fuel Islamophobia but Media Silent on British Crimes." London: *Arab Media Watch*, July 18, 2005.

Kayser, Christian, ed. *Asyl in Berlin*. Berlin: Auslaenderbeauftragte des Senats, 1999.

Khan, Uzma Aslam. *Trespassing*. New York: Metropolitan Books, 2003.

Karmi, Ghada. "The Arab Communities in Britain: A Population Map." Paper presented at Group 2: The Economic Conditions of the Arab Communities in Britain. The Third Arab Communities Conference. Arab Club of Britain, London, 1999.

———. *In Search of Fatima: A Palestinian Story*. London: Verso, 2002.

Kizilhan, Ilhan. *Der Sturz Nach Oben*. Frankfurt am Main: Medico International, 1995.

Ku, Leighton, Shawn Fremstad, and Matthew Broaddus. *Noncitizens' Use of Public Benefits Has Declined since 1996: Recent Report Paints Misleading Picture of Impact of Eligibility Restrictions on Immigrant Families*. Washington, D.C.: Center on Budget and Policy Priorities: 2003.

Kuecherer, Klaus-Peter, ed. *Kurdische Migranten in Deutschland: Problemfelder, Hintergruende, und dei Rolle der Nichtregierungsorganisationen.* Bonn: NAVEND— Kurdisches Informations- und Dokumentationszentrum, 1998.

Kuecherer, Klaus-Peter, and Maria Koch, eds. *Fluchtursachen in Kurdistan und die Situation kurdischer Fluechtlinge in Deutschland.* Bonn: NAVEND—Kurdisches Informations- und Dokumentationszentrum, 1997.

Kuecherer, Klaus-Peter, and Ulrike Schulte Overberg, eds. *Behoerden und Kurden: Begegnung mit Hindernissen.* Bonn: NAVEND—Kurdisches Informations- und Dokumentationszentrum, 1998.

Lahav, Gallya. *Immigration and Politics in the New Europe: Reinventing Borders.* Cambridge: Cambridge University Press, 2004.

McDowall, David. *A Modern History of the Kurds.* London: I.B. Tauris, 1996.

McRoy, Anthony. *The British Arab.* Stamford, U.K.: National Association of British Arabs, 2000.

Meehan, Elizabeth. "Citizenship and the European Union." ZEI Discussion Papers. Center for European Integration Studies, University of Bonn, 2000.

Meiselas, Susan, with chapter commentary by Martin van Bruinessen. *Kurdistan: In the Shadow of History.* New York: Random House, 1997.

Monitoring Minority Protection in the E.U.: The Situation of Muslims in the U.K. London: U.K. Home Office, 2002.

Mernisi, Fatima. *Islam and Democracy.* Boston: Addison Wesley, 1992.

Moore, Steven. *Immigration and the Rise and Decline of American Cities.* Palo Alto: Hoover Institution, Stanford University, 1994.

Muslims in the U.K. Budapest: Open Society Institute, 2005.

Nagel, Caroline. "Constructing Difference and Sameness: The Politics of Assimilation in London's Arab Communities." *Ethnic and Racial Studies* 25.2 (2002).

———. "Hidden Minorities and the Politics of 'Race': The Case of British Arab Activists in London." *Journal of Ethnic and Migration Studies* 27.3 (2001).

———. "The Role of Local Associations in the Creation of 'Arab Society' in London." Paper presented at Group 1: Cultural Identity of British Arabs. The Third Arab Communities Conference. Arab Club of Britain, London, 1999.

Nasrin, Taslima. *Meyebela: My Bengali Girlhood,* translated by Gopa Majumdar. Paris: Editions Stock, 1998.

Niessen, Jan and Yongmi Schibel. *E.U. and U.S. Approaches to the Management of Immigration: Comparative Perspectives.* Brussels: Migration Policy Group, 2003.

Nisbet, Erik C., and James Shanahan. *MSRG Special Report: Restrictions on Civil Liberties, Views of Islam, and Muslim Americans.* Ithaca: Media and Society Research Group, Cornell University, 2004.

Ottersbach, Markus, and Felix Weiland. *KurdInnen in der Bundesrepublik Deutschland: Ein Handbuch.* Bonn: NAVEND—Zentrum fuer Kurdische Studien, 1999.

Ozcan, Ertekin. *Tuerkische Immigrantenorganisationen in der Bundesrepublik Deutsch-land.* Berlin: Hitit, 1989.

Politische und soziale Partizipation von MigrantInnen. Bonn: NAVEND—Zentrum fuer Kurdische Studien, 2003.

Portes, Alejandro, and Ruben G. Rumbaut. *Immigrant America: A Portrait.* Berkeley: University of California Press, 1996.

Power, Samantha. *A Problem from Hell: America and the Age of Genocide.* New York: Basic Books, 2002.

Ramadan, Tariq. *Islam, the West and the Challenges of Modernity,* translated by Said Amghar. Markfield, Leicester, U.K.: Islamic Foundation, 2001.

Ratha, Dilip. "Workers' Remittances: An Important and Stable Source of External Development Finance." In *Global Development Finance 2003.* Washington, D.C.: International Bank for Reconstruction and Development / World Bank, 2003.

"Registration of Certain Nonimmigrant Aliens from Designated Countries." Notices: AG Order No. 2638–2002. *Federal Register* 67.243. Washington, D.C.: Department of Justice, Immigration and Naturalization Service, 2002.

Richards, Alan, and John Waterbury, eds. *A Political Economy of the Middle East.* Second edition. Boulder, Colo.: Westview, 1998.

Safieh, Afif. *On Palestinian Diplomacy.* London: Palestinian General Delegation to the U.K. and the Office of Representation of the P.L.O. to the Holy See, 2004.

Saggar, Shamit, ed. *Race and British Electoral Politics.* London: Routledge, 2003.

Salah, Salah, ed. "Non-Governmental Organizations in the Palestinian Refugee Camps in Lebanon." Beirut: Statistics and Documentation Office (Ajial Center), 2001.

Salamandra, Christa. "Globalisation and Cultural Mediation: The Construction of Arabia in London." *Global Networks* 2.4 (2002).

Sassen, Saskia. *The Global City: New York, London, Tokyo.* Princeton: Princeton University Press, 2001.

Schmidt, Susanne. *Kurdisch-Sein und Nicht-Sein: Einblicke in Selbstbilder von Jugendlichen kurdischer Herkunft.* Bonn: NAVEND, 1998.

Schiller, Nina Glick, Linda Basch, and Christina Blanc-Szanton. *Towards a Transnational Perspective on Migration: Race, Class, Ethnicity, and Nationalism Reconsidered.* New York: New York Academy of Sciences, 1992.

Segev, Tom. *One Palestine, Complete: Jews and Arabs under the British Mandate,* translated by Haim Watzman. New York: Henry Holt, 1999.

Seifert, Wolfgang. *Geschlossene Grenzen, offene Gesellschaften? Migrations- und Integrationsprozesse in westlichen Industrienationen.* Frankfurt am Main: Campus Verlag, 2000.

Semiannual Report to Congress: October 1, 2002 to March 31, 2003. Washington, D.C.: Office of the Inspector General, Department of Justice, 2003.

Sen, Amartya. *Development as Freedom.* New York: Anchor Books, 1996.

The September 11 Detainees: A Review of the Treatment of Aliens Held on Immigration Charges in Connection with the Investigation of the September 11 Attacks. Washington, D.C.: Office of the Inspector General, Department of Justice, 2003.

Sinai, Anne, and Allen Pollack. *The Syrian Arab Republic: A Handbook.* New York: American Academic Association for Peace in the Middle East, 1976.

Siddiqui, Tasneem. "Migration as a Livelihood Strategy of the Poor: The Bangladesh Case." Paper presented at the Regional Conference on Migration, Development and Pro-Poor Policy Choices in Asia. Dhaka: Refugee and Migratory Movements Research Unit, 2003.

Smith, Charles D. *Palestine and the Arab-Israeli Conflict.* Third edition. New York: St. Martin's Press, 1996.

Sowell, Thomas. *Migrations and Cultures: A World View.* New York: Basic Books, 1996.

Special Registration: Discrimination and Xenophobia as Government Policy. New York: Asian American Legal Defense and Education Fund, 2003.

el-Wafi, Layla M. "British Arab Muslims and the 'War on Terror': Perceptions of Citizenship, Identity and Human Rights." Stamford, U.K.: National Association of British Arabs, 2006.

Waters, Mary C. "The Second Generation in New York City: A Demographic Overview." Paper presented at Population Association of America Annual Meeting, New York, March 25, 1999.

Winkler, Beate, ed. *Zukunftsangst Einwanderung.* Munich: Beck'sche Reihe, 1992.

Wuensch, Roland, ed. *Rechtliche Situation und Integrationsperspektiven von Kurdischen MigrantInnen: Ein Handbuch.* Bonn: NAVEND—Zentrum fuer kurdische Studien, 2002.

Yavari, Neguin. "Muslim Communities in New York City." *ISIM Newsletter* 10. Leiden: Institute for the Study of International Islam, 2002.

"Young Muslims and Extremism." Draft report issued by the U.K. Foreign Commonwealth Office and Home Office.

GENERAL NEWS PUBLICATIONS, PERIODICALS, AND WEB SITES

Agence-France Presse

Associated Press

BBC News Service

Die Berliner Zeitung

The Financial Times

Foreign Affairs

The Guardian

Haaretz

The New York Times
Reuters Alertnet
Der Tagesspiegel
taz
The Times of London
The Wall Street Journal
Washington Post
Die Zeit

REGIONAL OR COMMUNITY-SPECIFIC NEWS PUBLICATIONS, PERIODICALS, AND WEB SITES

Arab Media Watch: www.arabmediawatch.org
Banglapedia: http://banglapedia.net
Hi Pakistan: www.hipakistan.org
Kurdistan Observer
Kurdistan Bloggers Union: kurdistanblog.blogspot.com
The Muslim News (News and Views of Muslims in the United Kingdom)
Palestine Monitor: www.palestinemonitor.org
Pakistan Link: www.pakistanlink.com
Sharq: British Arab Culture
SyriaComment: www.joshualandis.com/blog
The Third World View: http://rezwanul.blogspot.com

RESEARCH INSTITUTES, THINK TANKS, AND GOVERNMENTAL LIBRARIES

American Immigration Law Foundation, Washington, D.C.
Berliner Institut zur Foerderung der Kurdologie, Berlin
Berliner Auslaenderbeauftragte, Berlin
Brookings Institute, Saban Center on Middle East Policy, Washington, D.C.
Council on Foreign Relations (CFR), New York City
Europaeisches Migrationszentrum (EMZ), Berlin
   —Berliner Institut fuer Vergleichende Sozialforschung (BIVS)
   —European Research Forum on Migration and Ethnic Relations (EUROFOR)
The European Union
Federal Research Division, U.S. Library of Congress
   —Country Studies/Area Handbook Series (sponsored by the U.S. Department of the Army between 1986 and 1998): Bangladesh, Israel, Pakistan, Syria, Turkey
Imagining Global Asia, New York City

International Organization for Migration (IOM), Geneva
  —World Migration Report Series, Managing Migration
Migration Information Source, Washington, D.C.
Muslim Communities in New York City Project, New York City
Royal Institute of International Affairs/Chatham House (RIIA), London
Social Science Research Center (SSRC), New York City
United Nations Development Programme (UNDP)
United Nations Relief and Works Agency (UNRWA)
World Bank
  —"International Migration: Implications for the World Bank"

ADVOCACY, RIGHTS-BASED, SOCIAL JUSTICE, AND COMMUNITY-BASED ORGANIZATIONS

American Arab Anti-Discrimination Committee (ADC), Washington, D.C.
American Kurdish Information Center (AKIN) Washington, D.C.
Amnesty International
Arbeiterwohlfahrt (AWO), Berlin
Asian American Legal Defense and Education Fund (AALDEF), New York City
Arab Club of Britain, London
Al-Awda Right of Return Coalition, London
Council for Arab-British Understanding (CAABU), London
Council on American-Islamic Relations (CAIR), New York Chapter, Queens, N.Y.
Council on Pakistan Organization (COPO), Brooklyn, N.Y.
Desis Rising Up and Moving (DRUM), Queens, N.Y.
Disappeared in America/Visible Collective, Brooklyn, N.Y.
Human Rights Watch (HRW), New York City
Labour Middle East Coalition (LMEC), London
Kurdish Human Rights Project, London
Islamic Circle of North America (ICNA), Queens, N.Y.
Islamic Human Rights Commission (IHRC), London
Kotti, Berlin
Muslim Council of Britain (MCB), London
National Association of British Arabs (NABA), Stamford, U.K.
National Immigration Forum, Washington, D.C.
National Network for Immigrant and Refugee Rights, Oakland, Cal.
  —*Network News* (magazine)
Palestinian Peace Coalition, Ramallah, West Bank
Palestine Solidarity Campaign

INDEX

abaya, 29. *See also* Gulf states;
  migration
Abdelahad, Jamil and Nura: exile of,
  27–28, 33; long-distance marriage of, 31,
  33; and pan-Arabism, 26–27 (*see also*
  pan-Arabism); political views of, 28–29;
  social attitudes of, 28, 31–32; as target of
  secret police, 28, 30–31
Abdelahad, Muna. *See* Nashashibi, Muna
  Abdelahad
agha (landowner). *See* Dogan, Mehmet
ajanib (foreigner). *See* Kurds;
  statelessness; Syria
al-Aqsa mosque. *See* Intifada: Second
  (al-Aqsa)
Aleppo: Aleppo Chamber of Commerce,
  32; descriptions of, 29–30; Ford Motor
  Company, 30; Syrian Teachers' Institute,
  32; University of Aleppo, 32, 217. *See also*
  Nashashibi, Muna Abdelahad;
  Suleiman, Nezir
American Dream, 91, 92–93, 156, 162
antiterrorism activities and policies. *See*
  terrorism
Arab-Israeli conflict: and the annexation
  of Arab lands, 28, 34, 38; and the
  creation of Israel, 26, 33; and Israeli
  military occupation, 38, 100, 101, 108,
  117–118, 120, 122, 124, 193, 196, 199, 202,
  203; and Israeli settlements, 100, 101, 118,
  120, 122, 192, 202; and the 1948 War,
  25–27, 29, 34, 101; and the 1967 War, 28,
  34, 38, 101; and the peace process, 110,
  115, 119; and the "separation wall," 193,
  194, 195, 202. *See also* Intifada

Arabization, 214. *See also* ethnic cleansing
  or genocide; Kurds; statelessness; Syria
Arab League, 97
Arab Media Watch, 120, 121, 122, 123, 124,
  183, 184, 185, 186, 188, 191, 203, 204, 205.
  See also Arabs; London; media;
  Nashashibi, Sharif; United Kingdom
Arabs: Christians, 26, 187 (*see also*
  Abdelahad, Jamil and Nura; Nashashibi,
  Muna Abdelahad); collective identity of,
  26–27, 28, 39 (*see also* United Kingdom);
  in the diaspora (*see* diaspora); and
  Kurds (*see* Kurds); and pan-Arabism
  (*see* pan-Arabism); in the United
  Kingdom (*see* United Kingdom). *See*
  also specific character
Arafat, Yasser, 45, 106, 117, 120, 122
Ashrawi, Hanan, 187, 203. *See also* Arabs
asylum. *See* asylum seekers
asylum homes. *See* asylum seekers; Dogan,
  Mehmet; Dogan, Sukriye; Germany
asylum seekers: definition of, 35; in
  Germany, 136–138, 148–153, 210, 211, 226,
  227, 235–236, 238 (*see also* Germany;
  Kurds); and psychotherapy, 150–151, 211,
  232–233
Auslaendergesetz (foreigner law). *See*
  Germany
Auslaenderregelklassen (foreigner classes).
  See Germany

Ba'ath party, of Syria: ascent to power of,
  30; and influence of Marxist socialism,
  28; and Syrian Socialist National Party
  (SSNP), 28, 30

ABOUT THE AUTHOR

Kavitha Rajagopalan has studied international relations theory, and has done graduate work in international affairs, specializing in international communications and migration policy, at Columbia University. She was a recipient of a Fulbright scholarship to study political science in Berlin, Germany. She has worked in international development and finance, and as a journalist in India, Germany, and the United States. She lives in Brooklyn, New York, with her husband.